REGNUM STUDIES IN GLOBAL CHRISTIANITY

Civilisations in Conflict?

Islam, the West and Christian Faith

REGNUM STUDIES IN GLOBAL CHRISTIANITY

(Previously GLOBAL THEOLOGICAL VOICES series)

Series Preface

In the latter part of the twentieth century the world witnessed significant changes in global Christian dynamics. Take for example the significant growth of Christianity in some of the poorest countries of the world. Not only have numbers increased, but the emphasis of their engagement has expanded to include ministry to a wider socio-cultural context than had previously been the case. The *Regnum Studies in Global Christianity* series explores the issues with which the global church struggles, focusing in particular on ministry rooted in Africa, Asia, Latin America and Eastern Europe.

Not only does the series make available studies that will help the global church learn from past and present, it provides a platform for provocative and prophetic voices to speak to the future of Christianity. The editors and the publisher pray particularly that the series will grow as a public space, where the voices of church leaders from the majority world will contribute out of wisdom drawn from experience and reflection, thus shaping a healthy future for the global church. To this end, the editors invite theological seminaries and universities from around the world to submit relevant scholarly dissertations for possible publication in the series. Through this, it is hoped that the series will provide a forum for South-to-South as well as South-to-North dialogues.

Series Editors

REGNUM STUDIES IN GLOBAL CHRISTIANITY

Civilisations in Conflict?

Islam, the West and Christian Faith

J. Andrew Kirk

Foreword by Bishop Kenneth Cragg

First published 2011 by Regnum Books International

Regnum is an imprint of the Oxford Centre for Mission Studies
St. Philip and St. James Church
Woodstock Road
Oxford, OX2 6HR, UK
www.ocms.ac.uk/regnum

09 08 07 06 05 04 03 8 7 6 5 4 3 2 1

British Library Cataloguing in Publication Data
A catalogue record for this book is available from the British Library

ISBN - 978-1-506475-32-5

Typeset by RBI

Distributed by 1517 Media in the US and Canada

Contents

Foreword

They are frequently found in books but are they not unnecessary? An old English proverb says that 'Good wine needs no bush'. The reference is to the cluster of wine branches, or even of grapes, which innkeepers or vintners hung outside their premises to advertise their wines. No amount of publicity will avail if the product does not satisfy. Let the commodity advertise itself by its own inherent quality. Yet advertising persists as a large industry since popularity needs to be aroused.

So, it would seem, books welcome forewords, when all these can do is commend what must still justify itself. It seems now that the word 'Foreword' is often mistaken for the word 'forward'. It is a happy confusion since the business of any 'foreword' is to send the book on its way, or to 'forward' its progress.

Andrew Kirk's study of Islam as 'the rale of two cities' certainly achieves its own 'forward' movement into wise readership, expounding the essentials of Islam and engaging with Samuel Huntingdon's now notorious 'The Clash of Civilizations and the Remaking of World Order'. It explores the entanglements of a 'West-centred' concern with contemporary expressions of Islam, political and dogmatic, and how the Qur'an's verdict, via the angels in *Surah* 2.30, and their protest about the entrustment on Allah's part of his good earth to the tenancy and tenure of humankind who will 'corrupt in the earth and shed blood' (*yuf'sidu fīhā wayasfiku l-dimāa* – almost a play on words) which has become the angry charge of Al-Qu'idah and the Taliban against the West in Iraq and Afghanistan. Part One of Andrew Kirk's study examines these conflicts and tensions. Part Two offers a useful comparison of the origins of Islam and Christianity and carries the resulting issues further in Part Three into the vocation of Christian faith vis-à-vis both Islam and the West and the religious sense of the 'secular' and its relevance for both faiths and their mutual relations. There is an extensive biography where the several writings of Daud Rahbar, David Marshall, and Christian Troll might have been included. Taking the Mecca/Medina relation contrast as a defining clue is only to accord with the Qur'an's own identification of all its *Surahs* by that criterion, astride the all important *Hijrah* which committed the prophetic faith to the politics of power. How now to understand their inter-duty is the urgent question to which Andrew Kirk's book offers a lively and perceptive access and a competent 'forwarding'.

Bishop Kenneth Cragg
July 2010

Preface

This book has taken some time to gestate. This has been largely due to the kind of material that it tries to wrestle with. The nature of the discussion is complex and controversial. It has been necessary, therefore, for me to read as widely as is feasible. Also I have consulted with a number of people more expert in the details of Islamic history and belief than I am. In the latter category, my primary thanks goes to Colin Chapman, who agreed – probably in a rash moment – to read through the whole text, and make critical comments. It is impossible to over-estimate my appreciation for this labour of friendship. His comments have been perceptive and have led me to make a number of changes and additions. I have also learnt much in conversation, particularly with David Singh, David Shenk and Ida Glaser. I have been invited to present different parts of the book to seminars at the International Baptist Theological Seminary in Prague, the Oxford Centre for Mission Studies and the Oxford Centre for Muslim-Christian Studies. In each case the subsequent discussion was most helpful in both affirming and challenging certain conclusions I had come to. To all the people involved in these sessions I would like to say thank you for being willing to listen and to respond graciously and with insight.

Inevitably there are a number of Islamic terms incorporated into the text that are transliterations from Arabic. For the sake of consistency, I have almost always used the spelling that has been adopted by The Oxford Dictionary of Islam. The same is true for the spelling of proper names. I have not, on this occasion, tried to compile a glossary of terms: partly, because such a task is hazardous, but mainly because there are excellent Dictionaries around that do a far better job than I could. In addition to the one named above, I would recommend The Penguin Dictionary of Islam. The details of both can be found in the Select Bibliography at the end of the book. With regard to Qur'anic citations, I have consistently used the relatively new translation by M.A.S. Abdel Haleem, Professor of Islamic Studies at the School of Oriental and African Studies, University of London. It is both meticulous in its accurate rendering of the original and also fresh and clear in terms of language and style:

'It is written in a modern easy style, avoiding where possible the use of cryptic language or archaisms that tend to obscure meaning. The intention is to make the Qur'an accessible to everyone who speaks English, Muslims or otherwise'.[1]

---

[1] *The Qur'an* (Oxford: OUP, 2005), xxix.

Quotations from the Bible are taken from the New Revised Standard Version.[2]

I would like to thank the publishers for being willing to take the risk of bringing this study out in print. The subject is extremely topical. Therefore, as well as appealing to those engaged deeply with the vital issues being considered, I hope it will also attract interest among those who may not be so well-versed with the material covered, but who are aware that there are questions being debated here that may have a profound effect on future relations between large communities on our planet. Judging by the local community where I live, I would say that the subject attracts considerable interest among quite ordinary people. In the last three years, or so, various open meetings on aspects of the alleged conflict between the West and Islam have been well attended, and followed by lively discussions.

My desire is to contribute to this discussion by trying to identify fundamental problems and suggest tentatively some possible solutions. Those who live by strong convictions may have to agree to disagree about fundamental questions of belief. And yet, somehow they have to learn to live without rancour and resentment against those they feel lack sympathy towards and understanding of the beliefs that shape and direct the people they are. It is right, I believe, to bring into the open the strong opinions that seem to divide communities and to address them frankly, as long as this is done with the willingness to listen carefully to the other and to reconsider one's own position. This is the spirit with which I have tried to write this book. I hope I have succeeded, at least in part. Readers will judge for themselves.

J. Andrew Kirk
Easter, 2010

---

[2] (Oxford: OUP, 1995), copyright by the Division of Christian Education of the National Council of the Churches of Christ in the United States of America, and are used by permission.

Abbreviations

BCE	Before the Common Era
CE	Common Era
CUP	Cambridge University Press
IVP	Intervarsity Press
OUP	Oxford University Press
SPCK	Society for the Promotion of Christian Knowledge

Introduction

Soon after the demise of communism in Eastern Europe and the former Soviet Union, some people were identifying a new, potential threat to Western culture, values and way of life. In 1993, an obscure academic teaching political science in the USA, Samuel Huntington, wrote an article, later expanded into a book, in which he promoted the idea that the real cause of friction between different parts of the world was to be found not so much in political ideologies as in cultures. He contended that the most crucial and formative aspect of a culture was religious belief and practice. Although he identified seven different culture-types, which he referred to as civilisations, a large proportion of the book is devoted to a consideration of only one of them: Islam. His concern was to analyse the ways in which contrasting civilisations could engender serious hostilities, leading possibly to violent confrontation, and to suggest the means by which such civilisations could learn to live in peaceful co-existence.[1]

At the time that Huntington's thesis appeared, many commentators were inclined to dismiss his analysis as ideologically biased and alarmist. In the case of Islam, there was a fear that his thesis might hinder resolute attempts to encourage Muslims living in the West to integrate into its culture and institutions. Nevertheless, since the events of September 2001 in New York and Washington, some have been willing to reassess his arguments. Since then, a number of other incidents appear to confirm, rather than deny, the opinion that Western and at least some Islamic world-views are on a serious collision course.

Given the geopolitical realities of the contemporary world, it would be difficult to imagine an issue much more pressing than the one Huntington has outlined. There are serious disagreements about what is required today in the concourse of the nations. Fundamental political, social and moral issues to do with basic human freedoms and rights, the rule of law, democratic governance, peaceful co-existence, accountability, self-determination, common security, economic justice, the environment and mutual respect have not been solved. Protagonists of different core beliefs tend to talk past each other; none more so, perhaps, than Christians, Muslims and secular Western liberals.

This potential conflict is a major (though not exclusive) part of the present world order. It is, therefore, a crucial context for considering the contemporary calling of the Christian community. My research in this area follows an

---

[1] *The Clash of Civilisations and the Remaking of World Order* (London: Simon and Schuster, 1998).

extensive study, which I have fairly recently undertaken, of some of the main determining factors that shape contemporary Western culture and the challenge these pose to Christian faith.[2] It will, therefore, be a natural progression to explore and compare how another faith tradition deals with the all-encompassing challenge of a secular, pluralist society.

The research also repays a debt that I owe to several years of Muslim hospitality. Whilst I lived and worked in Birmingham (England's second city), I was part of a Muslim-Christian encounter group that met monthly for discussion and the sharing of a meal in the premises of a Muslim centre. We set out, in an atmosphere of trust and mutual respect, to learn more about each others' beliefs and practices and how the other community viewed them. One of my abiding memories is the seriousness with which Muslim leaders, living in Sparkbrook and Sparkhill (two neighbourhoods in Birmingham), viewed the challenge of secularism to their community. They were intensely interested in how Christians handled the tensions between religious and secular values, particularly as those affected young people.

The Focal Point

Huntington's thesis on the conflict of civilisations has set many hares running. There are numerous aspects of the debate that could be explored. I will limit my focus to the way in which Western social and political policies have constrained and shaped the social engagement of Christianity and also challenge the Islamic tendency to think in terms of theocratic rule. A primary concern, therefore, will be to do a comparative study of current attempts within Islam, ranging from extreme radical movements to modernising tendencies, to come to terms with the pressures of the Western world.

This is still a large arena. Obviously, it is necessary first to review the issues raised by Huntington in the light of events subsequent to the publishing of his book. In addition to these, I believe it is relevant to the discussion to raise the question of 'manifest destinies', understood as a profound sense of calling to remodel the world order, that seem to be latent both in Islam and certain sectors of the West.[3]

At the same time, in order to make the subject-matter manageable, I will concentrate on exploring the origin and early history of Islam as determinative of the way in which Muslims approach the relationship between their

---

[2] *The Future of Reason, Science and Faith: Following Modernity and Post-modernity* (Aldershot: Ashgate Publishing, 2007).

[3] In the case of the USA, see Frederick Merk and Kerm Lois Bannister, *Manifest Destiny and Mission in American History* (Grand Rapids: Eerdmans, 1995); Rosemary Radford Reuther, *America, Amerikkka: Elect Nation and Imperial Violence* (London: Equinox, 2007).

convictions and political power. I will compare this with the early history of the Christian movement, in order to show what resources, in terms of its original thought and context, each faith tradition possesses for confronting the current challenges of the Western cultural heritage.

I believe that this type of comparison has not been attempted hitherto in any systematic way. There is, therefore, a considerable potential for some fresh perspectives on the basic elements used for debating the relation between religion and modern society. Until now, this discussion has been undertaken largely within the parameters of the Christian faith for the obvious reason that Western culture has been hugely influenced by its long association with Christianity, and Christianity in the West has had to come to terms with the influence of modernity and post-modernity. Now, however, sizeable Muslim populations have begun to settle within Europe, North America and Australasia for the first time in their histories, coming mainly from the Middle East, North Africa, Turkey and South East Asia.

This influx of immigrants influenced by a totally different history, social context and set of cultural values has caused Western nations to rethink the kind of societies they wish to be. The advocacy of multiculturalism is one response to this new phenomenon.[4] In response to changing and variable global political realities, I will therefore attempt to compare the current ways in which each faith community interprets and applies its respective sacred writings and subsequent early traditions to contemporary matters of political engagement. From the Christian side, a re-evaluation is also necessary because of the increasingly post-Western nature of the world Christian movement.

Purpose of the Study

The reality of diverse, if not divergent, ways in which different faith communities are actually assessing the public relevance of their beliefs poses for the Christian community a new context for working out its mission priorities. The alleged current conflict of civilisations is undoubtedly a new context for Christian mission. I wish to contribute, if I can, to an analysis of its significance.

I come with the supposition that the circumstances out of which Christianity and Islam were born, which gave rise to distinctive communities with both related and contrasting core beliefs and practices, have moulded their respective views of the relationship between the exercise of political power and belief in

[4] Two fairly recent Christian commentaries on multiculturalism have been written, from different perspectives, by T.J. Gorringe, *Furthering Humanity: A Theology of Culture* (Aldershot: Ashgate Publishing, 2004), 239-256 and Vinoth Ramachandra, *Subverting Global Myths: Theology and the Public Issues Shaping our World* (London: SPCK, 2008), 127-168.

God. In the case of Islam, I base this assumption on the transition of Muhammad's band of followers from being a persecuted minority in Mecca to forming the ruling and guiding force in Medina.[5] In Islamic thought, it is generally agreed that this was a legitimate (indeed necessary) development of Muhammad's prophetic vocation. According to the argument, God revealed his desire that his messenger take full political responsibility for the governance of a city-state, demonstrating how the teaching, which he had received directly from God, should become a reality within a social community.

I also assume that the early history of the Christian community shows that for the first 300 years of its existence it had no direct influence on the exercise of state power. On the contrary, there is considerable evidence to indicate that its stance towards the Roman Empire and its religious underpinning was highly critical. In distinction from Islam's self-assessment, much contemporary Christian thought, both then and now, sees the transition of the Christian community from being a persecuted sect to representing the official religion of the Empire as jeopardising its mission.[6]

However, the hypothesis remains at the level of two major generalisations. First, even though a general repudiation of the Constantinian settlement in the context of current Christian thinking appears to be relatively unproblematic, some historians see it as an inevitable and necessary historical progression, given the changed historical circumstances of the early 4th century.[7] It has been argued, for example, that in spite of persecution by state officials, the growing Christian church at the end of the third century was already exercising a strong influence in various aspects of the social life of the Empire. This being so, some commentators believe that a form of accommodation between the state and the new religion was historically inevitable.[8]

Secondly, the direction that the early Islamic community took is less straightforward. Muhammad's governance of Medina, if it is taken as following divinely approved plans, is ambiguous. Muslim historians may be caught in the trap of having to exonerate all Muhammad's activities, because of a perceived

---

[5] The main group of Muslims left Mecca on 20 June, 622 (the *hijrah*). This date marks the beginning of the Muslim calendar.

[6] This is argued in a particularly passionate way by Stuart Murray, *Post-Christendom: Church and Mission in a Strange New World* (Milton Keynes: Paternoster, 2004). David Bosch, in his book *Transforming Mission: Paradigm Shifts in Theology of Mission* (Maryknoll: Orbis Books, 1991), chapters 6 and 7, summarises some of the negative effects of the Constantinian settlement. However, he does also recognise that there were some positive benefits; see 237.

[7] See, for example, the comments of Lesslie Newbigin, *Foolishness to the Greeks: The Gospel and Western Culture* (London: SPCK, 1986), 100-101.

[8] See, Robert Forrest, 'Loving the Political Enemy: The Church and Rome AD 33-400' in Craig A. Smith (ed), *The Cross at the Crossroads: Loving our enemies in the Twenty-first century* (Manila: Overseas Missionary Fellowship, 2008), 96-138.

need to defend either the absolute integrity of the Qur'anic text as the pure word of God [9] or the sayings and deeds of Muhammad as having exemplary authority. However one views the political situation during Muhammad's short rule in Medina (a mere 10 years), the events that followed his death, with a succession of political assassinations, divisions and wars between rival Muslim groups hardly speak of a successful transition from political impotence in Mecca to the effective exercise of political power in Medina and beyond.

In the case of both histories, however one interprets the developments of the respective communities, it is not immediately obvious what implications can legitimately be drawn from the historical reconstruction. A considerable part of this research, therefore, will be dedicated to a review of the significance of the respective origins. The basic research question can be formulated in the following way: in the light of an alleged 'clash of civilisations' between Islam, the West and Christianity, how does an examination of the origins of Islam and Christianity contribute to an understanding of their respective approaches to contemporary dominant political systems and ideologies and to the exercise of political power in a globalised world?

The Treatment of Sources

With regard to the interpretation of texts and the implications of historical events, a diversity of views undoubtedly exists. Most writers on Islam point to three major groupings amongst contemporary Muslims: revivalists (variously called fundamentalists, Islamists, extremists, radicals); neo-traditionalists and modernists.[10] Each group has its own way of approaching, interpreting and applying the authoritative sources: the Qur'an, and the *sunnah* (the collection of non-Qur'anic acts and sayings of Muhammad). There is a considerable debate within Islam about the exact relevance of the texts and the history within which they were written.[11] As a result, this piece of research has to be open-ended. It will also be inconclusive, partly because at best it can only take a cross-section

---

[9] A notable *crux interpretum* occurs in what appears to be a revelation *ex eventu*, which justifies the apparent breaking of a sacred tribal practice. Authority was given for the armed forces of Medina to raid a wealthy caravan on its way to Mecca during the sacred month of Rahab, when such an action was strictly forbidden by the accepted protocol of the time. *Surahh*s 2.217 and 22.39 of the Qur'an legitimated the breaking of the convention, on the basis that 'persecution is worse than slaying.' See, David Norcliffe, *Islam: Faith and Practice* (Brighton: Sussex Academic Press, 1999), 22.

[10] See, for example, Jon Armani, *Dynamic Islam: Liberal Muslim Perspectives in a Transnational Age* (Lanham: University of America Press, 2004), 11-13.

[11] See, for example, Abdullah Saeed, *Interpreting the Qur'an: Towards a contemporary approach* (London: Routledge, 2006); Jane Dammen McAuliffe, 'The tasks and traditions of interpretation' in Jane Dammen McAuliffe (ed), *The Cambridge Companion to The Qur'an* (Cambridge: CUP, 2006), 181-209.

of opinions within a given time frame, partly because the literature is immense and varied and cannot, therefore, be consulted in its entirety.

A further problem raises its head. Is it possible for a non-Muslim to enter empathetically into the intra-Muslim discussion and fully appreciate its essential features? Muhammad Abdul-Rauf, for example, believes that non-Muslims may legitimately study Muslim history, but will inevitably distort their study of the true nature and origins of the faith, for they will never truly understand it. He believes that critical historical analysis of the foundation documents is inapplicable:

> It is dangerous, when in the name of being scientific, the origins of Islam are explained as arising out of economic and other cultural phenomena...Its unique and well-testified claim upon its adherents cannot be explained away.[12]

On the other hand, Fazlur Rahman believes that

> The observer of an experience need not share it, in order to make sense of propositions about it. In the case of Islam it is preferable to aspire to an intellectual understanding or appreciation.[13]

He then sets out various criteria for an honourable approach to the study of Islam: a lack of prejudice against the object of study; a rejection of historical reductionism (i.e. the attempt to explain the origin of Islam by reference to cultural and historical conditionings alone); an acknowledgement of the distinction between a study of religious communities as the bearers of religious cultures and the normative or transcendent truths of religions. He concludes by saying that an intellectual understanding and appreciation of Islam is quite possible for a non-Muslim who is unprejudiced, sensitive and knowledgeable:

> I welcome the phenomenological approach with the provision that its users recognise the Qur'an and sunna as normative criterion-referents for all expressions and understandings of Islam.[14]

The difficulty of being as fair as possible to the subject-matter of Islam should not be underestimated. Islam represents an integrated world-view that makes absolute demands on those who choose to follow its teachings. Those who do not, particularly those who follow an alternative revelation of the reality of God, have clearly rejected its claims as at best unreliable, at worst

---

[12] 'Outsiders interpretation of Islam: A Muslim's Point of View' in Richard C. Martin (ed), *Approaches to Islam in Religious Studies* (Oxford: One World, 2001/2), 185.

[13] 'Approaches to Islam in Religious Studies: Review Essay' in Richard C. Martin (ed), *Approaches to Islam*, 192.

[14] Fazlur Rahman, 'Approaches to Islam...', 198.

false.[15] The temptation, therefore, to look for and emphasise the weak points in its claims is immense. Of course, this temptation exists for all researchers, when dealing with topics with which they are not largely in sympathy. In the case of a Christian looking at Islam, I would propose the application of the golden rule to the research exercise: 'In everything do to others as you would have them do to you' (Mt. 7.12). In other words, conduct your research with the same due respect for the beliefs of others and the integrity of the documents on which they are based as you would expect of those studying the New Testament and early Christian writings.

Having said that, it may also be argued that sometimes the outsider's penetrating analysis may reveal aspects of a religious community's belief and practice that have become hidden, unacknowledged, repressed or ignored. As Rahman says, not all members of a religious community understand their faith adequately. It is one thing to claim absolute truth for a particular revelation (and this is also open to dispute), it is quite another to claim that a particular interpretation is divinely revealed. In reality neither in Christianity nor in Islam is there an over-arching, definitive teaching authority recognised by all followers of the faith. In both cases, we find a conflict of interpretations, sometimes about quite weighty matters. It just might be the case, therefore, that a sympathetic outsider can throw light on internal controversies or anomalies in another's faith convictions, or even uncover some hitherto unacknowledged insight. Some Christian scholars, most notably Kenneth Cragg, have dedicated their life to this ministry or mission.[16]

This motive becomes more plausible in the case of the subject of this study, namely the relation between origins and present political and social stances, where the debate is by no means foreclosed within either community. Therefore, with all the caveats expressed, the attempt to throw new light on the theory of a clash of civilisations by trying to determine the role played by origins is, prima facie, a worth-while exercise.

Questions of Method

Part of this study, then, will delve into a historical reconstruction of the early Christian and Muslim communities. Clearly, it will need to represent as fairly as may be possible the actual events as they happened. Its main interest, however, will be on the way the communities developed and what that implies

---

[15] Andrew Rippin says, 'The Qur'an pictures those who interact with the text as either accepting its divine status and its witness or not; the idea that one could simply be 'curious' about the book without responding to its truth claims does not seem to be entertained', 'Western scholarship and the Qur'an' in *The Cambridge Companion to The Qur'an*, 237.

[16] See, the bibliography at the end for some of his most important writings.

about their respective beliefs. This aspect of the research project is not meant to be original: there are many studies of the life of Muhammad and histories of early Christianity. However, making a comparison between the two histories and relating it to the question of an alleged conflict of civilisations, though fraught with difficulties, is intended to offer an original contribution.

In the first place, then, I shall rely on some of the standard histories of the early Church. These usually contain a fairly long historical lead in, beginning either with the story of the Maccabees in the 2nd century BC, or with Pompey's invasion of Palestine in 63 BC. They assume (quite rightly) that the life and witness of the early church cannot be understood without a thorough grasp of the ministry and mission of Jesus of Nazareth within his historical context, and in particular the reasons for his death by crucifixion at the hand of the Roman authorities. Within the last forty years or so, there has been renewed interest in the Jewish background and context of Jesus' life work. A number of studies have appeared that emphasise Jesus' Jewish integrity, arguing against those who have stressed his radical break with his Jewish past.[17]

Even more recently the attention of historians of the period has turned to the immense influence exerted by the Roman Empire on the social, political, cultural and religious life of the time. There have been a number of attempts to show how much the early Christian communities saw themselves as a definitive alternative to life in the polis under the aegis of Rome.[18] As you would expect, not everyone is equally convinced of the degree to which the New Testament writings contain polemical remarks aimed against the oppression, exploitation and divine claims of the Imperium Romanum. However, there appears to be enough of a minimum consensus amongst historians to re-evaluate the life of the early Church within this context.

Another question concerns the span of history that should be included in a survey of the early Church, in order to make comparison with the early history of Islam viable. There seem to be good arguments for continuing up to the

---

[17] For example, G. Vermes, *Jesus the Jew* (London: Collins, 1973); J. Riches, *Jesus and the Transformation of Judaism* (London: Darton, Longman and Todd, 1980); E.P. Sanders, *Jesus and Judaism* (London: SCM Press, 1985); J.H. Charlesworth, *Jesus within Judaism* (London: SPCK, 1989)

[18] See, for example, Christopher Bryan, *Render to Caesar: Jesus, the Early Church and The Roman Superpower* (Oxford: OUP, 2005); Warren Carter, *The Roman Empire and the New Testament: An Essential Guide* (Nashville: Abingdon Press, 2006); Rodney Stark, *The Rise of Christianity: A Sociologist Reconsiders Christianity* (Princeton: Princeton University Press, 1996); Richard A. Horsley (ed), *Paul and Empire: Religion and Power in Roman Imperial Society* (Harrisburg: Trinity Press International, 1997); Richard A. Horsley (ed), *Paul and Politics: Ekklesia, Israel, Imperium, Interpretation* (Harrisburg: Trinity Press International, 2000); Seyoon Kim, *Christ and Caesar: The Gospel and the Roman Empire in the Writings of Paul and Luke* (Grand Rapids: Eerdmans, 2008).

transition period around the time of Constantine, when Christianity first became officially tolerated and then the preferred religion of the state. It is important not to adopt a simplistic reading of this period, as if from one day to the next Christian faith ceased being persecuted and began to be embroiled in the messy business of political power. The history is not quite so straightforward; albeit, a major shift in the status of Christianity did occur.

With regard to Islam there are other problems. We mention them briefly. There is, for example, a question of the reliability of the sources for the life of Muhammad (the sirah).[19] Inevitably, they were written from what Graham Stanton, referring to the stories of Jesus, calls 'a partisan point of view'.[20] Indeed, one may ask to what extent they tend to be hagiographical, given the immensely high esteem accorded to the messenger of Islam. It cannot be the work of this study to attempt a minute investigation of the reliability of the sources. I will have to rely on a general consensus among Muslim and non-Muslim scholars concerning the main features of the early history. The criterion of embarrassment is one methodological tool for judging authenticity, i.e. the inclusion of data that might seem to place the object of veneration in a dubious light. There are a number of instances of that recorded about the life of Muhammad, as that of Jesus and the early Church.

Another critical issue surrounds the attempt to place the various *surah* (chapters) of the Qur'an into specific moments in Muhammad's life. Although the practice of identifying the context of specific Qur'anic passages, known as *asbab al-nuzul* (translated as 'occasions of revelation'), was carried out in the early centuries after the prophet, traditional Islamic scholars seem reluctant to admit that the historical contexts in which it is alleged Muhammad received various revelations from God actually influenced their content. Here, modern scholars brought up to respect the academic conventions developed in the Western University system find themselves in difficulties. We are familiar with the historical-critical method as it has been applied to the study of the Bible for generations. Approaching the text with an interest in the process of its formation, it asks such questions as: What were the influences on the final redaction? What does the text tell us about the author and the historical context of his life, of which in many cases we know nothing apart from the writing in question?

In the case of the Qur'an, it is said by many traditionalist Muslims that this method is inapplicable. It is a firm part of doctrinal orthodoxy to affirm that Muhammad was no more than a conduit for God's speech. He was, it is alleged, unable either to read or to write. He heard the words being spoken and was told to 'recite' them, meaning to commit them to memory. At a later time, they were

---

[19] The first to write a comprehensive history of Muhammad was Ibn Khaldun (died 762), some 120 years after the former's death.

[20] *Jesus and the Gospel* (Cambridge: CUP, 2004), 128.

written down by an amanuensis. This theory is said to protect the absolute purity of the transmission process. Muhammad Arkoun describes well the place that the Qur'an occupies within orthodox Islamic faith:

> The object of research is a collection of initially oral utterances put into writing under historical conditions that are not yet elucidated. These utterances have then been elevated, by the industry of generations of historical figures, to the status of a sacred Book which preserves the transcendent Word of God and serves as the ultimate and inevitable point of reference for every act, every form of behaviour and every thought of the faithful, who themselves are to be considered as communally interpreting this heritage.[21]

There is a long-running dispute between Islamic scholars who wish to defend the divine provenance of the Qur'an and its immense, unprecedented place of authority within the religious, and cultural history of a living faith, and non-Islamic scholars who, following in the tradition of a previous generation of 'Orientalists',[22] are much more interested in the human dimensions of the writings and the concrete historical conditions which may have shaped its content.[23] This is a debate which, of necessity, will have to be reviewed, as the stance taken will affect the possibility of discovering as accurate a reconstruction of the origin of Islam as is possible to achieve. At the same time, fortunately, there is sufficient agreement on the basic elements of the life of Muhammad, amongst Muslim and non-Muslim historians, to be able to draw some conclusions regarding the way in which origins continue to affect contemporary socio-political perspectives.[24]

Outcomes

A study of the way in which the early history of each religion has shaped its attitudes to power is not intended to be an end in itself. Rather, it supplies indispensable data for assessing the inevitable tensions that exist between the current secular tradition of the West and the religious traditions of two major world religions. In the latter part of the study, therefore, it will be necessary to discuss how the two communities interpret and use their authoritative sources

---

[21] *Islam: To Reform or to Subvert?* (London: Saqi Books, 2006/2), 73.

[22] Such as William Muir, Richard Bell, Hamilton Gibb, Ignaz Goldziher and D.S. Margoliouth among others, see Albert Hourani, *Islam in European Thought* (Cambridge: CUP, 1991), 7-60.

[23] See, for example, Irving M. Zeitlen, *The Historical Muhammad* (Cambridge: Polity Press, 2007).

[24] Questions about the reliability of historical sources for the life of Jesus and the early church are touched on in chapter 6.

to confront the challenges of organising life in twenty-first century Western societies.

Within Muslim communities there is much debate about the way in which the injunctions of the Qur'an and the *sunnah* should be interpreted and applied in a world vastly different from 7th century Arabia. Islam is, in many ways, a religion of law. It is predicated on the belief that God has revealed his will for just about every aspect of life that could be imagined. The revelation came to be codified by jurists, during the two centuries following Muhammad's death, in the details of the *shari'ah* or divine law:

> God is the Transcendent Reality Who is all powerful and sovereign over human beings. He is the only ultimate sanction of law, and the laws of human society are the embodiments of His Will... In the Islamic perspective, Divine Law is to be implemented to regulate society and the actions of its members rather than society dictating what laws should be.[25]

This may sound straightforward. However, it is natural to ask whether human beings of subsequent generations have heard the divine word correctly. In particular, many contemporary Muslims query whether the word heard in the socio-political conditions of the 8th and 9th centuries, when the initial process of codification was being completed, can be the same as that heard 12 centuries later. Nasr contemplates a distinction when he says, 'The injunctions of Divine Law are permanent, but the principles can be applied to new circumstances as they arise'.[26]

In the early years the principles could be culled from the *sunnah.* Muhammad's actions are said to be a sure way of determining the meaning of the texts. However, what happens when circumstances arise not contemplated in the original texts? In many ways, the present divisions within Islam are the result of different answers to the questions that arise in unanticipated contexts. Traditionalists are inclined to assert that the early system of law is sufficient for all time, and that it is possible, therefore, to implement the injunctions within the contemporary world as they stand. Modernisers claim that 'the gates of *ijtihad*'[27] have to be reopened, meaning that there is ample room for a reinterpretation of the Divine Will, in order that human beings may be faithful,

---

[25] Seyyed Hossein Nasr, *The Heart of Islam: Enduring Values for Humanity* (New York: HarperCollins, 2002), 116-117.

[26] *The Heart of Islam*, 117.

[27] 'The concept of exercising independent judgement concerning a legal or theological question... The concept has been interpreted by many modern Muslim thinkers as an intellectual tool for dealing with modern and contemporary issues in the light of Muslim sources,' Azim Nanji, *The Penguin Dictionary of Islam* (London: Penguin Books, 2008), 74.

not to past interpretations, but to the divine intention in the contemporary world:

'Since the last century', writes Nasr, 'a great debate has taken place in the Sunni world about opening 'the gate of *ijtihad*' again, and in both the Sunni and Shi'ite worlds, fundamental discussions are taking place today about the future development and application of the *Shari'ah* to Islamic society facing new challenges, including those issuing from biotechnology and all the problems it poses for ethics'.[28]

Christians will recognise here a familiar debate. They call it hermeneutics or the way of interpreting and applying the texts of Scripture and the writings and practices of the early Christian communities. There are parallel questions for both faiths. However, the methods for deriving answers will differ considerably, precisely because of the divergent nature of the origin of each.

Clearly, the answers will also differ due to the substantially contrasting content of the core message of each faith. At the risk of over-simplifying a complex reality, it would generally be true to say that for Islam, although the word of God came at precise moments in the life of Muhammad, it is not so much about identifiable acts of God within those historical circumstances as about God's requirements for human action in order to deliver a society patterned after God's immutable will. For Christians right and wrong action is discerned ultimately on the basis of the nature of God's rule as shown in the life of Jesus and interpreted through his sayings and the apostolic interpretation of the meaning of his death and resurrection as the inauguration of a new order in the world. Kenneth Cragg puts it this way:

> ...distinctive theologies we certainly possess – the one turning on an 'eternal Scripture' sufficiently educating humankind into a moral regime via a structured discipline...the other turning on an eternal Christology as to 'God in Christ' inaugurating a moral regime of redemption and grace in the fellowship of a new people of God to serve humankind in that Messianic meaning.[29]

The two contrasting understandings of the way in which God's revelation is transmitted and the content of that revelation will produce different approaches to the apparent triumph of liberal values in Western societies.

---

[28] *The Heart of Islam*, 123-124. It has to be said that any attempt to reinterpret the injunctions of the *shar'iah* cause enormous controversy within world Islam. One example was the case of Hassan Turabi, who became the Attorney General and Minister of Justice in the Sudan in 1988 and sought to review thoroughly the legal enactments of his nation, see 'Abdelwahab El-Affendi, 'Hassan Turabi and the Limits of Modern Islamic Reformism' in Ibrahim M. Abu-Rabi (ed), *The Blackwell Companion to Contemporary Islamic Thought* (Oxford: Blackwell, 2006), 145-156.

[29] *Muhammad in the Quran: The Task and the Text* (London: Melisende, 2001), 180.

Also, of immeasurable importance is the historical trajectory of each faith in determining attitudes to current, prevailing, social and cultural assumptions in the West. These will be explored early in the project by seeking to explain some of the historical events that have given rise to frictions and misunderstandings between Muslims and the West. At a later stage, I will seek to assess whether the twin notions of 'manifest destiny' and 'manifest success' as these have been developed into religiously inspired ideologies by certain groups within the USA and Islam, are valid, or invalid, interpretations of the core beliefs of each faith.

The ultimate objective of this research is to suggest proposals for Christian life and work and for Christian-Muslim understandings as one small response to the second part of the title of Huntington's thesis (often overlooked by commentators), namely 'The Remaking of World Order'. This can only happen as the reality, or otherwise, of the first part, 'The Clash of Civilisations', is thoroughly scrutinised.

Chapter 1

Interpreting the Terms

There can be little doubt that the meaning of each word used in the title of this book is hotly contested. Given the nature of the topic under discussion, broad generalisations will not suffice. I will attempt, therefore, to bring a certain amount of precision to the terminology that has become common in the discussion around the relationship between Islam and the West, since Huntington launched his thesis on the world. I will take each term in the order in which it appears in the title of this book.

Civilisation

Leaving behind the 'barbarian'

According to Huntington, the idea of civilisation arose in France at the time of the Enlightenment as a way of distinguishing a cultured society from barbarism. The latter was a way of describing social groupings that had not produced any notable advances in terms of scientific discovery, technology, political organisation, sophisticated philosophical thought, architecture, literature and the arts. Such societies could be referred to as primitive in the sense that they were undeveloped. They belonged to an early stage of advancement.

The word itself comes from the Greek *barbaros*, generally taken to mean someone who speaks an unintelligible language and, therefore, a foreigner (1 Cor. 14.11). In a neutral sense it could refer simply to anyone who was not Greek. It is used in this sense in the New Testament by Luke of the inhabitants of Malta (Acts 28.2, 4) and by Paul of all non-Greeks (Rom. 1.14). However, it was also used in the Hellenistic world as a word of contrast, for all societies that lacked the sophisticated refinement of the Greek city states.

Embracing progress

Implied in the term is the notion of history moving in an upward direction, from ignorance, inexperience and innocence to knowledge, expertise, proficiency and ingenuity. Enlightenment thinkers were enamoured with the idea of progress. According to them, human populations made advances in their manner of living by stages, by overcoming ignorance and superstition, based on irrational beliefs regarding the unknown. All societies could be measured by the comparative stage of enlightenment they had reached, certain parts of Europe leading the way. It became self-evident to the European elite that they were at the pinnacle of a way of life most sharply distinguished from the brute forces that generally prevailed at a lower level of existence.

This confidence in their superior achievements led some European states to believe it was their duty to share the benefits of their society with the benighted peoples of other continents through education, modern health care, new agricultural methods, the creation of industries and 'benign' governance. There were also other motives, not least the need for both cheap raw materials to feed the growing industrial expansion taking place in Europe and markets to sell the goods being produced. In the middle of the 19th century, Karl Marx observed:

> The need for a constantly expanding market for its products chases the bourgeoisie over the whole surface of the globe...The cheap prices of its commodities are the heavy artillery with which it batters down all Chinese walls.[1]

Western people may think today that such attitudes have long since been abandoned. So-called Western progress took an enormous battering in the twentieth century because of the devastating wars and attendant brutalities ('barbarisms') unleashed on the European continent. The ideological struggle between 'East' and 'West', lasting for forty years from the end of the second World War, has had a devastating negative impact on many nations in Africa, Asia and Latin America. The reluctance of the European colonial powers to allow self-determination to their colonies, and the ensuing armed struggles to achieve this end, distorted the emerging nations' possibilities of advancement.

At the beginning of a new millennium, people living in the West may believe that, having learned from the errors of the past, they have now achieved a certain level of understanding with regard to how other peoples should be treated. In part this may be true. There is certainly less ignorance about the outstanding achievements of other cultures. There is also a greater willingness to recognise the intrinsic dignity and equality of all people, whatever their present situation or past history, now enshrined in a number of conventions on human rights. At the same time, speaking in general terms, Western peoples still consider their way of life, technological achievements, forms of government, legal codes, educational systems, health care and much more to be more advanced than any others and, therefore, worthy of being emulated.

---

[1] *The Communist Manifesto*; see, Robert C. Tucker, *The Marx-Engels Reader* (New York: W.W.Norton, 1972), 338, 339.

Developed and developing

So, behind the prevailing development terminology, as used frequently in the Western media and political circles, there still lies an implicit, unspoken perception that Western societies are in the vanguard of progress. Although sophisticated commentators no longer speak about under-development, which gives the impression of backwardness, the use of the euphemism 'developing' suggests that in terms of the image of a race, non-Western nations still have a lot of catching up to do:

> The 'civilizational' identity (is) the sense people have of the basic order by which they live, even imperfectly, as good, and (usually) as superior to the ways of life of outsiders, be they 'barbarians', or 'savages', or (in the more polite contemporary language) 'less developed' peoples.[2]

To be developed, then, means to be in more or less the same place that Western nations have reached. It also means to reproduce the same technological, economic and political means of getting there: borrowed technological achievements, free-market economies and democratically authenticated governments. In other words, the common view of many Western people is that their societies represent everybody else's future. These are the benchmarks and models of desirable ways of organising human communities in the contemporary world. Outside of these reference-points the 'barbarians' still live.

Cultures writ large

Huntington understands a civilisation to be the overall way of life of a particular people, the sum total of their values, norms, institutions and modes of thinking. A civilisation is a 'particular concatenation of worldview, customs, structures and culture which forms some kind of historical whole and which coexists with other varieties of this phenomenon'.[3] One might define a civilisation as a society or culture that has reached a certain level of complexity. This is marked by a number of changes in the way large communities organise themselves: for example, in the growth of settled urban life, resulting in part from the development of new forms of agricultural production, such as crop rotation, irrigation and the ability to store surplus crops, in an expanding bureaucracy and in an increasingly diverse division of labour.

---

[2] Charles Taylor, *A Secular Age* (Cambridge, MA: Harvard University Press, 2007), 455 (emphasis added).

[3] Huntington, *The Clash of Civilisations*, 41.

Civilisations surpass cultures in terms of their high level of social elaboration and organization, and by their varied economic and cultural activities. When speaking about civilisations, complexity is usually related to the political and economic organisation of society.[4] In the past this has usually meant a stratified society headed by a ruling elite, supported by a civil service and standing army. Civilisations have emerged when economic conditions have allowed the accumulation of wealth. This, in turn, has permitted certain segments of society to develop scientific research and artistic and literary activities. Civilisations possess intricate cultures, including literature, professional art, architecture, technological advances, organized religion, and complex customs associated with the elite. Many civilizations comprise large cultural spheres containing many nations and regions. The civilisation in which someone lives is that person's broadest cultural identity.

Some historians, like Oswald Spengler, have focused on these broad cultural spheres and have treated civilisations as single units. He maintained that a civilisation's coherence is based around a single primary cultural symbol. Civilisations experience cycles of birth, life, decline and death, often supplanted by a new civilisation with a potent new culture, formed around a compelling new cultural symbol.[5] According to Toynbee, civilizations generally decay and eventually fall, due to moral or religious decline, rather than economic or environmental causes.[6]

Civility

One aspect of civilisation highlighted in recent times is the rise of civility. In the context of European history, notable shifts in behaviour expected of the nobility and those who associated with them began to take place from the time of the Renaissance onwards. This has been well documented by Norbert Elias in the first volume of his work, *The Civilizing Process.*[7] He charted the development of conduct and etiquette in matters to do with eating habits, ablutions and other concerns about hygiene. Standards of conduct in 'polite' society were being raised for those who aspired to achieve upward social mobility.

---

[4] There are other forms of complexity, even in primary communities, such as kinship relations and religious rituals. So, complexity of itself does not determine the existence of a civilisation.

[5] Oswald Spengler, *The Decline of the West,* (eds. Arthur Helps and Helmut Werner; trans. Charles F. Atkinson; New York: OUP, 1991).

[6] Arnold Toynbee, *A Study of History* (Oxford: OUP, 1946).

[7] Norbert Elias, *The Civilizing Process, Vol. I: The History of Manners* (Oxford: Basil Blackwell, 1978).

According to Charles Taylor, 'Renaissance 'civility' is the ancestor of our 'civilization', and has much the same force'. It included 'taste, manners (and) refinement'.[8] Crucially it marked out life in the city from life in the jungle, a cultivated life from one which followed the raw impulses of nature. It is cultured, elegant, polished and urbane (a life fit for the sophistication of the city).

Above all, a civilised existence was marked out by discipline and self-control. It implied the need to tame the lower nature, in order that the higher forms of life could flourish. Thus, a civilised society is one in which rowdiness, coarseness, crudity and indelicacies in the general population are gradually eliminated:

> Delicacy...became the virtue of polite society.... Civilization is a game we play together...maintaining the standards: when we violate one of these tabus, we not only arouse disgust, but we feel terrible shame. Civilization is in a sense a matter of feeling shame in the appropriate places.[9]

As modern society became more complex, through the rise of new technologies and radical innovations in the means of production, so it had to become more ordered. As modern society became much more differentiated in terms of class structure, so it became necessary to realise a common, unified sense of what was appropriate social behaviour throughout the whole populace. The various conventions of civility came to take on the force of moral codes. Civilisation became all the more distinguished from every kind of philistinism.

Conflict

There may be at least three ways of looking at the reality of conflict within and between societies. First, there is the element of strife, in which some kind of physical encounter takes place. This may encompass anything from open war between nations to violent civil demonstrations (such as organised protests at G8 summit meetings) to hostile confrontations between gangs to domestic violence. Secondly, there is the element of discord and disagreement, in which two or more parties act in animosity towards each other. This aspect of conflict does not necessarily imply physical violence, though it might entail a level of coercion in the form of sanctions, embargos or other kinds of punishment. It could involve a breakdown of relations following a profound difference of opinion about policies, objectives, underlying convictions, values or lifestyles, and lead to verbal abuse and threats. Thirdly, there is the element of incompatibility, in which there seems to be no way of resolving contradictory

---

[8] Taylor, *A Secular Age*, 99, 100.

[9] Taylor, *A Secular Age*, 142.

views on particular issues between two or more protagonists (for example, in the case of abortion, between those who are 'pro-life' and those who are 'pro-choice'). Conflicts arise when consensus has broken down and a person or group of people feel threatened by the dominance of another person or group or by unfair competition. There are many possible causes. The following seem to be the major ones.

Misunderstandings

These may arise because people live at a distance from one another. They are not fully aware of the reality and the circumstances of the other. This can easily lead to false accusations, misrepresentation, generalisations, scapegoating, prejudice, stereotyping and demonising.

Estrangement

A barrier is created when people perceive that difference threatens their own identity or when they feel the threat of displacement by the potential removal of their jobs, attacks on their culture or removal of their political power by other 'strange' people who come from 'outside'. Such barriers can lead to a paranoid fear of the other and the belief that the only way to protect one's own interests is by mounting an aggressive pre-emptive strike.

Exploitation

Alienation happens on a massive scale when some human beings use others for their own ends. In order to justify the abuse of power, such people may go to great lengths to create ideologies, doctrines, myths and even religions that seek to give such practices a veneer of legitimacy. In such circumstances, the dominant group may delude itself into thinking that its security against the loss of power can only be achieved through the use of superior force. So, in order to prevent the weaker group ever gaining an equal standing in society it uses direct or indirect violence to suppress its aspirations and progress.

Islam

At this juncture, I will attempt only a brief summary of the main convictions that Muslims hold in common. As the study progresses, it will be necessary to introduce more nuanced distinctions between several branches of the faith, in order to show that there are a number of different ways of interpreting the foundation sources and history of Islam, particularly in response to the impact of the West.

Islam is a comprehensive view of human existence in the universe that has sprung from messages that Muhammad was convinced he had received directly from God during the years 610-632 CE. This period began when he was about 40 years old and continued until just before his death. Muhammad received the messages through the angel Jibril (Gabriel), memorised them and instructed his followers to commit them to writing. (Tradition asserts that Muhammad did not know how to read or write). After his death, the messages were collected into one volume, now known as the Qur'an, meaning 'recitation'.

The essence of Islam is summed up in the basic confession of faith (*kalima* or *shahada*) - 'There is no God but Allah and Muhammad is the messenger of God' (*La ilaha illa'Llah Muhamadun rasul Allah*)'. This affirmation can be further explained by reference to two central doctrines of Islamic faith. Firstly, there is *tawhid*, the doctrine of the unity of the one and only God, equivalent to the Jewish *she'ma*: 'The Lord our God, the Lord is one' (Deut. 6.4). No created thing can be made equal to God, for that would mean committing the cardinal sin of idolatry (*shirk*). Muslims affirm that Allah is the sovereign creator of all that exists and that human beings have been given the responsibility of being his vice-regents (*khulafa*) on earth (Q. 2.28). Secondly, there is the belief that Muhammad is 'the seal of the prophets' (*khatam al-Nabbiyin*) (Q. 33.40), that is he is the last in the line of prophets, which include, among others, Adam, Noah, Abraham, Moses, Job, David, Jonah and Jesus (Isa).[10] All the prophets were sent by God in his mercy to remind humankind of its essential duty to worship the one and only God truly, live in accord with his laws and look after the needs of the vulnerable. What Muhammad received and was written down in the Qur'an is God's final word to humanity. The content of all previous revelations is now fully incorporated into the Qur'an. It is absolute truth and the measure of all that we can know about God and his will.

The Qur'an is given, then, as divine guidance to tell all people how to submit (islam) to Allah. This guidance is supplemented or interpreted by the *hadith* – the sayings of Muhammad – and the *sunnah* – Muhammad's entire way of life. *Hadith* records the traditions that have come down of Muhammad's teaching, exemplified in his actions. *Sunnah* is the path to be followed because of the *hadith*; it is the way the latter enjoins.

As the Muslim community grew, a need was felt for an extensive compendium of ethical stipulations for daily living. In the course of the first two centuries after the founding of Islam, Muslim leaders developed what is known as *shari'ah* (generally translated, 'law', or 'path'). It incorporates rules that regulate the Muslim believer's relationship with God. It also directs every aspect of social, economic and family life. It is considered to have been derived directly from the Qur'an and the *sunnah*, and therefore is sacred law. It is a detailed code of conduct for every aspect of private and public life. In many ways it characterises Islam as a religion of revealed law given to inform every

[10] See, David E. Singh, 'Muhammad, The Prophet like Moses?' *Journal of Ecumenical Studies* 43:4 (2008).

action. On account of *shari'ah*, Islam has been able to evolve into a civilisation, which has created its own type of social order.

The basic duties of the Islamic faith are summed up in the 'five pillars' (*arkan al-Islam*). The first is the *shahadah*, the basic confession that Allah alone is worthy of worship and that Muhammad is the one supremely chosen to make known his requirements for human living. This declaration of faith (*iman*) is required for a convert to become a part of the Muslim community (the *ummah*). The second is salat, the obligation to pray to God five times a day, in the direction of Mecca. Each session of prayer is preceded by ablutions to signify ritual purity. The third is *zakat*, charitable giving. A Muslim family is expected to donate about 2.5% of its entire income to representatives of the state or the mosque as a tax. The money collected is used to share with those in need, to support Muslim mission (*da'wah*) and to defend the faith. The fourth is *sawm*, the observation of the fast from dawn to dusk during the month of Ramadan (the ninth month of the Islamic lunar calendar). It is a discipline through which physical desires are kept in check for the sake of inducing a more concentrated awareness of the need of God. The fifth is the *hajj*, the pilgrimage to Mecca that takes place during the first ten days of the twelfth month (*dhu al-hijja*). All Muslims who are physically and financially able to make the journey are required to make the *hajj* once in their life time.

Islam arose out of Muhammad's reforming zeal, following on the messages he was convinced came to him from Allah. He reacted strongly to polytheistic beliefs and the corrupt religion of his fellow tribes-people in Mecca. He was strongly critical of what he believed was the indifference shown by both Jews and Christians to the debased religion of the region. Islam, therefore, has always seen itself called to a strongly purifying mission against any form of idolatry, including the corruption of religion for financial or other forms of personal gain. It sees itself in terms of the definitive return to the long tradition of prophetic struggle against false worship. Muhammad's destruction of the 360 idols in the *kaaba* in Mecca is reminiscent of Elijah's contest with the prophets of Ba'al (1 Kings 18.16-40).

Muhammad's life was characterised by his struggle to see the message accepted and adopted in the whole of Arabia and made into a common basis for the communal existence of the different tribes. After the migration of Muhammad and his followers from Mecca to Medina (the *hijrah*) in 622 CE, the Muslim community, through a series of military exploits, became the rulers of the whole peninsular and Islam the guiding principle for society. From there it expanded north to Asia Minor, west along North Africa and East into the Indian sub-continent, central and south-east Asia, as far as China, Indonesia and the Philippines. The adherents of Islam form about one-sixth of the world's population.

The West

In broad terms, the West as a concept is roughly coextensive with European civilisation. However, in order to be more precise, it is necessary to look at a number of different aspects which today help to define loosely the boundaries of this notion. Geographically, the West encompasses the continent of Europe, although there may be some dispute as to whether this extends as far as the Ural Mountains to the East. However, the geographical extension of the West has not always coincided with that of Europe. Notably at the time of the 'cold-war' the West would have been restricted to those nations that stood opposed to the Soviet-bloc countries, namely the nations of Northern, Western and Southern Europe (and even here there were exceptions, as in the case of the former Yugoslavia).[11] Since the end of the communist regimes in Central and Eastern Europe, the 'West' may be said to have moved East politically, at least to encompass all those countries within the European Union (as well as Norway, Switzerland and nations likely to join the EU in the near future – Iceland and some of the Balkan states).

Clearly, the West has expanded geographically beyond the limits of Europe, incorporating those peoples who live in North America, Australasia, South Africa and parts of Central and South America whose origins lie in the European continent. So, another way of conceptualising the West is by speaking of all societies which identify with the cultural heritage that has marked the European populations. This heritage stretches back to the Greek civilisation and is marked by a number of highly significant events over the course of 2,500 years. Greek philosophy (Plato, Aristotle, the Stoics, Sceptics, Cynics and Epicureans) flourished in what has become known as the Hellenistic period and has strongly influenced European thought ever since. Bernard Williams' bon mot bears this out: 'the legacy of Greece to Western philosophy is Western philosophy'.[12] The Greeks also introduced the incipient idea of democracy, although without equating government by the people with universal suffrage. More important was the idea that rulers should be guided by virtue and subject to the rule of law.

The main heritage from the Roman Empire is the system of law known as the Corpus iuris civilis, based on the Theodosian Code and constituted by the emperor Justinian in 534 CE. It was at the beginning of the Roman Empire, that the Christian faith was born. Subsequently, this faith in its many forms has been the dominant force shaping the reality of the Western world. In time the Christian faith became seriously divided into three main traditions - Orthodoxy in the Eastern part of the continent, Roman Catholicism in the Central and

---

[11] Hence, the joke repeated in former Communist nations: Question, why is the sun so happy today? Answer, because it knows that by this evening it will be in the West!

[12] 'Philosophy' in M. I. Finley (ed), *The Legacy of Greece: A New Appraisal* (Oxford: Clarendon Press, 1981), 202.

Southern parts and Protestantism in the North and West. Despite these ruptures, Christianity has strongly influenced the moral value systems of the European peoples. It has also been at the forefront of pioneering education and medical services, social reform (as in the abolition of child labour and the slave trade) and the protection of the rights of individual conscience.

In the last two and a half centuries, parts of Europe have been deeply influenced by secularising forces. Under the influence of the so-called 'Enlightenment' many institutions, hitherto managed by Christian churches and organisations, have been turned over to the state and 'laicised'. Laws have been enacted, which have removed privileges accorded hitherto to one officially recognised church. In the West, religious beliefs, or a lack of them, are generally considered to be a matter of private choice. There is a tacit understanding that, as far as possible, they are to be kept out of the arena of public affairs.

So, Western nations now subscribe to the ideal of a plurality of beliefs and lifestyles. They also have signed up to contemporary conventions on human rights, which protect a number of individual freedoms, such as freedom of religion (including the liberty to change one's religion), association, speech and the press. The notion of rights also includes strong legislation against discriminatory practices, such as those based on differences of gender, race, religion, ethnic background, age and disability. So, the ideal of an absolute equality of all citizens is enshrined in national constitutions.

Another aspect of Western societies that has been strongly emphasised is the rule of law. By this is meant, among other things, the democratically accountable enactment of laws, the administration of law by bodies wholly independent of government influence and coercion, and free from possible financial corruption and other means of extortion, equal access to the law by all citizens, the presumed innocence of people accused of crime, until proved guilty, and proportionate sentencing.

Finally, the West is known for its championing of liberal democracy. Democracy is understood as implementing government 'of the people, by the people, for the people'. It generally takes the form of the delegation of elected politicians who represent designated constituencies. Governments, at national, regional and local levels, are obliged to seek the renewal of their mandate through formal elections on a regular basis (usually 4 or 5 years). Elections must be seen to be free (from any coercive pressure on individuals to vote in a particular way) and fair (in principle any citizen is eligible for election and no political party is given any advantage by the state over another).

The term the 'West' is, for a number of important reasons, also used in a pejorative sense. First, in the light of a tendency by Westerners to consider their societies more developed and progressive than any others, there is the accusation that they too quickly ignore the dark moments of their own history. Some of the greatest crimes against humanity have been committed in the twentieth century within the bounds of Europe: for example, the mass slaughter of military personnel in two major wars between European powers; the attempted extermination of minorities under the Nazis and, more recently, in the Balkans and of ideological enemies under Stalin.

Secondly, some Western nations have arrogated to themselves the right to conquer other nations, subdue them and seize their lands, capital and primary sources. Colonialism became a means of securing the domination of Western industry and financial power and the accumulation of wealth on a massively unequal scale. Subsequently, the metropolitan centres, because of their wealth and technological development, attracted people from the colonised nations, depriving the latter of some of their best human resources. Imperialism became a means whereby the Western powers maintained their spheres of influence and advanced their vested interests, especially during the ideological conflict with the Soviet Union and China. It also shows itself in the attempt to dictate who can and cannot acquire nuclear capability. Imperialism now takes the more subtle form of globalisation, in which Western business, financial institutions, trade arrangements and technological advances are all used to dominate and control world markets.

Thirdly, there is a general dislike of the overpowering imposition of Western popular culture through television, video games and the internet. This is seen often as indulging debased moral values (gratuitous violence and licentious sexual pursuits) that undermine healthy human relationships within and between social groups, families and individuals.

Fourthly, the West is seen as often adopting an attitude of superiority and condescension towards other civilisations, with a view to improving their moral, social and cultural traditions and institutions. This critique is depicted most forcefully by Edward Said in his study on Orientalism.[13] In this he condemned what he saw as essentialist, partisan and derogatory interpretations of Eastern cultures and peoples by scholars who saw little of value in their history or contribution to universal civilisation in comparison with that of the West.[14] He charged them with constructing an image of the East that arose, not from genuine historical and empirical research, but from a prior conviction that Eastern thought and ways of life were antithetical to and dangerous for the West. The self-image of the West is, thus, one of having achieved the highest possible form of social, political and economic success. This conviction then leads to the further assumption that all other parts of the globe need to catch up with the Western performance.[15]

---

[13] Edward W. Said, *Orientalism* (New York: Pantheon Books, 1978).

[14] In his book, *The House of Wisdom: How the Arabs transformed Western Civilization* (London: Bloomsbury, 2008), Jonathan Lyons shows, as the subtitle suggests, how much Islamic thought and learning contributed to medieval Europe.

[15] We will look more closely at these claims and counter-claims in chapters 3 and 4.

Christian Faith

As with Islam, it is relevant at this stage only to refer briefly to those beliefs and practices that are held in common by all the mainstream sections of the Christian church. This does not imply that alternative interpretations are unimportant. Rather, the approach starts from the premise that the greatest justice is done, when Christianity is construed according to its prevailing, established self-understanding. Christianity as a recognised, separate religion could be said to have originated at the time of the Jewish war against the Romans (66-73CE), when Christians definitively broke with the Jewish community by refusing to support the Jewish insurgence. Before that time, in the minds at least of the public in general, it remained a curious sect of the Hebrew religion.

However, in reality, some years before that event, it was already clearly espousing beliefs that set it on a collision course with Judaism. This reality may be illustrated from the events that occurred in Thessalonica, when Paul and his companion Silas preached in the synagogue there (Acts 17.1-9). The core of Paul's message was that the Old Testament scriptures spoke clearly of God's specially anointed servant (the) having to suffer to bear the sins of the people, and that having died he would be resurrected to new life (Acts 17.3). As Jesus of Nazareth died by crucifixion and also rose again, thus fulfilling the ancient prophecies about the Messiah, he should be identified as the Messiah whom God promised to send to his people at the right time (Acts 17.4). The controversy between the early Christians and the Jewish people centred on this way of interpreting the fulfillment of prophecy.

The preaching of the very first generation of Christians, as recorded in the Acts of the Apostles, bears out the difference of opinion between Jews and Christians about how to understand the meaning of the life and mission of Jesus. On the first Pentecost after Jesus death, Peter spoke to crowds in Jerusalem about the significance of the events that were taking place among them. His message emphasised the following points: (i) Jesus of Nazareth (probably born shortly before the death of Herod in 4 BCE) was shown to be God's special emissary to bring deliverance to his people by the deeds of power that he did among them (Acts 2.22); (ii) His death by crucifixion was not an accident, but happened according to God's plan and purpose (Acts 2.23); (iii) God raised Jesus from the dead, in order to demonstrate once and for all that Jesus was the means of salvation (Acts 2.24,38); (iv) The resurrection of Jesus is not just a nice theory or a comforting message about how hope can triumph over despair, but an event in history, whose factual credentials can stand up to rigorous examination (Acts 2.32); (v) This same Jesus, now exalted to the most intimate presence with God (his right hand), is the Lord (ruler) over everything created (Acts 2.36).

These major features of the significance of Jesus are reiterated in a number of other speeches given by the apostles soon after Jesus died and rose again in (probably) 30 CE. The meaning of the Jesus event is further elaborated to include his continuing healing power (Acts 3.16), the final restoration of all things to their God-given purpose and integrity (seriously damaged because of sin) (Acts 3.21), and the fact that he alone is God's means of salvation (Acts 4.12).

So, the first group of disciples, who had followed Jesus during his three-year ministry in Galilee and Judea, had come to believe that this man was indeed the Messiah, promised in the Hebrew Scriptures. Everything about him confirmed this impression: his preaching of the coming of God's righteous rule; his healing of the sick; his compassion for the excluded and despised people (tax-collectors, prostitutes, and others who failed to keep the rigorous demands of the law); his intolerance of religious hypocrisy; his demand for an inner transformation that included total reliability of character, purity in sexual relations, and a willingness to do only good to one's enemies (Mt. 5.27-45). Jesus gave many hints that he considered himself to be the Messiah. These were often in veiled form for fear that, since his understanding of the role of the Messiah differed markedly from the most prevalent views of the time, he would be (as he was) misconstrued.

The preaching of the first band of Jesus' followers brought an enormous division of opinion among the Jewish people, both in Judea and in the Diaspora. Many accepted the identification of Jesus with the Messiah and all that implied in terms of the nature of salvation. They were baptised in the name of Jesus and became members of this new, self-consciously distinct community. Others rejected the claims being made on behalf of Jesus. The problem for them was that they had identified the Messiah with a figure who would restore the good fortunes of Israel, so that once again it could become an independent nation, free to follow the law of the Lord and thus be a light to the nations. For them, the Messiah's task was to deliver God's special people from foreign domination and teach them how to walk again in holiness before God. Jesus had done neither of these things. Therefore, the claim that he was the Messiah had to be spurious.

The conflict between the Christian community and the synagogue focused, then, on three major disagreements. First, there was the interpretation of the significance of the Messiah's mission. To many Jews it was inconceivable that the Messiah, rather than delivering his people from the power of the Roman Empire, allowed himself to suffer the most shameful death possible at the hands of one of its governors.

Secondly, there was the understanding of God's ultimate purpose for the people he had called to be a special community of his possession (Ex. 19.6). After the incident of the conversion of the Roman centurion, Cornelius (Acts 10), the early Christians began to understand that the message of salvation in Jesus was for the whole world; there was to be no distinction on the basis of race, ethnic origin, social status or gender (Gal. 3.28; Col. 3.11). The new Jesus community was to be inclusive of every kind of human being. For the Jews, however, especially in the aftermath of the war against Rome, maintaining their national and ethnic identity was a top priority.

Thirdly, there was the realisation of how human beings could receive God's offer of salvation. For Jewish people this was based on the works of the law by which the covenant relationship with God could alone be sustained and renewed. For Christians it happened by believing in the efficacy of Christ's atonement for sins, being baptised as a sign of repentance, confessing Jesus as the only Lord and becoming part of God's new Messianic community.

After the fall of Jerusalem, the two communities went their own ways. The dispute about the meaning of Jesus was too great to be resolved. The rest, as they say, is history! The nascent church grew from being a persecuted, minority sect to becoming a powerful institution in the Roman Empire and the empires that succeeded it. Its history, like that of the ancient Hebrews, has known many periods of unfaithfulness and uncertainty. It has been rent asunder by as yet unresolved divisions, caused by both controversies over doctrine and conflicts over power and jurisdictions. However, its ability to renew itself is also notable. Without exception, every example of reform and revitalisation has been based on a desire to return to the pattern of early church life and the original preaching of the apostles as recorded in the pages of the New Testament. The apostolic preaching of the life, death, resurrection, ascension and coming again of Jesus remains the unrivalled authority for interpreting the nature of Christian faith in all ages and for all peoples.

Conclusion

The intention of this chapter has been to provide as accurate a guide as possible to the main terms that constitute the subject matter of this book, in order to avoid, as far as is achievable, the danger of talking at cross-purposes. As far as I am aware, the basic meaning of each of these is not particularly controversial. Others might have written the descriptions differently, perhaps emphasising additional points or explaining matters in other ways. Nevertheless, there should be a firm consensus that we are dealing here with broad categories that everyone can recognise to be as precise as is necessary for the purposes of this study.

Chapter 2

Huntington's Thesis under Review

Part I

Ostensibly, the year 1989 marked a turning-point in world history. Symbolised by the fall of the wall dividing the city of Berlin, Communist regimes throughout Central and Eastern Europe collapsed under the various forces clamouring for change. The process seemed to be complete in 1991, when the final bastion of the old system, located in Moscow, came to an end. The era of the cold war appeared to be over and a new epoch ushered in. In the long stand-off between East and West, the latter apparently had triumphed, not through force of arms, but through the success of its political and economic systems: political freedom prevailed over repression; the free-market over command economies.

The 'end of ideology' and the rise of religion

The euphoria, engendered by the site of fledgling democracies beginning to emerge in former totalitarian societies, had hardly subsided, when some analysts were predicting the arrival of another threat to the seemingly relentless imposition by the West of its ideas and objectives on the rest of the world. If the former clash of ideologies between communism and liberalism (inspired respectively by the titanic 19th century figures of Karl Marx and John Stuart Mill) now appeared to be obsolete, a new force was arriving on the world scene: cultural identity. Samuel Huntington in a highly significant study predicted that the universalising pretensions of Western civilisation would clash with local and regional cultures not prepared to be absorbed into the value systems and patterns of life predominant in the Western world. The rivalry of the superpowers was being replaced by the clash of civilisations.[1]

Huntington advanced the thesis, already declared dead by many Western secularists, that of all the elements that define civilisations, the most important is religion. There never has been a great civilisation that has not been empowered by a major religion.[2] Moreover, although all the most important

---

[1] Huntington, *The Clash of Civilisations*, 20-28.

[2] Huntington, *The Clash of Civilisations*, 42.

ideologies of recent times – liberalism, socialism, anarchism, corporatism, Marxism, communism, nationalism, fascism, social and Christian democracy – have been products of Western civilisation, the West has never itself generated a major religion. Religions have shown themselves to be much more resilient than ideologies. Just when many Western commentators thought that the struggle between religious and secular forces had been decisively won by the latter, the 'gods' are taking their revenge. On a world scale, ideologies are in decline; their place is being taken by resurgent religions.[3]

The new imperialism

What is happening, according to Huntington, is that perceptions of human development are changing across the world. The penetration of Western values, institutions and lifestyles into every corner of the globe is no longer being viewed as a benign process, but as a malignant growth. The non-West sees as peculiarly Western what the West sees as universal. What the West sees as a benevolent and beneficial global integration, for example the proliferation of a world-wide media operated by Western agencies, the non-West denounces as imperialism.[4]

Ever since the impingement of the West on the other continents of the world, from the time that some European nations – Spain, Portugal, France, England and Holland – took control of the seas, the non-West has been forced to come to terms with this alien force. Through many vicissitudes and in numerous, different ways, the non-West has had to respond to the compelling forces of modernisation. Some nations, like Japan, began by rejecting the encroachment of the West utterly and completely. Others sought to receive the material benefits of modernisation whilst rejecting the culturally destructive influences of Westernisation. Yet others (like Turkey under Kemal Ataturk), at least for a time, embraced both. Over time, all non-Western civilisations have adjusted in their own ways to the apparently insatiable Western will to conquer – territories, markets, space, ideas.[5]

The revitalisation of cultures

Now, however, says Huntington, the West is in decline.[6] Surprisingly, perhaps, he believes that Western domination reached its height in 1900. He has

[3] Huntington, *The Clash of Civilisations*, 53-54.
[4] Huntington, *The Clash of Civilisations*, 66.
[5] Huntington, *The Clash of Civilisations*, 72-78.
[6] This is, of course, not a new idea. Both Spengler and Toynbee, as mentioned in chapter 1 (see notes 5 and 6) had cogently advanced the thesis that all civilisations in the past,

measured this in terms of territorial possession, population and the ability to impose its own interpretation of human rights, liberalism and democracy on others. Certainly the processes of decolonisation that followed the Second World War were not envisaged in 1900, nor was the form they took planned for by the former colonial powers.

The rise of the Tiger economies in the East (Japan, Korea, China, Malaysia, Singapore and India) has redressed the commercial balance on the world's markets. They will become increasingly powerful, whilst the West's share of industrial output and wealth steadily dwindles. In recent years in India there has been a notable resurgence of Hinduism, in China of Confucianism, in Japan of forms of Buddhism, and in Russia a kind of pan-Slavism aligned to a renewed Orthodox Church has come to the fore. All these are connected with a revitalisation of cultures, once thought to have succumbed to the persistent onslaught of Western precepts and criteria, in their own terms.

The awakening of Islam

By far and a way the most potent form of resistance to the hegemony of the West in the contemporary world is Islam. As Huntington sees it, the fairly recent revival of an assertive Islamic religion is inextricably linked to a renewed search for identity in a rapidly changing and bewildering world. No longer is the Islamic world prepared to be defined in its history, culture, institutions and values by outside criteria. It is seeking to rediscover in a different kind of world the correspondence between the law of God and social and political life that has always marked its belief. It finds that many of the assumptions of Western, secular culture are incompatible with its understanding of the primary reality of God. Modernism is deemed to have failed, because it has cut itself off from the ultimate source of human life: it has separated itself from the living God. Therefore, some are calling the Islamic community worldwide not so much to 'modernise Islam but to islamise modernity'.[7]

Revival movements within Islam are a 'way of coping with the experience of chaos, the loss of identity, meaning and secure social structures, created by the rapid introduction of modern, social and political patterns, secularism, scientific culture and economic development'.[8] Communism is seen as the latest secular god to have failed and, in the absence of compelling new secular deities, we may now turn with relief and passion to the real thing. Religion takes over from ideology and religious nationalism from secular nationalism.

---

although they had risen to a position of apparently unassailable predominance, were doomed eventually to fade away.

[7] Huntington, *The Clash of Civilisations*, 96.

[8] Huntington, *The Clash of Civilisations*, 98.

The revival is not a wholesale rejection of modernity, but of the West and its secular, relativistic and degenerate culture. Huntington foresees the possibility that a purified Islam will play a role in the contemporary era comparable to that played by the Protestant ethic in the history of the West.[9]

The resurgence definitely encompasses a lot more than a negative reaction to the cultural, economic, political and military aggression of the West. It is built on the supposition that rightly understood and implemented, Islamic principles of jurisprudence and statecraft, underpinned by Islamic moral values, will create a more cohesive, participatory, satisfying and flourishing society than Western liberal secularism. So, in some ways, a renascent Islam is not advocating mere modifications in Western attitudes and social arrangements but a whole new social order, built from the ground up on firmly established Islamic principles. The old order has failed; the time has come to introduce a different social arrangement.

In this sense, as Huntington affirms, the resurgence is mainstream, not extremist. This is highly important. The desire to see a fully fledged society that is based on Islamic principles of jurisprudence, economic management, codes of social behaviour (such as female dress and abstinence from alcohol) and education arises from a general perception in many countries with an Islamic majority, and especially among the educated young, that Islam provides a superior way of organising human society. The resurgence addresses in particular issues of identity, meaning and morality.[10]

So, Huntington reckons that new alignments are being forged in the contemporary world. Those that used to be defined by ideology and relations between the super-powers (the USA and the Soviet Union) are giving way to those founded on historic cultures and civilisations. The central fault lines of potential conflict are now those that exist between civilisations.[11] Since the 1970s, springing in part from a reassessment of the global political scene, based to some extent on growing economic power, many Muslims have decided that the time has come to assert the independence of Muslim states from Western intrusion. The fall of the Shah in Iran, together with the accession to power of the mullahs (people with authority to interpret Islamic law), heralded a new assertion of Islamic consciousness.

After the First World War, the territories of the Ottoman Empire were divided among the Western powers. New nations (like Iraq) were created, formed according to a Western model of statehood. However, these states were alien to deeply-embedded Islamic traditions: 'The idea of the sovereign nation-

---

[9] Huntington, *The Clash of Civilisations*, 100-101.

[10] Huntington, *The Clash of Civilisations*, 109-121.

[11] Huntington, *The Clash of Civilisations*, 125-129.

state is incompatible with belief in the sovereignty of Allah and the primacy of the *ummah*'.[12]

Since that time, no Muslim country has had both sufficient power and cultural and religious legitimacy to assume the role and be accepted as a leader of Islam by other Islamic states. Huntington believes that the absence of an Islamic core state is a major contributor to the pervasive internal and external conflicts which characterise Islam: 'Consciousness without cohesion is a source of weakness to Islam and a source of threat to other civilisations'.[13]

The decline of the West

On the other side of the alleged clash of civilisations lies the West. Huntington believes that the West has always been 'missionary'. In recent times it has taken the form of spreading the 'good news' of liberal democracy, free markets, limited government, human rights, individualism and the rule of law. However, the central problem for the West has been its declining ability to promote for the future what it believes must be a universal culture for all peoples. Non-Westerners point to the many gaps between Western principles and action: for example, the hypocrisy and double-standards of promoting democracy in Islamic countries, but only if it does not lead to Islamic parties gaining power, or of enforcing the non-proliferation of nuclear weapons on Iran, but not Israel, or of agitating about human rights' abuses in China, but not in Saudi Arabia.[14]

One of the major problems the West has to face, according to Huntington, is the acceptance that it is a civilisation in decline. Echoing Fukuyama,[15] he says that 'history ends' at least once and occasionally more often in the history of every civilisation. As the global reach of civilisations emerges, people are often blinded by the 'mirage of immortality' (Toynbee), convinced that their form of society, whether the Roman, Christendom, Abbasid, Mughal or Ottoman, was the final form. He then asks the pertinent question: 'Is Western civilisation a new species, in a class by itself, different from all others that have ever existed?'[16]

His answer is no, because there are numerous indicators that Western civilisation is steadily decaying. Individual and collective consumption has taken priority over the creation of capabilities for future economic growth. Standards of morality are degenerating: seen, for example, in a marked increase

---

[12] Huntington, *The Clash of Civilisations*, 175.The *ummah* is the whole Muslim community that transcends artificially created geographical borders.

[13] Huntington, *The Clash of Civilisations*, 177.

[14] Huntington, *The Clash of Civilisations*, 184.

[15] Fukuyama, Francis, *The End of History and the Last Man* (London: Hamish Hamilton, 1992).

[16] Huntington, *The Clash of Civilisations*, 301.

in anti-social behaviour, the use of drugs, fraud and violence, and in a lessening of trust at all levels of society. Family life is crumbling through increased divorce, unstable partnerships, illegitimacy, teen-age pregnancy and single parent families. The work ethic is weakening and the cult of personal indulgence is rising. A commitment to learning and critical intellectual enquiry is lessening. Above all, Western civilisation is being undermined by the weakening, in many cases the outright rejection, of its central component, Christianity.[17]

The idea that Western culture embodies 'the highest, most enlightened, most liberal, most rational, most modern and most civilised thinking of humankind' is, says Huntington, false, immoral and dangerous. Western leaders have a responsibility not to try to shape other civilisations in the image of the West. Western intervention in the affairs of other civilisations is probably the single most dangerous source of instability and potential global conflict in a multi-civilisational world.[18]

A clash of civilisations is real

With regard to present and projected future relationships between Islam and the West, Huntington quotes three expert opinions:

> This development (the contest between Islam and the West) is partly due to secular versus religious values, partly to do with the historical reality between Christendom and Islam, partly to do with jealousy of Western power, partly to do with resentments over the Western domination of postcolonial political structuring of the Middle East, and partly to do with the bitterness and humiliation of the invidious comparison between the accomplishments of Islamic and Western civilisation in the last two centuries.[19]

> There is no less than a clash of civilisations, that is perhaps irrational but surely the historical reaction of an ancient rival against our Judeo-Christian heritage, our secular present, and the worldwide expansion of both.[20]

> There are unmistakeable signs of a growing clash between the Judeo-Christian ethic and the Islamic revival movement, which is now stretching from the Atlantic in the West to China in the East.[21]

---

[17] Huntington, *The Clash of Civilisations*, 303-305.

[18] Though prescient of the future, one has to remember that this analysis was written a few years before the West's intrusions into Iran and Afghanistan.

[19] Barry Buzan, 'New Patterns of Global Security in the Twenty-First Century', *International Affairs* 67 (July 1991), 448-449.

[20] Bernard Lewis, 'The Roots of Muslim Rage', *Atlantic Monthly*, 266 (September 1990), 60.

Huntington adds his own comment:

> The underlying problem for the West is not Islamic fundamentalism. It is Islam, a different civilization whose people are convinced of the superiority of their culture and are obsessed with the inferiority of their power.[22]

Huntington finishes his whole treatise, of which the above summary is only a small sample, on a deeply pessimistic note. He says that law and order, which is the first prerequisite of civilisations, seems, on a world-wide basis, to be yielding to barbarism, generating the image of new, global Dark Ages possibly descending on humanity.

Part II

Problems with the thesis

In this second part of our analysis of Huntington's thesis, we turn to some of the many reactions that it has provoked. As can be imagined, with a thesis as controversial as Huntington's, commentators have responded in every way imaginable. The furore that his study has evoked demonstrates, at the least, the significance of the subject.

Abdolkarin Soroush points out that 'The term civilization is a construct of the historians, Moslems, for example, were never aware that they were building or had built a 'civilization' until the last century'.[23]

Fouad Ajami reckons that the notion of civilisations has been created by the West: 'Huntington found his civilisations whole and intact, watertight under an eternal sky'.[24]

The idea of civilisations is promoted at a time when the hegemony of the Western world is being seriously challenged and its 'civilisation' is in decline. It enables the West to draw boundaries, demarcate a series of values, and thus to define itself in opposition to other major players on the world scene (also described as civilisations). However, Ajami believes that the concept of an Islamic civilisation is greatly exaggerated: 'Islamism is less a sign of

---

[21] Mohammed Sid Ahmed, 'Cybernetic Colonialism and the Moral Search', *New Perspectives Quarterly*, 11 (Spring 1994), 19.

[22] Huntington, *The Clash of Civilisations*, 217.

[23] Mahmoud Sadri and Ahmad Sadri, *Reason, Freedom and Democracy in Islam: The Essential Writings of Abdolkarin Soroush* (Oxford: OUP, 2000), 24.

[24] 'The Summoning' in *The Clash of Civilizations? The Debate* (New York: W.W. Norton, 1996), 26.

resurgence as of panic, bewilderment and guilt that the border with the 'other' has been crossed'.[25]

In other words, there is a genuine (and understandable) fear within Islamic communities that the purity of faith is under threat of contamination by being mixed with the ideals and ideology of modernity, transmitted worldwide by Western cultural artefacts. However, he chides Huntington for failing to see just how much the Western way of life attracts as well as repels. He believes that nation states are still key players in terms of international relations and that economic factors are much more likely to shape political engagement than vague concepts like civilisations: 'States will consort with any civilisation, however alien, as long as the price is right and the goods are ready'.[26]

He asserts that states control civilisations, seeing brotherhood, faith and kin as important only when in their interests to do so.[27]

Kishore Mahbubani continues to explore the argument that the putative clash of civilisations is the result of a certain degree of panic on the part of the West. He maintains that Huntington's thesis is bound to resonate in the West, where there is a deep sense of unease about the future. In many ways, the notion of a clash is a self-fulfilling prophecy, because it stirs up a certain paranoia that results in the West almost deliberately pursuing policies designed to aggravate the Islamic world.[28] The events that have happened since Huntington's treatise was published certainly seem to bear out Mahbubani's claim. The invasion of Iraq and the subsequent political meddling in the internal affairs of a sovereign state by the euphemistically named 'coalition of the willing' have been deeply problematic and highly resented. Earlier, in the events surrounding the abdication of the Shah of Iran, the Iran-Iraq war and the struggle of the Mujahidin to remove the Russian army from Afghanistan, Western intrusion has been both manifest and inept.

Mahbubani wonders why, if civilisations have been around for centuries, they are only posing a challenge now. He surmises that the perceived threat springs from the need to deal with the image of itself that the West sees in the mirror and shrinks from. He believes that the West may have developed structural weaknesses in its core value systems and institutions: for example, the work-ethic is eroding, and people are demanding too high wages in spite of uncompetitiveness, low savings and investments.[29]

---

[25] 'The Summoning', 28.
[26] 'The Summoning', 31.
[27] 'The Summoning', 34.
[28] 'The Dangers of Decadence: What the Rest can teach the West' in *The Clash of Civilizations?* 37.
[29] 'The Dangers of Decadence', 39-40. Although written a dozen years before the economic crisis that came upon a largely unsuspecting world in 2008, his perception

Albert Weeks believes that Huntington, in attempting to construct another 'grand theory', is too dependent on the work of historians like Spengler and Toynbee. Resurrecting a controversy from the past may be symptomatic of the failure of globalism specifically to establish a genuinely 'new world order'. He does not think that the fault lines exist between large entities like civilisations but occur as borders that encompass every nation-state, thus chopping the alleged civilisations into small pieces. In our times, the major phenomenon on the international scene is the heterogeneity of the state, not supranational aggregations.[30]

He might have added, from another point of view, that any truth that there may be in the clash of civilisations thesis is not so much a failure of globalism as its direct result. The coming of globalism in economic terms has accentuated the growing gap between affluent populations and poverty–stricken ones. Using euphemistic terms like 'emerging economies' and 'developing nations' may have a certain ideological force, but hardly hides a reality only too visible on the ground. The coming of globalism in terms of communication networks, whilst bringing an enormous increase in available information, also helps to emphasize differences. Globalism in both senses may, then, be a factor in increasing tensions and creating conflicts.

Amartya Sen is convinced that 'there are two distinct difficulties with the theory of civilizational clash'.[31] 'The first relates to the viability and significance of classifying people according to the civilizations to which they allegedly 'belong'. Sen argues that there are many ways in which people can be classified. There is no justification for privileging the notion of civilisation over say nationality, class, occupation, language or political outlook. Seeing people primarily in terms of belonging to a given civilisation with its accompanying religious identification is unreal and dangerous:

> In partitioning the world into to those belonging to 'the Islamic world', 'the Hindu world', 'the Buddhist world', the divisive power of classificatory priority is implicitly used to place people firmly inside a unique set of rigid boxes.[32]

He calls this a reductionist view of world populations and attacks it as

> A pervasively intrusive phenomenon in social analysis, stifling other – richer - ways of seeing people. It lays the foundations for misunderstanding nearly

---

appears to be born out by that train of events. In fact, the situation has proved to be far more serious than he might have imagined.

[30] 'Do Civilizations Hold? in *The Clash of Civilizations?* 53-54.

[31] Sen, *Identity and Violence: The Illusion of Destiny* (London: Penguin Books, 2007), 40.

[32] Sen, *Identity and Violence*, 11.

> everyone in the world, even before going on to the drumbeats of a civilizational clash.[33]

The second problem that Sen finds with the thesis is

> The crudeness with which the world civilizations are characterized, taking them to be more homogeneous and far more insular than tends to emerge from empirical analyses of the past and the present.[34]

Quite simply, the concept of civilisation gives the impression of a largely uniform set of factors that describe and determine similar ways of believing and behaving that cross national or regional boundaries; whilst the reality on the ground points to considerable diversity: 'The civilizational approach has tended to suffer also from ignoring the diversities within each identified civilization'.[35]

What appears, perhaps, to be a monolithic system, on closer scrutiny shows considerable variance. Sen illustrates this from the notion that India is a Hindu civilisation, showing in actual fact just how diverse are the cultures and religions of the sub-continent, often (as in the case of Indian classical music or Bollywood) crossing the religious boundaries. Later, he discusses the case of Islam. Within the categorisation, there are numerous variations. Islam covers a multitude of different ways of interpreting the history of Muslim communities and different understandings of what Muslims should adhere to in the contemporary world:

> The idea of ijtehad, or religious interpretation, allows considerable latitude within Islam itself,...an individual Muslim has much freedom to determine what other values and priorities he or she would choose without compromising a basic Islamic faith.[36]

The very fact that some Muslims would endorse Sen's statement here, whilst others would disagree, precisely confirms what he is saying.

Sen's quarrel with Huntington's thesis has a sharp pragmatic edge to it. The idea of a clash of civilisations can easily lead to identity politics, which in turn (as has been the case in India, for example) result in sectarian passions and violence. This follows from identifying Islam per se with certain political ideals, and then debating whether these political ideals belong to the essence of Islam or represent some kind of cultural accretion. This, Sen believes, has led to the tragic consequence of identifying acts of terror with one particular

[33] Sen, *Identity and Violence,* 42.
[34] Sen, *Identity and Violence*, 45.
[35] Sen, *Identity and Violence,* 46.
[36] Sen, *Identity and Violence*, 65

interpretation of Muslim identity. Abdolkarim Soroush puts the same matter in a different way:

> I fear that Moslems, in their confrontation with Western civilization, wish to turn to Islam as an identity...I recently reviewed Mr. Huntington's thesis and noticed that he has invoked a number of civilizations, including Islamic civilization. His notion of 'a crisis of identity' in the Islamic world made me even more confident of the veracity of my own judgment. I think one of the greatest theoretical plagues of the Islamic world, in general, is that people are gradually coming to understand Islam as an identity rather than a truth. It is true that Moslems did have an Islamic identity and civilization, but they have not adopted Islam for the sake of identity or civilization...So, I believe that the Islam of identity should yield to the Islam of truth. The latter can coexist with other truths; the former, however, is by its very nature, belligerent and bellicose. [37]

The point at issue, which may have far-reaching repercussions in contemporary geo-politics, is that the core beliefs and practices of Muslims are distinct from specific social and political commitments. About the former, there may be little room for disagreement; about the latter, there is much latitude of interpretation.

Sen makes one other (common-sense) remark about this whole controversy: in spite of the apparently great dissimilarities between the cultures of the world, underneath, especially in personal contact, 'people are much the same the world over'. In a world, where people seek to manage the confusion of diversity by labelling, classifying and shoving vast swathes of people into carefully catalogued boxes, it is refreshing to discover how much people of different races, religions and cultures have in common.

The thesis defended

It can be seen from this brief survey that there are strong arguments pitched against Huntington's main idea. Nevertheless, he remained convinced that the thesis stood up against all its critics. He continued to believe that the paradigm of inter-civilisational conflict was the best way of explaining the turn that world politics has taken after the end of the ideological conflict between communist and non-communist regimes. He cites the issues of human rights and multiculturalism as two of the main examples of the shift in perspectives between different peoples the world over. The question of rights is culturally determined and hotly disputed in the various fora of the United Nations. He might have added that the acutely divergent views often follow a pattern which separates peoples' outlook according to whether their cultures are guilt-oriented

[37] Mahmoud Sadri and Ahmad Sadri, *Reason, Freedom and Democracy*, 24 (emphasis added).

or shame-oriented. The particular alignment has a lot to do with the religious beliefs and values that underpin cultural conventions. In other words, the most basic motivating force for human life resides in the fundamental reference-point for life. In the vast majority of human societies this is tied up with a basic religious world-view:

> What ultimately counts for people is not political ideology or economic interest. Faith and family, blood and belief, are what people identify with and what they will fight and die for.[38]

Huntington's thesis has some sympathisers among the Muslim community. Mohammed Arkoun, for example, states that

> S. Huntington is right in trying to identify competing logospheres,[39] which might develop violent clashes if they remain indifferent, if not openly hostile, to any intellectual or cultural attempt to cross the ideological frontiers and create historical opportunities for sharing transnational, multicultural solidarities.[40]

Tariq Ramadan says that

> Huntington's thesis on the 'clash of civilizations' has been much criticized, and progressive, optimistic thinkers en masse have rejected this prophecy of doom. My many visits to the Muslim world and to European and American societies, especially after shocks like that of 11 September 2001, indicate that if the clash is not a reality, the ingredients that could lead to it are very present in current mentalities: on both sides, the lack of knowledge of the other (and of self), the acceptance of simplistic and absolute caricatures and final judgements, not to mention conflicting political and geostrategic interests, are objective features that could lead to the breakdown.[41]

Conclusion

In fairness to Huntington, much more has been made of the first part of the title of his book than the second. If the first part is an attempt at a diagnosis, it is done with the purpose of providing the necessary background for attempting to launch the positive policies needed in order for there to be 'a new world order'. Huntington points out the absolute requirement for separate communities with divergent core beliefs, different values and varying histories to find ways of living together, which preclude the resort to offense, hostility and violence.

---

[38] Samuel P. Huntington, 'If not Civilizations, What?' in *The Clash of Civilizations?*, 67.

[39] By this term Arkoun seems to mean self-interpretations.

[40] *Islam: To Reform or to Subvert?* (London: Saqi Books, 2006), 36.

[41] *Western Muslims and the Future of Islam* (Oxford: OUP, 2004), 226.

The thesis about a 'clash of civilisations' is bound to be controversial. On both sides of the debate there are those who wish to accentuate the profound, and possibly irreconcilable, differences between the cultural perspectives of Western societies and other societies with different historical trajectories. They will be inclined to endorse the thesis that the core secular beliefs of Western nations,[42] increasingly enshrined in laws that actually discriminate against religious communities, are severely at odds with the core beliefs of other societies. There are others who for reasons of peaceful co-existence or interreligious dialogue, or because they have come to appreciate the enriching nature of diverse ways of looking at life, see the thesis, at best, as profoundly exaggerated, and, at worst, as distorted and prejudiced.

In actual fact, both parties may be correct to a certain degree. Because the thesis is bound to be all-encompassing, it is quite possible to find convincing evidence on either side and then to ignore the contrary signs. The thesis has aroused enormous interest, not least because of the stances that have been taken and the events that have transpired since September 2001. This would suggest that the thesis cannot be ignored; it may be a case of both smoke and fire. Perhaps, the word 'clash' seems overstated to some people; 'contention' or 'contest' might be more nuanced ways of describing distinctions and contrasts. Perhaps, the 'clash' is more apparent than real, more potential than actual. Nevertheless, it would be foolish to adopt the stance of the ostrich. There is sufficient evidence to indicate that what Huntington describes as fault-lines between profoundly different ways of believing and acting in the contemporary world do exist. These are held with sufficient conviction that they can and, in limited cases, do explode into serious conflict and violence. Therefore, the attempt of this study to explore the origins of the two world faiths that have shaped the main protagonists involved in the alleged 'clash', and draw out some tentative judgements regarding current cultural, political and social engagements, does have a rationale. It merits consideration as one way of understanding better where and why the fault-lines may continue to exist.

It is still an open question whether the three entities with which this study is concerned - Muslim peoples, the West as an ideological creation and Christian communities - have the capacity and resources to live together in relative goodwill and co-operation, or whether there is something fundamental in their self-understanding which inclines them to discord and even confrontation. In the next chapter, we will examine some of the points of tension that have led to what one might call a stand-off between the parties.

[42] Magisterially portrayed in Charles Taylor, *A Secular Age*.

Chapter 3

Muslims in Dispute with the West

Huntington maintains that the expansion of the West, begun in the late 15th century, has come to an end, to be replaced by a new 'revolt against the West'.[1] Other parts of the world are gradually exerting their own autonomy: they are reinterpreting their place in the global arena. In particular, the elements of political, social and moral life that the West sees as having universal validity (for example, human rights, free markets, secular society and limited government), and therefore being an integral part of everyone else's future, other nations identify as Western.

Whereas the Western world at one time controlled much of the world's economic and military resources - technology, banking, hard currency, markets, weaponry, sea-lanes, space, and much more -[2] its share is now declining at a steady rate. Its ability to superintend the affairs of other nations, if not by economic means, then by military intervention is seriously diminished. The failure in 2002 of the USA and Great Britain to persuade the Security Council of the United Nations to authorise military intervention in Iraq is symptomatic of the resistance of nations, including some that are normally allies, to the dominating influence of the West. Within this general picture of a growing opposition to the so-called Pax Americana, substantial sectors within Islam, understood as a self-consciously non-secular approach to political and social life in all its phases, has begun to reassert its claim to offer a comprehensive alternative to the liberal, secular, pluralist ideal of Western societies.

The background to the alleged present conflict is constituted both by the ascendency of the European nations in terms of territorial conquest, control of international trade and dominance of international institutions, since the middle of the 18th century and by the simultaneous weakening of the once proud and powerful Islamic caliphate.[3] The former in particular has given rise to a whole

---

[1] Huntington, *The Clash of Civilizations*, 53.

[2] Huntington, *The Clash of Civilizations*, 81-82.

[3] See, for example, Ibrahim M. Abu-Rabi, 'Contemporary Islamic Thought: One or Many?' in Ibrahim M. Abu-Rabi (ed), *The Blackwell Companion to Contemporary Islamic Thought*, 15-17.

raft of grievances on the part of the Muslims world-wide,[4] of which this chapter will investigate what are probably the four most substantial.

The West's Alliance with Revisionist Islamic States

The seeds that ended colonial rule after the Second World War were sown in the Atlantic Charter of 1941, in which Roosevelt and Churchill declared, among other things, that 'We respect the right of all peoples to choose the form of government under which they will live'.

Although this sentiment was originally intended to refer to those countries ruled at that time by the Axis powers, Roosevelt insisted that political self-determination included the colonies still under the administration of Britain, France, Belgium and Holland. Thus, in the immediate aftermath of the war, beginning with the Indian sub-continent, nations gradually acquired independence from the metropolitan powers. Amongst the first tranche were Pakistan and Indonesia, two nations with an overwhelmingly Muslim population. The former colonial powers negotiated the establishment of constitutions that would follow Western democratic principles. They also sought to maintain their influence by means of fostering regimes sympathetic to their interests.

The same had happened earlier in the Middle East: new states were created after the First World War out of the collapsed Turkish caliphate: Iran, Iraq, Jordan, Saudi Arabia and Egypt. It was hoped that each new nation would remain friendly to the West, indeed in a sense under its patronage and within its sphere of influence. The cause celebre was Iran during the last years of the Shah, ending in 1979 with his eventual overthrow by revolutionary forces loyal to the Ayatollah Khomeini. The newly independent nations with a Muslim majority had to decide by which ideological tenets they were going to govern themselves: according to the principles of liberal democracy or by the historical tradition of *shari'ah.*

Ever since that time, and right up to the present, many Islamic countries have witnessed an internal struggle between those advocating pro-Western policies and those who wish to see the creation of some kind of Islamic Republic, independent in its internal affairs of any Western influence. The latter believe that Islam, as a complete socio-religious way of life, cannot accommodate the Western secular ideal of a separation of spheres of influence between the public-political and the private-religious. There is a doctrinal opposition between liberal, democratic values based ultimately on the notion of a natural law somehow embedded in 'the inherent dignity and...equal and

---

[4] See also the list suggested by Peter G. Riddell and Peter Cotterell, *Islam in Context: Past, Present and Future* (Grand Rapids: Baker Academic, 2003), 152-162.

inalienable rights of all members of the human family',[5] and self-evident to all right-thinking people, and belief in a divine law that is not subject to the will of the majority through some kind of social contract.

This has led to a continuing debate within the Muslim community about the compatibility between Islam and democratic ideals.[6] To this we will return later. Suffice it to say, at this juncture, that although there may be an underlying tension between Islamic traditionalists[7] and the modernistic tradition of the West, this is not the most immediate reason for Islamic contention with the West. This lies, rather, in the overt support that Western nations (particularly the USA) give to regimes that, in fact, are neither democratic nor properly Islamic. In other words, the West stands accused of bolstering governments that are corrupt, that oppress their people, violate elementary human rights, and do not allow for the democratic will of the majority to stand (as on various occasions in Algeria, Pakistan and Indonesia). In this way, the West stands indicted of gross hypocrisy by adopting a foreign policy that, whilst it serves its supposed strategic interests, denies its much vaunted moral principles.

The two most cited examples are Saudi-Arabia and Iraq. In the former case, one of the main causes of conflict lies in the permission given by the ruling House of Saud for the USA to maintain troops on Saudi soil. In the eyes of many, this is tantamount to a kind of pollution, in that the USA is treated as a Christian nation and, therefore, its troops belong to the category of infidel (the realm of *jahillyyah* –unbelief). It has to be remembered that Saudi-Arabia is guardian of the most holy shrine in Islam, the *kaaba* located in Mecca. Moreover, the ruling powers in the nation are condemned as maintaining an autocratic and feudal regime, in part by means of an intelligence service trained in the West. The US policy towards Saudi Arabia convinced Osama bin Laden that the survival of Islam was in jeopardy.[8]

In the case of Iraq, the West has notoriously meddled in its internal affairs for many years. Following the Iranian revolution in 1979, a number of Western nations directed their foreign policy to supporting the supposedly socialist and 'secular' regime of Saddam Hussein as a kind of counter-weight to the radical Islamic forces unleashed in the neighbouring state. In spite of Saddam Hussein's ethnic cleansing policy against the Kurds in the north of the country

---

[5] 'Preamble' to the *Universal Declaration of Human Rights* (emphasis added).

[6] See, for example, Michael Nazir Ali, *Conviction and Conflict: Islam, Christianity and World Order* (London: Continuum, 2006), 132-134.

[7] This description is used in a neutral, descriptive sense to identify one movement within contemporary Islam that has as its main goal to turn Islamic societies towards the arrangements pioneered in the early years of the emergent Islamic state, namely the rule of Muhammad in Medina and that of the early caliphs. It is not intended as a value-judgement between so-called 'conservatives' and 'progressives.'

[8] Phil Rees, *Dining with Terrorists: Meetings with the World's Most Wanted Militants* (Basingstoke: Pan Books, 2006), 270.

and persecution of the Shi'ite majority (both considered sympathetic to the Iranian cause), his regime was supplied with plenty of weapons to prosecute the war against Iran during the 1980s. This was part of the US policy of dual containment against Iran and Iraq, both considered volatile nations in an oil-rich area of the world.

The war ended in a stalemate in 1988. In 1990, Saddam Hussein invaded Kuwait, with a view to using its oil wealth to restore his own ailing economy. The subsequent invasion of Iraq by Western armed forces in 1991 and again in 2003 – the first under a UN mandate, the second in spite of its opposition – helped to radicalise further certain revolutionary Islamic groups. Meanwhile, the armed overthrow of the Taliban regime in Afghanistan by a coalition of Afghan opposition forces backed by heavy strategic support from the US air force in October 2001 further alienated large sections of the Islamic world. Under the pretence that this was part of a global 'war on terror', NATO forces became heavily involved, together with a reconstituted Afghan army, in seeking to contain the subsequent Taliban insurgency, especially in the south of the country.

Western military and political intervention in Muslim nations has caused alarm.

Apparently, with or without UN authorisation, the so-called 'coalition of the willing' has treated territorial integrity with contempt, justified its pursuit of a highly dubious 'war' against shadowy organisations with loose networks in different parts of the globe, and defied the opposition of most of its own citizens to these policies. Although the ideology and actions of the Al Qaeda network and other militant groups, in using Islam as a justification for a campaign of hate and the indiscriminate killing of defenceless civilians, are abhorrent, the notion that it constitutes a well-defined enemy against whom a war is appropriate is ludicrous. Other terrorist groups, with a variety of ideological motives, have appeared and disappeared in various parts of the world over the last half century. They have rightly been treated as criminals, within the respective territories were they have operated, rather than as enemy combatants. Advocating a war against terrorism has proved to be immensely counter-productive. The means used to prosecute such a 'war', detention without trial, torture (euphemistically called 'special rendition') and the unauthorised invasion of sovereign territory (as in NE Pakistan) do not even conform to the normal, universally agreed conventions on war. The coalition has failed miserably to win the hearts and minds of those Muslims, living in Iraq, Iran and Afghanistan, who may actually admire certain aspects of Western social organisation:

> Fanaticism and obscurantism are not healed by being merely deplored or rebuked. The anxieties they shelter have to be patiently allayed. The factors that induce them need to be resolved.[9]

The State of Israel and the Question of Palestine

There is, perhaps, no other issue so contentious in relationships between Islam and the West than the present situation of hostility and apparently irreconcilable standpoints evident in the Israeli-Palestinian conflict. Andrew Rippin warns that 'the insult that Israel represents to the Muslim world cannot be underestimated'.[10] From an Arab perspective, the nation of Israel was created on the basis of a double fiction: that the Jews represent 'a people without a land' and that Palestine constituted 'a land without a people'.[11]

Although it is undoubtedly true that the Jews are a people in the sense of forming a distinct ethnic and religious group, it does not follow that they thereby qualify for the right to govern themselves in their own territory. Such a right could not be accorded to every distinct ethnic group without causing an unsustainable fragmentation of the world. It is also dubious in the extreme that this particular people, although once they inhabited a parcel of land at the Eastern end of the Mediterranean, have any abiding claim upon it after two thousand years. If such a privilege could be established, it would mean that all migrating peoples would have the right to return to the lands they originally left.

Palestine was hardly an uninhabited land at the end of the 19th century. In a study of the demographic reality of the period,[12] Sergio DellaPergola estimates that the population of Palestine west of the River Jordan was approximately 530,000 in 1890 and 690,000 in 1914. According to Ottoman statistics, studied by Justin McCarthy,[13] the population of Palestine in the early 19th century was 350,000, in 1860 it was 411,000 and in 1900 about 600,000 of which 94% were Arabs. In 1914 Palestine had a population of 657,000 Muslim Arabs, 81,000 Christian Arabs, and 59,000 Jews.[14] In 1920, the League of Nations' Interim

---

[9] Kenneth Cragg, *The Qur'an and the West: Some Minding Between* (London: Melisende, 2005), 9.

[10] *Muslims: Their Religious Beliefs and Practices* (London: Routledge, 2001), 177.

[11] The phrase, which may have been incorrectly ascribed to Zionist propaganda, was first used in the mid-19th century by Christian 'restorationists' (i.e. those who believed that a return of Jewish people to the land of Israel would be a fulfilment of prophecy). Whatever its origin and early use, the phrase sums up a strong sense of Palestinian and Arab grievance. On the history of the phrase, see, Diana Muir, 'A Land without a People for a People without a Land', *Middle East Quarterly*, Spring 2008, 55-62.

[12] 'Demography in Israel/Palestine: Trends, Prospects and Policy Implications', 2001, 5.

[13] *The Population of Palestine* (New York: Columbia University Press, 1990).

[14] McCarthy, *The Population*, 26.

Report on the Civil Administration of Palestine stated that there were 700,000 people living in Palestine:

> Of these 235,000 live in the larger towns, 465,000 in the smaller towns and villages. Four-fifths of the whole population are Moslems. A small proportion of these are Bedouin Arabs; the remainder, although they speak Arabic and are termed Arabs, are largely of mixed race. Some 77,000 of the population are Christians, in large majority belonging to the Orthodox Church, and speaking Arabic. The minority are members of the Latin or of the Uniate Greek Catholic Church, or--a small number--are Protestants. The Jewish element of the population numbers 76,000. Almost all have entered Palestine during the last 40 years. Prior to 1850 there were in the country only a handful of Jews. In the following 30 years a few hundreds came to Palestine. Most of them were animated by religious motives; they came to pray and to die in the Holy Land, and to be buried in its soil. After the persecutions in Russia forty years ago, the movement of the Jews to Palestine assumed larger proportions.

Even allowing for some migration into the area designated Palestine, after the first wave of new Jewish settlers arrived, a much disputed supposition, these numbers hardly add up to a land without a people.

Some will argue that mere inhabitants do not constitute a people, and therefore there was no self-consciously united community with an established sense of common origins and destiny. However, one has to remember that this territory was under the governance of the Ottoman Empire, a regime that would not have allowed any ethnic political awareness to have manifested itself. There was, therefore, no immediate historical cause to stimulate such a perception. It was tragically ironic that first the arrival of Jewish settlers and, secondly, the creation of the State of Israel provided just such a stimulus.

Another argument that could have been used to justify the assertion that there were no people in the land might have borrowed from the historical occasion of the arrival of the 17th century pilgrims in New England. On learning from the indigenous peoples themselves that no-one owned the land, on the grounds that in a tribal society the land belonged to everyone, they thought they had a right therefore to take it for themselves. This justification was further strengthened by a curious and capricious theological argument put forward by the philosopher, John Locke. According to him,

> The Indian had a right to venison and to the uncultivated fruits of the land, (but) the soil itself, the very land, belonged not to the Indians, who because they were uncivilised and lacking in industry had failed to cultivate it, but to those who through their labour had tilled and enclosed a portion of the land for agricultural production. Locke's justification for this view was theological. He argues that although God had given 'the world in common to all Mankind', God also commanded man to work the land and it was only those who 'in Obedience to this Command of God, subdued, tilled and sowed any part of it' who had a right therefore to annex it to their own persons as their own property, and to hold title

> upon it…. In this way Locke took the biblical injunction in Genesis 1.28 to 'subdue the earth' as the basis for the colonial claim to dominion over the particular portion of the earth that is America, and the supplanting thereby of the native inhabitants' claim to this same portion…Land held in common, as by the native Americans, is unproductive valueless land and cannot rightly be said to belong to anyone.[15]

Certainly the original advocates of a separate homeland for the Jewish people argued that Palestine was inhabited only by nomadic tribespeople; there was no settled agricultural or urban community seeking to create wealth out of the natural resources and thereby to develop an economy and advance the welfare of the people.

In spite of the creation of a new state, with the historically evocative and highly provocative name of Israel, Palestinians in the majority have come to accept that it would be possible for two separate states to live side by side in peace. However, a minority on both sides has done all it could to disrupt such a prospect. Jewish extremists have anachronistically appealed to certain Bible verses to press the case for a 'greater Israel', i.e. one that at least absorbs all the land from the coast to the Jordan. In pursuit of this claim they have built numerous settlements on land designated as Palestinian territory, with a view to establishing a situation difficult to reverse. Palestinian extremists continue to withhold any recognition of the de facto existence of a new nation and some are still vowed to destroy it, in order to replace it with an Islamic state. There is, therefore, a tremendous sense of injustice, on the part of Arabs in particular, at the creation of a separate state for Jewish people. Some believe that Zionism is an assault on the territorial integrity of the Muslim, Arab people.

Whatever the gross mistakes made in the past in dividing up this piece of land between Jews and Palestinian Arabs, and whatever the complexities of working out a solution acceptable to the majority on both sides,

> We can hardly escape the fact that, in the eyes of most Muslims all over the world, Israel today is closely associated with the West and totally identified with the US, and that we are dealing here with one of the most important and the most bitter of all the complaints that Muslims direct towards the West.[16]

Much of the anger is directed against the consistent support given by the USA to Israel in defying successive UN Security Council resolutions,

---

[15] Michael Northcott, *An Angel Directs the Storm: Apocalyptic Religion and American Empire* (London: SCM Press, 2007), 48.

[16] Colin Chapman, 'Israel as a Focus for the Anger of Muslims against the West' in Ron Geaves , Theodore Gabriel, Yvonne Haddad and Jane Idleman Smith (eds), *Islam and the West Post 9/11* (Aldershot: Ashgate Publishing, 2004), 195.

concerning the occupation of Palestinian territory.[17] This is in contrast to the hypocrisy of the USA in enforcing UN resolutions against Iraq by force, or even invading Iraq without the sanction of the Security Council. The refusal of the USA to bring sufficient pressure to bear on Israel to exchange territory for security through the creation of a viable Palestinian state is seen by some as a Zionist plot to keep Arabs divided and weak.

The Threat of Secularism

There is a general fear abroad among Islamic communities that the West is trying to undermine Islamic culture by asserting such Western values and beliefs as individual freedoms, human rights, the privatisation of faith, a liberalisation of moral practices and the gratutious critique of Muslim sacred symbols, such as the Qur'an (in the case of Salman Rushdie's The Satanic Verses), Muhammad (in the incident of the Danish cartoons) and even Jesus (in the instance of Scorcesi's film, The Last Temptation of Christ). If secularism can be best defined as a view of life which denies that there is any reality beyond the material world and which seeks to reduce and weaken the influence of religion on public life,[18] it will surely conflict head on with a belief system that affirms the reality of God in every detail of human existence.

Charles Taylor understands that the coming of modern secularity

> ...has been coterminous with the rise of a society in which for the first time in history a purely self-sufficient humanism came to be a widely available option. I mean by this a humanism accepting no final goals beyond human flourishing, nor any allegience to anything else beyond this flourishing.[19]

In the main, people living in the West have come to accept that normal life can be experienced without any need to refer to a transcendent, personal Being who has created all things and is the ultimate reference-point for meaningful human existence: 'The great invention of the West was that of an imminent order in Nature, whose working could be systematically understood and explained on its own terms'.[20]

The imminent order, open to the natural senses, provides a sufficient context for most people most of the time to make sense of their reality. Only in times of

---

[17] Among others, 242, 338, 478, 607 and 608; see, 'Israel, Palestine and the Occupied Territories' at www.globalpolicy.org/security-council/israeli-palestine-and-the-occupied-territories.

[18] See, J. Andrew Kirk, 'Mission as Dialogue: The Case of Secular Belief' in *Mission under Scrutiny: Confronting Current Challenges* (London: Darton, Longman and Todd, 2006), 32-39.

[19] Taylor, *A Secular Age*, 18.

[20] Taylor, *A Secular Age*, 15.

emergency – for example, during a prolonged and life-threatening illness, in the face of death or in the time of a great tragedy – may they turn to some kind of supreme being. Such a reaction might be considered akin to concocting a 'god-of-the-gaps'. 'God' is brought into the equation only as a last resort, because important gaps still remain in all non-religious attempts to give an adequate account of the whole of experience.

Such a truncated view of reality is obviously disturbing for anyone who believes in the existence of a personal, infinite Being, without whose sustaining presence life is ultimately meaningless and would disintegrate and descend into chaos. Christians living in the West have become accustomed to the secular outlook, for secular assumptions in education, medical ethics, the making of law, economic matters and the dissemination of news prevail and have become part of the cultural air that is breathed on a daily basis.

For Muslims, such a state of affairs is incompatible with their deepest sense of what is true. The whole of life, in its most intricate features, is related to the will of Allah, to whom every living being is accountable. It is unthinkable to imagine that there can be any separation between a presumed secular and sacred realm of life. Islam is more than a programme of political action. It is a system of beliefs and morals, a social doctrine, a call to righteousness in all individual and communal concerns. For traditional orthodoxy at least it is a complete self-contained ideology, which regards all aspects of existence as parts of an indivisible whole of human life. Because the ideology is so complete and self-contained, adherents cannot live a truly Islamic life merely by holding Islamic beliefs. The coordination of attitude and endeavour is impossible unless the whole community is subject to the socioeconomic laws of Islam:

> And so it is only within the framework of an independent ideological state built on the principles of Islam and endowed with all the machinery of government legislation and law enforcement that the ideals of Islam can be brought to political fruition.[21]

If this is one way of authentically interpreting Islam, it is not surprising that Muslims have a hard time understanding and coming to terms with secularism. Some of the attempts to do this by Muslims living in the West will be explored later in this study.[22]

Thus, a substantial corpus of Muslim writings has been dedicated to combatting secularism as an ideology, seeking to show that the Western world, because it has been severed from the one true source of its existence, now floats

---

[21] Muhammad Asad, *The Principles of State and Government in Islam* (Gibraltar: Dar al-Andalus, 1980/2), 95-96.

[22] See chapters 9 and 11.

on the raft of unsustainable rationalist and materialist assumptions.[23] Out of this critique, some Muslim writers have constructed a kind of Occidentalism (the mirror image of the Orientalism so heavily criticised by writers such as Edward Said).[24] The West is now identified as the land of the 'setting' sun, i.e. a civilisation in decline, the zenith of whose splendour is now past. It represents a new barbarism, motivated by the lust for power, pleasure and riches. It is aggressive and arrogant in believing that its own form of political and social life is superior to any other and should, therefore, be dissemminated by all means possible (including military force).[25]

The 'West' may also be a symbol of the ever-beckoning frontier that holds out the illusion of new borders to cross in pursuit of human constructed enterprises that have little sense or purpose beyond the glorification of the human creator. Human enterprise and autonomy is venerated. Both culturally and geographically, the West ends in Hollywood! Here life is trivialised, and apathy and boredom are alleviated by 'larger doses of unreality, whether administered by drugs or novels or soap-operas that diminish a lively personal zeal for existence'.[26]

In some of the polemic against the perceived moral relativism and abandonment of God, the Christian faith is seen as one of the main culprits. Christianity, according to this narrative, has colluded with a society that has sought to express itself in 'godless' terms. It is, therefore, responsible (at least by omission) for an immoral society, since in the absence of God, anything becomes permitted.[27] This Muslim view of Christianity is based on the assumption that, because the latter makes a distinction between the kingdom of God and the world, it has abandoned society to the ungodly forces of 'Caesar'.[28] Thus, according to this interpretation, Christianity, through its reform movements, and its tendency to formulate its core message in terms of

---

[23] See, for example, Jacques Waardenburg, 'Reflections on the West' in Suha Taji-Faraki and Basheer M. Nafi, *Islamic Thought in the Twentieth Century* (London: I.B. Taurus, 2004), 281-282.

[24] In his book, *Orientalism*, he strongly criticises a certain perceived bias in the study, by Western academics using certain critical, historical tools, of the history, culture and religion of the Middle East. They are accused of making false claims of objectivity and of treating living realities as fossilised theories. Even more serious is the impression given of having adopted an attitude of superiority by contrasting Western institutions and achievements with those of Islam. This attitude is said to arise out of the underlying assumption that Muslim belief still adheres to the intellectual conventions and moral values of pre-modern societies.

[25] See, Waardenburg, 'Reflections on the West', 266-268.

[26] Cragg, *The Qur'an and the West*, 42-43.

[27] See, Ron Geaves, *Aspects of Islam* (London: Darton, Longman and Todd, 2005), 28.

[28] In chapters 6 and 10, we will examine the relationship between church, world and the kingdom of God in mainstream Christian thought.

an individual, spiritual salvation, has produced, or at least hastened, the coming of the secular world-view.[29] That this is a gross misreading of Christianity's genuine understanding of the relastionship between God, the world and the church is one of the major subjects of dialogue between Christians and Muslims.[30]

The Domestication of Islam

Within the current set of relationships between Western societies and Muslim communities, especially since 9/11, Western scholars and governments have been energetically engaged in trying to define (and promote) what might be called an 'ideal Islam'. They have hit upon the notion of 'moderate Islam' in stark contrast to traditionalist, radical, or extremist versions. By moderate Islam is understood a version of the faith that is prepared to review its unchanging and intransigent nature. It represents an interpretation of the foundation texts and traditions which is flexible, making room for contemporary, independent judgements on the way these should be applied in circumstances that differ so vastly from their original context. This approach to the past would allow for a certain amount of reconstruction (*islah*) of the form that Islam should take in the modern world.[31] Thus, although the principles for right living may be adduced directly from the Qur'an and the *sunnah*, the specific and detailed legal prescriptions that have become codified in the various law schools in the early years of the spread of Islam are not necessarily binding. It is hoped that moderate Islam will find ways of accommodating acceptable aspects of Western culture, just as other world religions have succeeded in doing. Indeed, the 'creation' of 'moderate' Islam might become a 'virtuous' self-fulfilling prophecy.

According to this way of thinking,[32] it can be shown that the Qur'an calls for human progress. The revelation was never intended to lay down a set of immutable laws, valid for all time and all places. On the contrary, it assumes that the injunctions will be faithfully, but creatively, related to changing situations.[33] As has often been pointed out, the Qur'an contains remarkably few specific laws. Therefore, it is the responsibility of every generation of Muslims to discover the abiding moral purpose of the texts, i.e. their true universal

---

[29] See, for example, David Martin, *On Secularization: Towards a Revised Grand Theory* (Aldershot: Ashgate Publishing, 2005), 3-6.

[30] See, Nazir Ali, 'Some Issues in Dialogue Today I: Religion, Democracy and the State' in Nazir Ali, *Conviction and Conflict.*

[31] Andrew Rippin, *Muslims: Their Religious Beliefs and Practices*, 185-186.

[32] To which I will return in more detail in chapters 9 and 11.

[33] See, Jon Armajani, *Dynamic Islam: Liberal Muslim Perspectives in a Transnational Age* (Lanham: University of America Press, 2004), 11-12.

intent, and to work out from them appropriate forms of ethical conduct. Thus, reforming thinkers have taken pains to distinguish between the absolute truth of the divine text and the relative authority of interpretative traditions adopted by legal scholars over the centuries.[34]

So, Western governments and other institutions hope that a rejuvenated Islam will arise, more alert to the benefits gained for human flourishing by Western societies, less inclined to polarise issues and find fault. They will point out that leading Muslim thinkers of past generations[35] have already set a precedent in welcoming the positive advantages of adopting some crucial Western values, such as the emphasis on individual liberty, the equal dignity and rights of men and women, the representative channelling of the will of the people through democratic instruments, and an open society, which tolerates diversity and freedom of speech.

Now, this attempt from outside the faith to encourage a sanitised version of Islam is interpreted by some as the desire to redefine Islam so that it fits into the typical Western understanding of what it means to be a liberal, secular and pluralist society. As one writer has put it,

> Muslims… might well be convinced that the secular/liberal worldview contains an iron hand inside a soft glove as they watch the bombs drop on Afghanistan and Iraq and the conditions of the prisoners held in the camps on Cuba, and see that being a moderate Muslim is simply defined as sharing the world view of the powerful.[36]

This stratagem is interpreted as yet another example of the desire by Western leaders to control the threat of a new Islamic invasion of Europe. Western governments and opinion-formers are locked into a struggle to isolate and discredit radical Islam by co-opting another form of Islam for consumption in a secular society. Emphasis on moderate Islam becomes, then, an ideological tool to deal with the Muslim world and incorporate it into the superior values of allegedly tolerant and pluralist societies. At its best, such a strategy is deemed to be somewhat condescending and patronising. At its worst, it is seen as an attempt to neutralise any radical criticism of the social, political and economic status quo of the Western establishment.

If moderate Islam is ideal Islam, Islam as it was always intended to be, then every other form is a deviation, a misinformed interpretation that needs to be

---

[34] See, Talal Assad, 'Europe against Islam: Islam in Europe' in Ibrahim M. Abu-Rabi, *The Blackwell Companion to Contemporary Islamic Thought*, 309.

[35] Such as Sayyid Ahmed Khan (1817-98) and Muhammad 'Abduh (1849-1905), see Malise Ruthven, *Islam in the World* (London: Granta Books, 2006/3), 296-299, 301-305.

[36] Ron Geaves, 'Who defines Moderate Islam 'post'-September 11?' in R. Geaves, *Islam and the West*, 69.

corrected by Islamic scholars and imams educated in Western, liberal, educational establishments.

Any self-respecting Muslims, however, would want to ask by what right Western politicians and other opinion formers can dare to suggest what constitutes authentic Muslim belief and action. They would almost certainly see this as a strategy to tame a phenomenon that does not easily abide by the secular rules that Western societies seem to have laid down to oblige religions to play the game properly. Nevertheless, whatever suspicion there may be of motives and intentions does not preclude different strands of Islam from engaging in a vigorous debate as to what represents its authentic faith in present circumstances. Thus, as we shall discover later, there are strong impulses towards change and integration coming from within migrant Muslim communities resident in the West

If there is a 'clash of civilisations' between the West and Islam, and as we have seen opinion is divided on the issue, then the grievances that we have traced here would certainly be some of the main factors that would contribute to such antipathy and friction on the side of Muslims. In the next chapter, we will investigate some of the causes of dissension from the other side, namely negative perceptions of Islam in the West.

Chapter 4

Westerners' Concerns about Islam

The notion that there might be a conflict of civilisations depends on there being substantial evidence of tensions, suspicions and nervousness between two (or more) separate entities. Present relationships are never forged in a vacuum, but are deeply affected by historical memories on both sides. In this chapter we will trace four major areas where many contemporary Europeans, brought up in a secular, liberal culture, believe they are right to be distrustful of Islam as both a faith and a political force.

The History of Europe

Islam is the only external civilisation that has threatened the territorial integrity of Europe. From the 7th to the 15th centuries Europe was surrounded by Islamic empires and for much of this time significant parts of the European continent were ruled by Islamic powers. Only in the 16th century did European nations gain control of the seas and, thereby, manage to outflank the Islamic encirclement:

> Some Westerners...have argued that the West does not have a problem with Islam, but only with violent Islamist extremists. Fourteen hundred years of history demonstrate otherwise. The relations between Islam and Christianity, both Orthodox and Western, have often been stormy. Each has been the other's Other. The twentieth-century conflict between liberal democracy and Marxist-Leninism is only a fleeting and superficial historical phenomenon compared to the continuing and deeply conflictual relation between Islam and Christianity.[1]

In the early years of the new faith (roughly 630-750 CE), Muslim armies swept across North Africa, once the scene of flourishing Christian communities, and into Spain. They also conquered the Middle East, Persia and as far east as India. The conquered peoples' political status (unless they converted to Islam) was known as *dhimma*, a system in which the state gave some freedom of religion and communal self-government to minorities in return for the payment of an obligatory tax (the *jizyah*); however, they had no

---

[1] Huntington, *The Clash of Civilizations*, 209.

influence on the nation's governance.[2] To them the subjugating armies appeared to herald just another marauding empire, on a par with those of Byzantium or Persia of an earlier period.

In 732, Charles Martel halted the advance of the Umayyad caliphate's armies between Poitiers and Tours. So, the Islamic occupation of the European continent was confined for several centuries to Spain. In 1492, the same year that Columbus sailed to the Caribbean, the Moors, who had originally conquered Spain in 711, were finally driven out of the peninsular. Meanwhile, attempts to recapture the Christian 'holy' places in Palestine from the Muslims began in 1095. The various crusades eventually ended in 1291, when the last European stronghold at Acre fell. The whole episode was disastrous from many points of view, not least in embittering relations between the Eastern and Western churches and causing profoundly resentful and acrimonious relations between Christians and Muslims for centuries to come.

The Ottoman Empire, the domain of the Muslim Turks, was established in 1299 (and lasted until 1922). It began in northern Anatolia and then expanded to include all of Asia Minor, the Middle East and parts of North Africa. In 1453, Constantinople, the centre of Eastern Christianity, was captured by the Turks and made into the capital city of their empire. From there they advanced into SE Europe, occupying much of present day Bulgaria, Hungary and the Balkan states. Twice they reached Vienna and besieged it: the first time in 1529 and the second and last time in 1683. Their failure to capture such a crucial city in the heartlands of Europe was the beginning of a dramatic decline in the power and influence of the Ottoman Empire.

At the conclusion of the First World War, the Ottoman Empire was decimated and many of its territories handed over to France and Britain to administer as protectorates. At this time, and up to the period after the Second World War, only four hitherto Islamic states – Afghanistan, Iran, Saudi Arabia and Turkey – remained free of some kind of non-Muslim rule. Meanwhile, Turkey became a secular state under the government of Mustafa Kemal, who was renamed Ataturk ('the father of the Turks'), when he was elected the first president of the new Republic. His main achievement, perhaps, was the abolition of the caliphate in 1924. In doing this he broke the inextricable link in one country between the religion of Islam and political power.

The European peoples are also well aware of the consistent and persistent Islamic claim that it has a mission to institute its civilisation in all parts of the globe.[3] There is, therefore, a long residual historical consciousness of the peril of being subjected to Islamic dominion as an alien force. This has led to the fear that the present Muslim populations of Europe are acting as a kind of fifth

---

[2] See, Nazir Ali, *Conviction and Conflict*, 66-68.

[3] This claim will be explored further in chapter 5.

column.[4] Their presence is viewed with suspicion, because it is assumed that their primary allegiance is not to their adopted country, but to the wider universal Muslim people (the *ummah*).

Thus, in the context of the historic reality that at distinct moments of its history Europe was under threat of Muslim subjugation, it is not surprising that the indigenous European populations are nervous about a kind of subversion from within. The situation is complicated by the fact that Europe is still identified by its residual attachment to Christianity, which in its present phase (having left behind much of its Christendom legacy) is seen as quite a distinct religious commitment from that of Islam. It can be argued, for example, that present-day democratic liberties owe their origin to the refusal of religious non-conformists to submit to the state religion. Eventually, they won the day and began the process of securing equal freedoms for all citizens in areas like assembly, education, universal suffrage and property rights.

Europe reckons that it has turned its back once and for ever on the oppressive, intrusive, power-hungry version of Christian faith that was medieval Christendom. It is anxious when it sees that at least some variants of contemporary Islam look exceedingly like the kind of pre-modern Christianity that was believed to have passed away. Needless to say, there is no appetite for a return to any kind of political arrangement remotely comparable to the political union between the state and religion. The notion of an 'Islamic Republic' in the heartlands of Europe, however remote, rightly fills Europeans with alarm and dismay. The immediate problem is that Islam is an alien faith, perhaps largely misunderstood, easily characterised by some extreme customs (like enforced marriages and 'honour killings') and aligned with politically-inspired violence, as in the phrase 'Islamic terror'.

The Refusal of Liberal Democracy

Islam is perceived as having a perennial yearning for the implementation of a theocratic state. One example of this desire can be seen in the approach of some Muslims to law and punishment. Western nations currently found their legal systems on the concept of natural justice, defined more or less in terms of the rule of law based on an implicit contract between all citizens that acknowledges their absolute equality, irrespective of the circumstances of their birth, and their reciprocal rights and duties. The Islamic ideal is to follow the alleged dictates

---

[4] This apprehension is exacerbated by the demographic factor: Muslim families on average produce more children than non-Muslim; immigration from Muslim nations continues to be substantial.

of revelation (contained in the Qur'an, *sunnah* and *hadith*).[5] In the Western mind, this equates with the imposition of the regulations of shar'iah[6] – the codified legal system developed during the first three centuries after the death of Muhammad. In particular, the West is dismayed by the lack of guarantees protecting human rights in various Muslim societies, such as religious liberty, understood among other things as the freedom to change religious allegiance. In the development of Western political consciousness, one of the touch-stones of a free and open society is the obligation to protect those citizens from harassment or persecution who may wish to change their beliefs.

Huntington lays out some of the main characteristics of Western societies that, in terms of the long history of humankind, make them distinctive. The two principal sources, in terms of ideals, are Greek philosophy and the Judeo-Christian religion: the first supplies a particular way of thinking; the second offers a distinct view of human beings' place in the universe, the meaning of life, the resolution of evil and a special set of values. Both have combined to produce a notable understanding of justice. Also, from the Romans Europeans have taken the centrality of law for regulating acceptable behaviour in community:

> The tradition of the rule of law laid the basis for the constitutionalism and the protection of human rights, including property rights, against the exercise of arbitrary power.[7]

Another characteristic is the existence of a plurality of social institutions in most Western societies which recognises and commends ethnic, social, political and religious diversity. These have tended to keep at bay the absolutism of a centralised state bureaucracy typical of social orders elsewhere. They also have given rise to a notable array of representative bodies to further the interests of the different sectors of society. These latter have come to be bound together by constitutions, setting out fundamental rights and obligations. Eventually representation in the political realm resulted in parliamentary democracy, government of the people by the people for the people; the absolute monarchs of former times became constitutional monarchs, or were abolished altogether: 'Le roi n'adminstre pas, ne gouverne pas, il regne'[8] (the king does not manage, he does not govern, he reigns).

---

[5] The *sunnah* reports on Mohammad's way of life; the *hadith* contains his teachings. The *sunnah* is the 'path' to be followed because of the *hadith*, i.e. it is the way it exemplifies and enjoins.

[6] *Shar'iah* is sacred law. It is derived from the Qur'an and the *sunnah*. It is a detailed code of conduct for every aspect of life, both public and private.

[7] Huntington, *The Clash of Civilizations*, 70.

[8] Louis Adolphe Thiers, *Le National* (4 February, 1830).

Democracy was supposed to indicate, through universal suffrage, the legal and moral equality of all human beings, irrespective of social status, gender, or economic prosperity. There are undoubtedly defects in the best of democracies: for example, the possibility of the tyranny of the majority; the distance between citizens and government; the difficulty of encouraging grass-roots participation in political affairs; the danger of money, educational privileges or social connections controlling access to political pursuits. Nevertheless, in the famous words of Winston Churchill:

> No one pretends that democracy is perfect or all-wise. Indeed, it has been said that democracy is the worst form of Government except all those other forms that have been tried from time to time.[9]

Finally, Huntington refers to individualism as perhaps the most distinguishing mark of Western societies. This trait slowly achieved prominence as the individual's preferences and choices became distinguished from those of the collective body of which he or she was part. It reflected the gradual rejection of a hierarchical and coercive political and social order and was bolstered by a doctrine of natural freedoms and rights. It represented a revolt against an authoritarian, collectivist way of viewing human communities. The individual is considered autonomous, in the sense of being responsible for taking control of his or her own life, free from the coercion of family, community or state direction. This has become a major default position in the potential conflict between civil liberties and the interests of the state.

One other distinguishing feature of Western societies, not mentioned by Huntington, is that, in general terms, they can be understood as guilt rather than shame-oriented cultures. In shame-oriented cultures the most important reaction to a sense of wrongdoing or being wronged is not to lose face. The opposite of shame is honour. The supreme good in a shame culture is to maintain one's honour intact. In order to achieve this, the individual has to accept the opinion of the community with regard to a perceived shortcoming, misdeed, or offence. In true shame-oriented cultures every person has a place and a duty in society. Thus, one maintains self-respect, not by choosing what is good rather than what is evil in absolute terms, but by choosing what is expected of one. Shame is removed and honour restored only when a person does what the society requires of him or her in the situation, including committing suicide if necessary.[10]

Guilt, on the other hand, is a sensation that is internalised within the conscience of the individual. The people concerned acknowledge to themselves

---

[9] Speech to the House of Commons (London: 11 November, 1947).

[10] See, Paul G. Hiebert, *Anthropological Insights for Missionaries* (Grand Rapids: Baker Book House, 1985).

the wrongness of what they have done or thought, irrespective of what the wider society may think. Thus, in the case of being accused unjustly of committing some particular crime or misdemeanor, as well as wishing to preserve one's reputation, it is important to clarify the real truth of the situation. A guilt society would seem to have a well-formulated sense, not only of what may or may not be conventionally acceptable within the culture, but what is right and wrong, irrespective of a society's consensus on the matter. We can refer to this as ethical realism: there exists for every human society an objective standard of right and wrong, good and evil. The positive aspect of a guilt culture is its concern for an independently administered system of justice. It also gives to individuals personal responsibility for their behaviour. They stand on their own, guided ultimately by their own conscience. Thus, they cannot fall back on a collective morality, which rewards or punishes according to whether a person conforms to its norms, or not.

Now, in the light of these general characteristics, there is a widespread perception abroad among many Westerners that Muslims are not equipped by their cultural background, including their religion, to understand properly or integrate into Western society. In almost every case, it is alleged, Muslims have a hard time coming to terms with the generally accepted mores of Western culture. Muslims as a whole are understood to have principled objections to democracy as it has been developed within the framework of a secular constitution. The idea of democracy is that people in a nation state decide what form of government is appropriate for them, who will represent them and, ultimately, by what laws they will be governed. By universal and secret ballot, the people will hold to account those they have elected. They expect politicians to listen to their views and respond to their interests and concerns. Muslims, on the other hand, are interpreted as preferring some kind of theocratic rule, i.e. the implementation of God's rule over people through the mediation of carefully codified law, to be interpreted by specially trained scholars. According to this view, ordinary people are not equipped, by and large, to understand fully the intricacies of legal processes and economic principles; they have to trust the experts to work out the best set of conditions for the orderly working of society. Thus, to take one case,

> Mawdudi's ideal system is one in which the most suitable person is entrusted with the position of khalif, or *amir*, 'the basic qualification for the election of an *Amir* is that he should command the confidence of the largest number of people in respect of his knowledge and grasp of Islam.[11]

[11] Syed Abu'l A'la Mawdudi, *The Islamic Way of Life* (Leicester: The Islamic Foundation, 1986), 34, quoted in *Muslims and Modernity*, 50.

Muslims are also seen to equivocate on the issue of fundamental human rights:

> Many believe that there is a fundamental clash between the Charter (The Universal Declaration of Human Rights) and Islamic practice and that the record of 'human rights' in the Muslim world suggests an inherent conflict between Islam and 'human rights.[12]

The issue that seems to have become a test case is that stated in Article 18 of the UDHR:

> Everyone has the right to freedom of thought, conscience and religion; this right includes freedom to change his religion or belief, and freedom, either alone or in community with others and in public or private, to manifest his religion or belief in teaching, practice, worship and observance.

In Muslim states this principle of religious freedom in respect of the liberty to change one's religion is not observed in practice. There are many documented cases of people who have left Islam to embrace another faith who have been harassed, victimised, threatened, and even murdered. It may be argued that the right to believe and practice any particular faith, as long as this does not threaten other people's freedoms and security, is the most fundamental right of all. Ultimately, it is the right to pursue truth for oneself and the freedom to err, which, as the saying goes, is human. In other words, freedom from external coercion to conform enhances human dignity; thus, it is a prerogative too precious to concede. [13] A society, which seeks to prevent error, defined as any thought or practice inimical to state ideology, through restrictive legislation or indoctrination is totalitarian.

Lamin Sanneh argues that wherever a state sponsors religion it confirms secular suspicions that religious belief is too weak to stand alone. It appears to show a fear of criticism, of equal rights under the law and of heresy. Moreover, it does not acknowledge fully the human integrity of other believers. If the state must procure the allegiance of believers, the truth claims of religion have no intrinsic, persuasive merit: 'threats corrupt, and absolute threats make absolute hypocrites'.[14] He goes on to argue that salvation by God's grace through faith alone, not by the coercive sanctions of state power, is not only a true response

[12] *Muslims and Modernity,* 62.

[13] See, Gavin D'Costa, 'Engaging with a 'Clash of Civilisations': Liberal Views of Religion in the Public Domain and Catholic Approaches', in *Studies in Interreligious Dialogue*, 17, 2007, 1, 36-39.

[14] 'Shari'ah Sanctions and State Enforcement: A Nigerian Islamic Debate and an Intellectual Critique', in *Islam and the West,* 161.

to God but also the foundation for social tolerance and democratic renewal: what the philosopher, Karl Popper, called 'an open society'.

In this context, it is interesting to note that in Tariq Ramadan's sympathetic attempt to bridge the gaps between Islamic and Western traditions and cultures, in his section on human rights, there is no mention of the rights to religious freedom, association, and speech, and to democratic government, based on free and fair elections. [15] It is true that he does not pretend to cover all possible rights. It is also true that he is emphasising what might be called social or positive rights. However, given the extreme sensitivities in the Western world, born out of its own history, that surround the question of the freedom to believe, change and practice faith, it is surprising that he does not grapple with the issue. The Universal Islamic Declaration of Human Rights, drawn up by the Islamic Council of Europe in 1981 states (in Article XIII) that 'every person has the right to freedom of conscience and worship in accordance with his religious beliefs'. However, as has been pointed out by commentators on the Declaration, 'no reference is made to the issue of conversion, whether a Muslim is free to change his or her religion'.[16]

It is not the intention of this section to leave the question of Muslims' response to the question of Western liberal values with a largely negative picture. There are plenty of Muslims who are trying to find a way forward that will, whilst maintaining the integrity of their own foundation documents and history, enable them to appreciate the reasons why Western societies set such a store by democratic structures and individual human rights.[17] This study will explore at a later stage how far some Muslims have been able to go in accepting Western liberal values. The concern here has been to look at perceptions. This chapter is seeking to set out the most usually expressed misgivings concerning the likelihood that Muslims can integrate into Western societies. Questions are asked about how far Muslims, where they find serious tensions between their beliefs and secular norms, are willing to be conciliatory, rather than belligerent.

A Pre-Critical Religion

Islam is seen as a religion that does not allow the free-play of critical, historical analysis of its early life, foundation documents and subsequent traditions. Traditionally-minded Muslims, whilst acknowledging that revelation was given in the specific circumstances of the original Muslim community, refuse to accept that events in the life of Muhammad could have influenced the content

[15] *Western Muslims*, 149-152.

[16] Clinton Bennett, *Muslims and Modernity An introduction to the issues and debates* (London: Continuum, 2005), 69.

[17] See the discussion in J. Andrew Kirk, *The Meaning of Freedom: A Study of Secular, Muslim and Christian Views* (Carlisle: Paternoster Press, 1998), 176-189.

of the various *surahs* (chapters) of the Qur'an. These are presented, not in chronological order, but according to their length. Non-Muslim scholars of the Qur'an are convinced that a much greater depth of meaning would be extracted from the text were it seen to be causally affected by the life and circumstances of Muhammad's leadership of his followers in Mecca and Medina. In other words, they propose that an historical approach to the formation of the Qur'an is a necessary presumption for gaining a clear understanding both of the origin of the sayings and their meaning in the contemporary world.

At issue here is the openness, or otherwise, of Muslim scholars to the academic conventions and procedures accepted as normative in Western educational institutions. This would mean, for example, as has long been the case for Christian documents, that dogmas and doctrines cannot be shielded from rigorous, critical scrutiny with regard to their origin, compilation and textual integrity. In other words, Western scholarship cannot set out from the premise that the only explanation for the existence of the Qur'an is that it came purely by divine disclosure, without any human influence. On the contrary, its first instinct is to find in the circumstances of Muhammad's life and work as prophet, statesman and warrior the real causes of the particular sayings of the Qur'an.

It is true that Muslim scholars acknowledge the significance of the 'occasions of revelation', i.e. the historical circumstances in which the divine word was transmitted. However, the tradition affirms that the particular revelation was given to illuminate and direct the course of action to be taken within the context. Western scholars, on the other hand, would tend to see the relationship between revelation and historical situation working in the opposite direction, namely that the latter informed and shaped the former.

Mohammed Arkoun, an Islamic scholar, sets out a detailed proposal for a responsible critical approach to Qur'anic and *hadith* studies. Commenting on a proposed Encyclopaedia of the Qur'an, he states that its methodology – 'conceived and produced for the critical order of rational processes' – confirms his belief that it is long overdue in order to redress the imbalance between

> ...philosophical and scientific reasoning as practised today in the West...and Islamic reasoning as its asserts itself in its positions on Islam...The task remains to produce an Encyclopaedia that would help to reconcile the requirements of critical knowledge and the legitimate irreducible ethos of a culture, postures of mind and existential styles of human expression.

He believes that it may become 'a scholarly, intellectual, scientific and hopefully spiritual answer to the ideological theory of the 'clash of civilizations'.[18]

[18] Arkoun, *Islam: To Reform or to Survive*, 90.

The question is whether the majority of Muslim leaders are prepared to open up their sacred texts to such scrutiny, granted that Western scholarly procedures are by no means wholly disinterested and neutral. Or, will they resist accepting that non-Muslim scholars, or even Muslim scholars who acknowledge that the use of critical tools is an indispensable means to knowledge and understanding, may be able to make important discoveries about the early history of Islam and the transmission of its heritage. They may suspect that such scholarship is unreliable on the grounds that the former are working within a framework of hostility to the Islamic experience and the latter are probably equivalent to apostates and unbelievers. We will explore these issues at a later stage, when we come to examine in more detail contemporary approaches to the interpretation of the foundation documents.

Another aspect of the suspicion that Islam is still operating in a precritical mode, is the apparent refusal of Muslims in general to take seriously both Jewish and Christian self-understandings and, in the latter case, of the quite ludicrous, a-historical attempts to demonstrate the corruption of the New Testament. The question of the origin of the sayings in the Qur'an, where these quite clearly contradict similar accounts in the Bible is not properly addressed. Instead, Islamic tradition has tended to assert a priori and dogmatically the unity of the prophetic message prior to the final revelation from God in such a way that any discrepancy is resolved by appeal to the principle of correction: whatever comes later puts right previous errors. By definition, where there are irreconcilable differences between the Bible and the Qur'an, the former has to be incorrect. Needless to say, this method of dealing with disparities and controversies is considered arbitrary and, therefore, unacceptable in institutions of higher, critical learning.

The figure of Jesus ('Isa), who emerges in the Qur'an bears some resemblances to the Jesus encountered in the four canonical Gospels of the New Testament.[19] He is called Messiah (*al-Masih*) nine times, was born of a virgin (Q. 19.20) and is called God's 'Word' (Q.4.171) and 'a spirit from God'. He was a miracle-worker (Q. 3.49, 5.110) and one of the greatest of the prophets who preceded Muhammad. He was sinless (Q. 19.19). He ascended into heaven, without dying, and is predicted to come again to this world. At the same time, there are major discrepancies: the most important being that he denied ever claiming deity and that he never died on the cross.[20] The latter assertion is, on any reputable canons of historical investigation, plain wrong. The attempts by Muslims to explain away a fairly conclusive historical datum demonstrate how solid evidence is made to yield to theoretical considerations,

---

[19] A good summary of the evidence may be found in Oddbjorn Leirvik, *Images of Jesus Christ in Islam* (Uppsala: Swedish Institute of Missionary Research, 1999), 23-27.

[20] See, Norman Anderson, *Islam in the Modern World: A Christian Perspective* (Leicester: IVP, 1990), 11-12.

namely that God (i.e. the God of the Qur'an) could not have allowed such a notable prophet to have finished his life in such an ignominious failure.

The Muslim conclusion that, wherever there are serious divergences between the New Testament and the Qur'anic references to Jesus, the former must have been falsified lacks historical evidence and scholarly integrity. The use of the pseudepigraphical, apocryphal, late 16th century, forged manuscript called the Gospel of Barnabas as in any way a reliable account of the life of Jesus shows to what lengths Muslim apologists may go in trying to undermine the authenticity of the New Testament narratives.[21]

The point at issue in this instance is not a discussion about the relative merits of the two widely divergent versions of Jesus, but the willingness to allow beliefs to be challenged and, if necessary, modified on the basis of sound historical evidence. In the light of the enormous amount of historical study undertaken around the life and times of Jesus of Nazareth, based on sources close to being contemporaneous, the picture of Jesus in the Qur'an lacks credibility. It is, what it looks like, a legendary account based on fragments of information that Muhammad might have gleaned from Christian contacts and passed through the prism of the revelations that he professes to have received. No Christian Arabic texts were available to Muhammad. His sources of information were oral and second-hand, a mixture of biblical and pseudo-biblical material.[22]

In order to maintain the truth of their account of Jesus and other Biblical figures and stories, Muslims have had to invent the historically wholly unjustifiable notion of textual corruption. From the point of view of carefully tested evidence, it is not acceptable to declare that wherever the Gospel accounts portray Jesus in ways that conflict with Muslim sensibilities (for example, 'that he drank wine…spoke harshly to his mother, or refused to obey the law of God…')[23] they must have been fabricated. Until and unless Islamic scholars are prepared to engage with the critical tools of historical and cultural analysis, admitting the likelihood that the text of the Qur'an and the traditions of the *hadith* were, at least in part, shaped by historical factors, it is difficult not to draw the conclusion that defence of the dogma is always the primary concern. When, for example, Muhammad Abdul-Rauf says, 'it is dangerous when, in the name of being scientific, the origins of Islam are explained as

---

[21] See, Anderson, *Islam in the Modern World*, Appendix: 'The so-called 'Gospel of Barnabas'', 223-234.

[22] See, Philip K. Hitti, *Islam: A Way of Life* (Minneapolis: University of Minnesota Press, 1970), 19.

[23] Geaves, *Aspects of Islam*, 30.

arising out of economic or other cultural phenomena',[24] one is prompted to ask, dangerous for whom and for what reason?

As a last resort, to defend historical anomalies or the textual integrity of the traditions, some scholars will resort to blatant ad hominem arguments, namely that Western and/or Christian scholars are driven purely by motives that seek to denigrate and find errors in the Muslim faith. Thus, to quote Abdul-Rauf again, 'given truths, accepted and upheld by all Muslims for fourteen centuries have been subjected to misguided critical analysis, sometimes ruthless and usually insensitive'.[25] The allegation that Islam represents a pre-critical religion will only be refuted when Islamic scholars confront the critical evidence that is produced by way of interpreting its origin and development and show that it is in fact, not just in imagination, biased, prejudiced, methodologically faulty or false.

A Resistance to Integration

At this point, in order to avoid, as far as possible, misunderstandings, it is necessary to reiterate that this chapter is about perceptions of Islam that pervade many ordinary people's impression of Islam. This is different from saying that all the perceptions are necessarily valid. The question of the integration of Muslims, who have come to Europe from countries where Islam is the dominant religion, into a predominantly secular culture is hotly debated. It is closely tied to the promotion, or otherwise, of multiculturalism.

We may understand multiculturalism as the peaceful and enriching mixture of peoples from different ethnic backgrounds and cultural traditions living together in one society. There is a positive and negative aspect to its practice. As an ideal it allows peoples from different historical and geographical settings to express their sense of identity in ways that they freely choose. It also means that the host nation may not unnecessarily or arbitrarily restrict this freedom (for example, by forbidding the use of original languages) or compel some kind of consensus or uniformity on all immigrants. The vision is of a society, where peoples not only experience liberty to be themselves, but are positively encouraged to share the riches of their cultural heritage with the rest of the population. The desire is that, as in the case of educational practices, people will widen their horizons, understand the reasons for difference and the way it can enhance appreciation of what it means to be human.

Nevertheless, multiculturalism is not without its drawbacks. Tim Gorringe mentions five of these.[26] First, it may hide an inverted kind of superior attitude

[24] 'Outsiders Interpretation of Islam: A Muslim's Point of View' in Richard C. Martin, *Approaches to Islam in Religious Studies* (Oxford: One World, 2001/2), 185.
[25] Abdul-Rauf, 'Outsiders Interpretation', 185.
[26] Gorringe, *Furthering Humanity*, 242-245.

by showing the exceptional benevolence and generosity of Western liberal societies, which practice an exemplary degree of tolerance towards difference. However, it is quite likely that such an attitude covers up (or is even an expression of) an ingrained racism and the perennial problem of access to power in society. He might have added that tolerance also tends to promote indifference, so that multiculturalism is a convenient theory that actually allows us to ignore other communities.

Secondly, multiculturalism can easily function as a form of ghettoization. Rather than immigrant communities being encouraged to participate fully in the democratic system, they are seen as the objects of special social policies. Their identity is confirmed first and foremost in terms of their distinctives, not in terms of being co-contributors to the development of a society of genuine equals. Moreover, the communities are usually dealt with as uniform collectives, which are often represented only by self-appointed (male) leaders. Thus, the real opinions and desires of the people themselves are mediated by these officially recognised spokespersons, and can therefore be manipulated for apologetic purposes.

Thirdly, following on from this, there is the question of who speaks for the community. Unless, the genuine voice of individuals within the communities can be expressed and heard, then its very culture can appear static, and eventually anachronistic. Moreover, the real abuse of human rights, particularly against women and girls in such matters as marriage, domestic maltreatment and property prerogatives may be hidden or even condoned on grounds of supposed cultural sensitivity. Multiculturalism, therefore, does not seem to envisage critical engagement, leading to modifications and progress.

Fourthly, 'multiculturalism fails to do justice to the complexities of minority situations'.[27] Cultures are not homogeneous. People may relate to their supposed communities in different ways. They may possess multiple identities, as we saw Amartya Sen arguing. Multiculturalism, therefore, tends to confine people within a circumscribed self, which precisely in a pluralist society does not represent reality. It can lead to identity politics, in which minority groups are encouraged by their leaders to acquire from the system as much as they can for themselves, rather than seeking to contribute to the common good.

Fifthly, multiculturalism challenges and dilutes the need for all citizens of a nation to share a cultural core. As well as being born within a community that acknowledges and celebrates a different history, language and cultural customs, every person also belongs to a nation that transcends all cultural differences. This is, perhaps, the nub of the question about integration: should not all peoples who want to live permanently within another nation acknowledge and live by the core values and expectations of that nation? The concern among many indigenous Europeans is that Muslims, who have come from outside

---

[27] Gorringe, *Furthering Humanity*, 244.

Europe to live in its heartlands, do not fully appreciate how these values have been arrived at. So that, in reality, they have not resolved the tension between a double allegiance: to the rules and standards of their adopted nation and to the principles and precepts of their religion. The perception is that, wherever a clash is perceived, the latter are always privileged. Derived, perhaps as a hangover from Orientalism, is the view that Islam is basically incapable of substantial change and adaptation, because Islamic modernism is an oxymoron: ''Islam reformed was Islam no longer' and modernism was irrelevant to any understanding of real Islam'.[28]

Such a concern was born out by the establishment of a so-called Muslim Parliament in the UK (1992), originally under the leadership of Kalim Siddiqui (who died in 1996), who envisaged it 'as an embryonic non-territorial state for British Muslims that could eventually run its own schools and hospitals'.[29] Such an institution, coupled with demands in some quarters that Muslims should be allowed to apply *shari'ah* to family matters within their communities, naturally has raised the fear that this was the first step to establishing a separate jurisdiction within the nation. Its Muslim Manifesto, published in 1990, 'explicitly rejects assimilation or integration as an option, and each section ends with (the refrain) 'we are Muslims first and last''.[30] However, the Muslim Parliament, which no longer has the high profile it once possessed, has changed its way of working from a confrontational to more consensual approach to community politics.[31]

---

[28] Bennett, *Muslims and Modernity*, 112.

[29] 'The Muslim Parliament during its early days under the leadership of Dr Kalim Siddiqui, whose brain-child the Parliament was, opted for a high-profile, confrontational approach in its championing of Islamic causes. The need for a 'Muslim Parliament' arose out of the frustration felt at the time of The Satanic Verses controversy as well as a wider feeling that governmental and policy-making bodies were adopting indifferent and at times discriminatory policies toward Muslim pre-occupations. The idea was instead to empower Muslims with their separate and distinctly Islamic institutions to meet their needs independently of the British government and local authorities. It also sought to discourage Muslims from entering mainstream politics or even from voting in elections; rather, the focus of debate was the need to create a 'non-territorial Islamic state' in Britain. ''The Muslim Parliament – a Historical Background;'' see, www.muslimparliament. org.uk.

[30] Bennett, *Muslims and Modernity*, 187-188.

[31] Under new leadership, it has revised its approach to political life in Britain: 'Its new leader Dr Ghayasuddin Siddiqui (no relation, but a close associate) began to introduce reforms into how the Muslim Parliament was to operate and engage with its social and political environment. Out went the ideologically-driven thinking and in came a more consensual, pragmatic modus operandi. Predictably this led to disaffection in the ranks of Dr Kalim Siddiqui's more ideological followers, some of whom seceded to form separate groups. The Muslim Parliament held the view that Muslim's grievances were best met by building alliances with other Muslim organisations, grass-root and national,

It would appear that the question of integration is bound to be hotly contested within the Muslim communities in Europe. A strong case can be made out for rejecting the two extremes of assimilation, where immigrant peoples lose all their distinctives and become more or less indistinguishable from the host culture, and isolation, which speaks of a studied and determined separation from the way of life of the majority. Integration is somewhere in between the two. It is a developing process, especially between generations, so that unless Muslim communities deliberately keep their children apart from non-immigrant children, younger people in time will become increasingly conscious that their roots are being extended into European soil, as they know no other reality first-hand.[32]

Conclusion

These four areas of concern, for the reasons that have been given, have the effect of causing a level of mistrust between Muslims communities living in the West and the host societies, which sometimes is based on solid evidence and sometimes is the stuff of oft-repeated myth or deliberate falsification. If conflict is to be avoided, it is imperative that all communities eschew superficial judgements and establish the real facts of any given situation. It is equally important that Muslims and non-Muslims meet as neighbours, work-colleagues, fellow-citizens and fellow human-beings, in order to appreciate first-hand what is the nature of cultural or religious differences (for example, over issues of dress or patterns of family life), why these differences exist, and also what are the many values that are held in common.

Christians, perhaps, have a particular role to play in seeking to interpret the recent history of the West regarding the secularisation of public life and the present situation regarding the place of religion in Western societies. This is not a one way process, as Christians can also learn from Muslims concerning the latter's more robust attitude to the centrality of faith in all aspects of life. At the same time, as this book attempts to achieve, Christians may be able to persuade Muslims that there are some aspects of a secular society that need to be properly appreciated and affirmed.

---

and – a radical move at the time – with non-Muslim groups entertaining similar welfare and civil rights objectives,' 'The Muslim Parliament – a Historical Background;' see, www.muslimparliament. org.uk.

[32] It is worth pointing out that questions about integration affect most immigrant communities, whatever their background and in whatever part of the world they have moved from and to. This can be illustrated, for example, in my experience by the many small ex-patriot communities from different parts of Europe that have settled in Argentina. In the case of Muslims, the predominance of the religious factor in their cultural heritage probably accentuates the problems. However, they are not an isolated case, and should not be seen as such.

Chapter 5

A Tale of Two Cities: Mecca and Medina

However a religion may develop in the course of a long history, there can be little doubt that it will for ever be shaped by the character and circumstances of its origin. This is particularly true for Christianity and Islam, both of which, although in differing ways, are religions of a sacred book that was compiled during their early years. It is the contention of this inquiry that the exact nature of the birth of these two faiths has a substantial bearing on how each one perceives itself in the contemporary world. Therefore, in this chapter and the next, I will attempt to focus on the most significant aspects of the early history of each faith community. I have chosen in both cases to highlight the significance of two key cities. Each of them had what today we might call geopolitical prominence; they also possess a highly symbolic quality.

In the year 610 a man of 40, a member of the Quraysh tribe in the city of Mecca on the Western side of the Arabian peninsular, claimed to have received through the angel Gabriel communications from Allah, the name of the one high God. The initial message spoke about the existence of only one God, God's hatred of idolatry, a call to care for the poor in Mecca and the reality of punishment for those who did not believe. Almost out of nowhere, a man in the prime of his life asserted that he had been chosen to be the instrument through which the one true God would make known his final will and testament to the whole world, beginning with Mecca.

Mecca

Now Mecca was an important city for two main reasons. First, it was a noted commercial centre. Due to its location and natural resources, including water, it attracted much business from the caravans carrying goods along the various trade routes that criss-crossed the Arabian peninsular. It was a strategic hub for trade between the Fertile Crescent to the North, Abyssinia to the South and West and India to the East. As a result, some merchants in the city amassed considerable wealth. However, this wealth was not well distributed, so there was a substantial contrast between the rich and poor. Meccan society, being based on tribal values, was supposed to be cohesive and egalitarian. However, the accumulation of wealth tended to undermine tribal solidarity. Care for widows and orphans grew less. They now became the objects of exploitation.

Clan rivalries became accentuated. The city, because of its wealth, became the object of attack from outside.[1]

Secondly, Mecca was the site of a prominent and popular shrine, the *Kaaba*. It attracted people from all the surrounding areas on an annual pilgrimage. This proved to be commercially profitable to the Quraysh clan, which had become the guardian of the sacred site. It benefited, for example, from the rules and regulations about food and clothing, which it imposed upon the pilgrims.[2]

> The pre-Islamic *Kaaba*, according to tradition, was an unpretentious cube-like (hence the name) structure of primitive simplicity, originally roofless, serving as the domicile for a black meteorite venerated as a fetish...The traditional pilgrimages were made there and special sacrifices offered. Muslim tradition maintains that the *Kaaba* was originally built by Adam according to a celestial prototype, and after the Deluge, rebuilt by Abraham and Ishmael (Q. 2.118-21).[3]

According to Islamic belief the *Kaaba* was originally a shrine built to acknowledge and worship the one true God, the creator and provider, who would look after those who worshipped him in times of danger or need. Later, however, the shrine fell into the hands of polytheists, who installed within it numerous idols. The pre-Islamic religion of the Arabs appears to share similar features with primal religions all over the world, namely a kind of transactional relationship with the deities whereby, in return for assiduous ritual practices and the maintenance of t raditional laws and customs, (presumed to be divinely approved), the gods would look favourably upon the people and bring them prosperity and safety from harm.[4]

It was within this context that Muhammad started declaring the message he claimed to have received directly from God. He was convinced that he was bringing to the Arabs a restoration of their original belief in the one high God. This was the original faith of Adam, and of Abraham the father of all the Semitic peoples. Religion had been corrupted from its original pristine purity. From time to time, Allah sent prophets to teach the people the right path from

---

[1] See, Montgomery Watt, *Islam and the Integration of Society* (London: Routledge and Kegan Paul, 1961), 7-10. The question of how much trade the Meccans were involved in and, therefore, how wealthy a city it had become is disputed; see Daniel Brown, *A New Introduction to Islam* (Oxford: Blackwell, 2004), 17. However, no one doubts that trade was widespread (Muhammad 's extensive business journeys on behalf of Khadija, a wealthy businesswoman, who became his first wife, are witnesses to this) nor that there was a severe discrepancy between rich and poor within the city.

[2] See, Ibn Ishaq, *The Life of Muhammad: Apostle of Allah* (London: The Folio Society, 2003), 27.

[3] Irving M. Zeitlin, *The Historical Muhammad* (Cambridge: Polity Press, 2007), 32-33.

[4] See, 'Religions in Primal Societies' in John R. Hinnells (ed.), *A Handbook of Living Religions* (London: Penguin Books, 1991), 392-449.

which they had strayed. Polytheism was a degenerate form of religion, which had the effect of weakening tribal unity.

Muhammad believed he had been given a divine commission to bring about a renewal of the Arab peoples by bringing them into submission to the one and only, true God. With their foolish idolatry they were living in a period of ignorance and barbarity. God would bring judgement upon them. In place of the perpetual conflicts and the neglect of the poor, he emphasised a sharing of wealth, care for the weak and vulnerable, a return to egalitarianism and a recovery of unity. Here was the last of the genuine prophets, who was in the process of receiving Allah's final word and testimony. Eventually, like the Jews and the Christians, some of whom he had met on his travels, the Arabs too would have a Scripture in their own language.[5]

His preaching received a mixed response: a few believed he was a true messenger from God; the majority, however, particularly the wealthy, opposed him. Clearly, this new message would have cut right against the vested interests of the Quraysh, especially the accumulation of wealth at the expense of the disadvantaged in the community and against the clan's esteem and influence on account of being guardians of the *Kaaba* shrine. His message posed a threat to the sacred (*haram*) status of the shrine.[6] Muhammad was, therefore, met largely by a wall of hostility, which his preaching did little to penetrate. The factors leading to this animosity were communal, commercial, traditional, and religious. For twelve years he endured ridicule, calumny and attempts to have him removed, either by exile or death.[7]

The initial attempts at silencing Muhammad did not prosper. The Quraysh leaders then decided on the expedient of banishing all the members of Muhammad's clan, the Banu Hashim. This meant setting up a total boycott: 'avoiding any contact with members of the clan – they would no longer marry their daughters and sons, trade with them, establish any other type of contract'.[8] The banishment lasted three years. It was finally revoked, when sufficient numbers of people in the various other clans believed it was futile.

In 615, some of his followers took refuge from persecution across the Red Sea in the Christian kingdom of Ethiopia, where they were treated with respect and kindness.[9] Despite the presence of a delegation sent from Mecca, the

[5] See, Karen Armstrong, *Islam: A Short History* (London: Widenfeld and Nicolson, 2000), 3-5.

[6] It was a place where certain profane acts, like carrying weapons and engaging in violence, were forbidden.

[7] See, Kenneth Cragg, *Muhammad and the Christian: A Question of Response* (London: Darton, Longman and Todd, 1984), 19-23.

[8] Ramadan, *The Messenger*, 66.

[9] Montgomery Watt suggests that the sending of Mohammad's followers to Abyssinia in 615 may have had commercial motives: to gain a livelihood through trade and break the monopoly of the Meccan merchants. See, *Islam and the Integration of Society*.

Christian king of Abyssinia, refused to send them back, but instead offered them sanctuary under his protection.

In 619 his wife, Khadija, and his uncle, Abu Talib, both died.[10] They were influential figures in the Meccan clan-based society, who had protected Muhammad against threats to his life. A new clan leader withdrew all support from him. Meanwhile, some Muslims were martyred for their faith. So, in 622, Muhammad and his followers, having been rejected by the people of the town of Taif as a false prophet (they reasoned that his failure to convince his fellow citizens of the truth of his message meant that God must have abandoned him in Mecca), emigrated to a city to the north of Mecca (in those days called Yathrib). He and his followers went at the invitation of an influential group there, to be their leader and establish the unity of the city (one God, one people).

There is some speculation about the exact nature of the invitation. Certainly, some Muslim believers (known locally as the ansar (helpers)) met Muhammad secretly at al-Aqaba to pledge their support. The following year they returned with a larger delegation to renew the pledge. Meanwhile, Muhammad had been given permission by Allah to fight, when necessary:

> To this point Muhammad had been required to bear opposition patiently, but the time for patience was past. 'Leave is given to those who fight…because they were wronged – surely God is able to help them – who were expelled from their habitations without right…' (Q. 22.4-42). The Muslims of Yathrib…were now no longer just religious supporters of Muhammad, but also military allies.[11]

It is possible that Muhammad was perceived by some of the Arabs living in Yathrib, where there was already a large population of Jews, as the future prophet foretold in the Jewish Scriptures. They hoped that by inviting Muhammad to go to their city they would have a powerful ally in their disputes with the Jews. They also hoped that he might act as a mediator to bring together the two mutually hostile Aws and Khazraj tribes.[12]

This migration is known as the *hijrah*. It brings to an end the first chapter in Muhammad's eventful life. This initial Meccan phase may be summarised in the following way: 'A new religion is announced, another religious leader climbs on to the stage of history, a few followers are gained, much suffering is nobly born'.[13]

---

[10] Khadija became the first person to accept Muhammad's message; Abu Talib, though loyal to his nephew, never became a Muslim.

[11] Brown, *A New Introduction to Islam*, 77.

[12] See, Zeitlin, *The Historical Muhammad*, 11.

[13] P. Riddel and P. Cotterell, *Islam in Context*.

Medina

Ruler of a city

Yathrib became *Madina-al-Nabi* (the city of the prophet). Muhammad became the governor. The *hijrah* marked the birth of Islam. This proved to be an emigration of a different order from that which took place to Ethiopia seven years earlier. The latter was intended as a temporary measure, and eventually the small band of Muhammad's followers returned (in 629). The move to Medina was designed to be permanent. From now on, a new community (the *ummah*) came into existence. It took control of the political process. Instead of being a small, persecuted minority in a hostile environment, it became the dominant force in a cosmopolitan city. It now won control of power. Islam was no longer the religion of a small group that had defied the polytheistic beliefs and practices of the majority, but became the state religion.[14] Ostensibly freedom of worship was allowed for the Jewish and Christian inhabitants of the city; later, however, this concession was denied to polytheists (*mushrikun*).[15]

From this event, the Muslim calendar has been dated. In other words, the history of Islam begins, not so much with the first revelations in 610 and the formation of a small band of the companions of the prophet, but with the establishment of a socio-political community.[16] By dating the Islamic era from the time of the *hijrah*, Muslims seem to be saying that the years of adversity in Mecca were, in effect, pre-Islamic.

> That migration...marks the major turning point in Islamic history, when Islam was transformed from a small group of devotees to a full-fledged community.[17]

Muhammad built the first mosque in Medina. Tariq Ramadan explains the significance of this event:

> Once built, the mosque becomes the axial space of the Muslim spiritual community in which it is situated, but it also expresses the reality of settlement, of acceptance of the hosting space, which is then turned into a space for oneself, a home.... Mosques tell of meaning, direction and settlement. Yathrib had become Medina.[18]

In other words, the incipient Muslim community did not regard itself any longer as a pilgrim people, for it had discovered here an abiding city.

---

[14] Rippin, *Muslims: Their Religious Beliefs and Practices*, 42.
[15] Abdullah Saeed, *Interpreting the Qur'an*, 141
[16] Esposito, *Islam, the Straight Path*, 10.
[17] Nasr, *The Heart of Islam*, 31.
[18] Ramadan, *The Messenger*, 84 (emphasis added).

Muhammad also produced a written constitution and law code for the inhabitants. In some ways this act was even more significant than the building of the mosque.

> On arriving in Medina, he (Muhammad) already possessed a symbolic and political power that none of the city's dignitaries could ignore. Many of Yathrib's inhabitants had converted to Islam and recognized him as God's messenger; those converts came from both the Aws and Khazraj clans, which had been at war for ages.[19]

> In Madinah he arrived as a ruler, laying the foundations of a nascent state and religion. He now began to establish his community. One of the first tasks was to provide the charter of Madinah – a sort of Magna Carta – which announced the rights and obligations of all citizens, Jews and Muslims.[20]

The principal purpose of the constitution was to bring about a sense of unity, by ending inter-tribal and inter-ethnic conflicts, whilst recognising diversity. The idea was to include within the city state all communities as equal participants and to ensure that, in the event of threats from outside, the different groups would stand together and protect one another.

Two aspects of the agreement are indicative of the way in which political life developed within Medina. First, the constitution was drawn up by Muhammad. It cannot be said to express the considered input of all the different communities. Perhaps this is not particularly important, since it provided a framework that appeared to benefit all the inhabitants. Secondly, however, the text stipulated that in the case of dispute, the Prophet would be answerable for the strict and equitable implementation of this agreement. In other words, in the light of the claim to be the one channel of divine revelation, he alone had the authority to discern the specific divine requirements. Hassan Turabi called Medina a federal state between Jews and Muslims. However, according to Abdelwahab El-Affendi, this is a disingenuous interpretation of what took place, since the arrangement in Medina began as more of a defence pact than a state. The Jews were never given any right to exercise authority over Muslims as part of the pact.[21]

---

[19] Ramadan, *The Messenger*, 88.

[20] Akbar S. Ahmed, *Discovering Islam: Making Sense of Muslim History and Society* (London, Routledge, 1988), 20.

[21] 'Hasan Turabi and the Limits of Modern Islamic Reformism' in Ibrahim M. Abu-Rabi, *The Blackwell Companion to Contemporary Islamic Thought*, 149.

> The prophet-preacher in him now recedes, and the man of practical politics comes to the fore. What becomes most salient in Medina is his role as political leader, military strategist and warrior.[22]

Once having taken the momentous decision to leave Mecca, with the prospect of being able to set up a situation, where he and his followers would be free of persecution and able to govern, he became the object of renewed hostility. Whereas in Mecca he proved an irritant in opposing the religious and economic monopolies of the ruling families, as an exile in another city he represented an external peril that threatened the very existence of the Meccan way of life. Thus, much of his activities and strategies in Medina have to be interpreted in the light of the aggression that his own people directed towards him.

External hostilities

Early on in the new environment, in order to survive, Muhammad sent out raiding parties to take goods from caravans passing close to the city. In one such raid, the party desecrated a sacred Arab convention that during certain months of the year the caravans were to be free from assault. Muhammad had misgivings about the raid, because bloodshed was forbidden during the sacred period. However, a new revelation (Q. 2.217-218) justified the attack in these words:

> They ask you [Prophet] about fighting in the prohibited month. Say, 'Fighting in that month is a great offence, but to bar others from God's path, to disbelieve in Him, prevent access to the sacred Mosque, and expel its people, are still greater offences in God's eyes: persecution is worse than killing.

With these words, *jihad* (in the sense of the justified use of armed force) was legitimated.[23] The raids led to 'more complex military enterprises and put the

[22] Zeitlin, *The Historical Muhammad*, 11.

[23] Other Quranic verses that appear to enjoin violence against non-Muslims are the following: 2.221; 3. 28, 85, 118, 142, 155-8, 169; 4. 84, 95-96, 100-101, 144; 5. 14, 36,51, 72-3, 116; 6. 149; 8. 12-14, 39, 55; 9.5, 14, 17, 23, 29, 39, 41, 73, 123; 22. 19-22; 25.52; 47.4; 98.6. *Jihad* is a divine institution, an instrument to be used for the purposes of advancing Islam. Muslims must strive and fight and, if necessary, kill in the name of God, see R. Peters, *Jihad in Classical and Modern Islam* (Princeton, NJ: Princeton University Press, 1996). 'The Quran refers to armed defence and justly executed warfare, for which Islam specifies the conditions of war and peace, the treatment of captives and the negotiation and resolution of conflict'. The idea was further developed by Muslim jurists 'as concerned with the defence of Muslim society and as an extension of its borders,' Azim Nanji, *Dictionary of Islam,* (London: Penguin Books, 2008), 90-91.

nascent Muslim community on its course of development as a militant dominating power'.[24]

Much of the next ten years of Muhammad's rule in Medina was taken up in dealing with various kinds of opposition, both internal and external. Externally, the Quraysh tribe in Mecca continued to be a potent threat. In the first armed encounter between the forces of Mecca and Medina, the battle of Badr (624), the latter prevailed. Naturally, this victory was interpreted by the Muslims as confirmation of God's guiding hand and protection of the newly fledged community: 'The solidarity of the Medinan Muslims was immeasurably strengthened by the meaning assigned to the victory as divine sanction of the new faith'.[25]

Muhammad's position as governor of Medina and commander of its army was consolidated by the success. It is open to speculation whether Muhammad would have survived as the leader of the city of Medina had his army been defeated.

Nevertheless, in the following year he did suffer a reversal, at the battle of Uhud. Although apparently winning the confrontation at the beginning, a tactical error by some of the archers led to a Quraysh counter-attack which threw the Medina army into confusion. Muhammad himself was wounded. Nevertheless, as the saying goes, Muhammad, aided by further revelations, was able to take some positive lessons from the defeat. The decision to leave Medina and fight in open country, rather than wait from within prepared fortifications for the enemy to attack, was taken by a majority decision after a process of consultation, for

> Revelation...states that the principle of deliberation, of majority decision making, is not to be negotiated and must be respected beyond historical contingencies and human mistakes in decisions.[26]

A revelation (Q. 3.136-7.) also gave the reason for the defeat: it was to distinguish between true and false believers, and to condemn those who disobeyed orders because of their desire to get their hands on the booty. Moreover, Muhammad was not killed, suggesting that God still had plans for his messenger.

A third major military encounter occurred two years later (627). A large force of Meccans, Bedouins, and Abyssinian mercenaries came together to invade Medina, with the aim of inflicting a defeat that would end Muhammad's governance of the city (Q. 33.9-25). Eventually, after a 25 day siege, the

---

[24] E. Landau-Tasseron, 'Features of the Pre-Conquest Muslim Army in the time of Muhammad' in A. Cameron (ed.), *The Byzantine and Early Islamic Near East* (Princeton: The Darwin Press, 1995), 307.

[25] Zeitlin, *The Historical Muhammad*, 12

[26] Ramadan, *The Messenger*, 127.

alliance against Medina was forced to withdraw. A new military strategy, that of digging a deep trench around the city to act as an impassable barrier to horses, was successfully carried out. Then, Muhammad agreed to a plan to sow confusion among the opposition alliance, which set them against one another. Finally, a lack of provisions and the extreme cold of the season made it impossible for the opposing army to continue.

The failure of the Quraysh to inflict a major defeat on the Muslims in Medina led eventually to a peace treaty. Muhammad attempted a pilgrimage back to Mecca in 628. Outside the city at a place called al-Hudaybiyya, the two parties negotiated an end to hostilities. Under the terms of the treaty, the Muslims were not to enter Mecca that year, but they would be permitted to return to Mecca for three nights in future years. The following year, Muhammad returned to the city with his companions for the first time since the *hijrah,* to make a pilgrimage to the holy site of the *Kaaba.* In 630, owing to a violation of the treaty by some tribal allies of the Quraysh, Muhammad marched on Mecca. The city surrendered and he entered as conqueror. His final pilgrimage was made in 632, the tenth year after the *hijrah.* Later that year he died in Medina at the age of 62 after a short illness.

Internal hostilities

In many ways, the opposition to Muhammad from within Medina was more difficult to deal with. Initially, when Muhammad accepted the invitation to go with his companions to the city, he had hoped that the Jewish population there would recognise him as the prophet spoken of in their Scriptures:

> The Lord said to me:..I will raise up for them a prophet like you from among their brothers; I will put my words in his mouth, and he will tell them everything I command him. If anyone does not listen to my words that the prophet speaks in my name, I myself will call him to account.[27]

As a result of receiving revelations from God that dealt with topics found in the story of Moses (idolatry, exploitation of the poor, neglect of widows and orphans, resistance to God's message) was he not entitled to think of himself as a new Moses?[28] Would it not have been natural to have likened the *hijrah* from Mecca to the exodus from Egypt? And, once he had entered the refuge of Medina, might he not have seen himself as a second Joshua, commanded to subdue the enemies of God's people?

However, the Jews in Medina refused to recognise Muhammad as an authentic prophet. For them, the age of prophecy was over. All that needed to

---

[27] Deut. 18.18-19.

[28] See, Singh, 'Muhammad, "The Prophet like Moses"?'

be known about God's will was already revealed in the Torah of the Hebrew Scriptures. They might well have suspected that Muhammad's claim to have received the final revelation from God was motivated by the desire to create a religion for the Arab peoples that would be on a par with that of the Jews and Christians. Moreover, they would have been suspicious of the way in which the history of the Jewish people was portrayed in these new revelations, sometimes totally at odds with the Biblical accounts. Although initially agreeing to the Medina constitution as a pact of mutual support and protection, the Jews came to resent the power and authority which, in their eyes, Muhammad had illegitimately taken to himself.

Up to the time of the Battle of the Trench (627), relations between Jews and non-Jews though tense had not broken out into open conflict. After the battle, Muhammad launched a campaign against them. A significant amount of the verses of the Qur'an that came to Muhammad in Medina have to do with a polemic against the Jews. In January 624, the congregation worshipping in the mosque, which hitherto had been facing in the direction of Jerusalem, was told to turn round and pray in the opposite direction of Mecca. Muhammad taught that the *Kaaba* had no connection with either Judaism or Christianity, and that Islam was a separate faith, associated with Abraham and Ishmael:

> Say, 'my Lord has guided me to a straight path, an upright religion, the faith of Abraham, a man of pure faith. He was not a polytheist (Q. 6.161).
>
> We made the House (the *Kaaba* at Mecca) a resort and a sanctuary for people...We commanded Abraham and Ishmael: Purify My House for those who walk round it, those who stay there, and those who bow and prostrate themselves in worship (Q. 2.125).
>
> Were you [Jews] there to see when death came upon Jacob? When he said to his sons, 'What will you worship after I am gone?' they replied, 'We shall worship your God and the God of your fathers, Abraham, Ishmael and Isaac, one single God: we devote ourselves to Him (Q. 2.133).

Richard Bell, in a highly illuminating study of Muhammad's relationship to Judaism and Christianity, proposes that it was in Medina, through the Jewish community there, that he discovered two salient facts about Abraham, which he used as the bedrock for considering Islam a wholly independent religion. First, Abraham preceded Moses (and, of course, Jesus). Secondly, Abraham had two sons, Ishmael as well as Isaac.

> Ishmael was the reputed ancestor of the Arabs, and having discovered that he was the son of Abraham, the prophet of the Arabs knew how to make use of the fact that Abraham came in time before Moses. It brought the Arabs and himself into the race...of the people of God, and into the line of descent in which the prophetic office was appointed to be, as stated in *Surah* 57.26: 'We...appointed the

> prophetic office and the Book to be among their descendents...' The priority of Abraham to Moses and also to Jesus, enabled...Muhammad at Medina, when his hopes for the Jews failed, to fall back upon a man of God, independent alike of Jews and Christians, whom he can associate with the Ka'aba and the new Arab faith.[29]

Irving Zeitlin comments:

> That was the thought-process, for Bell, by which Muhammad turned Abraham and Ishmael into the original Muslims. They could be made into the precursors of Islam, associated as they were with Arabia, because they represented in his mind the pure religion, which was eternal (din qayyim), and free from the corruptions which occasionally crept into it.[30]

We find here, therefore, a highly plausible account of how Muhammad was able to elaborate a faith that could stand on its own, without having to depend on already existing monotheistic religions. Moreover, although chronologically Muhammad was the last of the prophets, his message was a recapitulation of one that preceded, in his eyes, the religions of both the Jews (Moses) and the Christians (Jesus). He was simply reinstating a pure, original monotheistic faith that had become, in part, corrupted in the course of its transmission. The Arabs had a prophet and Scripture of their own in their own language, and their rediscovered faith predated that of the other communities in the Arabian Peninsular.

From early on in his governorship of Medina, Muhammad had to contend with the machinations of those called hypocrites (*munafiqun*). They were the people who professed to support the new constitution and the city against its enemies, but in reality were working behind the scenes to thwart efforts to bring order, unity and justice to the community. Among them, according to the Qur'an, were the Jews. From the beginning they resented the presence of Muhammad, in particular taking exception to his presumption that they would recognise his prophetic calling. They believed that privileges were due to them as the original settlers of Yathrib. Moreover, as those who had become successful city-dwellers as merchants and cultivators, they considered that their culture was superior to that of the nomadic, Bedouin tribes, which represented the background of the Meccan immigrants. Therefore, they were reluctant to accept a contract that implied that it was being concluded among equals.[31]

---

[29] Bell, *The Origin of Islam in its Christian Environment* (London: Macmillan, 1926), 130

[30] Zeitlin, *The Historical Muhammad*, 102.

[31] See, Barakat Ahmad, *Muhammad and the Jews: A Re-examination* (New Delhi: Vikas, 1979).

The leaders of the Banu Nadir Jewish tribe were accused of supporting a raid on Medina by Meccan forces under Abu Sufyan soon after the battle of Badr:

> The Jewish public rhetoric against Muhammad together with the B.Nadir's secret dealings with his enemies, compelled him to act decisively and to show that he was not weakened by the Meccan attacks.[32]

They also launched a propaganda campaign against Muhammad. When they refused to renew the mutual non-aggression pact, they were subdued and expelled from Medina. The tribe's land was redistributed to Muhammad's companions (the *Muhajirun*), who thereby became economically independent of the original Arab inhabitants of the city.

After the Battle of the Trench, Muhammad moved against the Banu Qurayza Jewish tribe, who represented the last major focus of opposition to his rule. He attacked their strongholds and crushed them; the tribe had no option but to surrender unconditionally.

Now occurred one of the most controversial episodes in the life of Muhammad. At his instigation, a judge was appointed to decide what should be done to the tribe. The man appointed was Saad b. Muadh, who served as Muhammad's personal bodyguard, a man with a reputation for harshness and bad temper. His decision was that the adult male members of the tribe should be killed and the women and children sold into slavery, in order to purchase horses and weapons for the Muslims.[33] About 700 people perished as a result. Gordon Newby believes that 'it should not come as a surprise that the massacre of the Qurayza took place as it did. The escalating tension between Muhammad and the Jews was bound to force a military confrontation'.[34]

The final campaign against Jewish communities in the vicinity of Medina took place in 629 against the fortified city of Khaybar situated some 80 kilometres north of Medina. The city had considerable wealth, built upon a highly successful agricultural system. Muhammad through the use of superior force was able to negotiate a treaty whereby the Jews could remain on their land on condition of paying to Muhammad the proceeds from half the annual harvest. It does not appear from the records that the people of Khaybar constituted a threat to Muhammad or that they showed any particularly belligerent gestures towards him. The expedition against the city must then be interpreted as a means of securing a regular income for the Muslim community.

---

[32] Zeitlin, *The Historical Muhammad*, 148.

[33] See, Zeitlin, *The Historical Muhammad*, 150-151.

[34] Gordon Newby, *A History of the Jews of Arabia* (Columbia, SC: University of South Carolina Press, 1988), 93.

It became the forerunner of similar treaties with conquered peoples during the military expansion of Islam subsequent to the prophet's death.

Assessment of the Origins of Islam

So far, we have presented a bare outline of the historical events of the epoch-making last twenty two years in the life of Muhammad. As we have already seen, there is a basic consensus among Muslim and non-Muslim historians about the essential episodes. However, how they should be interpreted either within the wider context of Muhammad's own day or as a guide to the present debate about the alleged clash of civilisations is a complicated question. Part of the problem lies with the understandable veneration accorded to Muhammad by the followers of Islam. Certain high profile affairs, such as the controversy over Salman Rushdie's book, *The Satanic Verses*, or the cartoons in a Danish publication depicting Muhammad as a terrorist, have highlighted the extreme affront and provocation that any kind of criticism of Muhammad can evoke. Andrew Rippin explains that 'Those who insinuate evil of Muhammad or who cast aspersions on him are considered to be insulting Islam'.[35]

There is an important historical dimension to this extreme sensitivity. Disparagement of Muhammad creates for contemporary Muslims images of the extreme polemic against him that took place in medieval times. Criticism raises the suspicion that such charges, particularly in relation to the use of war to bring about conversions, to the divine legitimising of polygamy and to the number of marriages that Muhammad consummated, are being laid once again. Moreover, because Muhammad is seen as an exemplar for every Muslim,[36] a person whose piety and behaviour is taken as a pattern to follow, denigrating Muhammad implies an attack on Muslims' way of life.

And yet, at the same time, Muhammad is not considered, except perhaps in extreme hagiographical writings, a faultless human being. Criticisms and correction of his behaviour are recorded in the Qur'an.[37] Early material certainly portrays Muhammad as a person who was capable of making mistakes. The idea that he was a 'perfect man' took centuries to become fully established in Islam. In the evolution of a religion, the founding figure tends to grow in stature, the apparent moral infelicities tend to become excused, and the original real life historical person is overtaken by the construction of an ahistorical pious substitute.

---

[35] Rippin, *Muslims: Their Religious Beliefs and Practices*, 49.

[36] See Q. 33.21.

[37] For example, *Surah* 80, is called 'He Frowned', because Muhammad became annoyed at the interruption by a blind man of a conversation he was having with an eminent member of the Quraysh clan. The Qur'anic text rebukes him for his partiality and injustice.

So, the major criticisms of Muhammad almost exclusively concern his life and policies as governor of Medina. They include his military ruthlessness, political opportunism, toleration of massacre, religious belligerence and marital excess.[38] The major issue that confronts every person attempting to explain the life of this man revolves around the compulsion to leave Mecca. Given the circumstances of persecution and the threat on his life and those of his followers, was the *hijrah* inevitable? Or, was there a way in which he could have remained in Mecca, acting perhaps as a reformer from within, without compromising the message that he was in the process of receiving? There is, also, a second question of nearly equal consequence: having decided to emigrate from Mecca, was it completely unavoidable that he should assume the reigns of political power in Medina? Would, for example, a situation of sanctuary, akin to that his followers enjoyed in Abyssinia, have been possible?

These questions are not merely historical anachronisms. The relative merits of a religion based on the revelations given during the sojourn in Mecca in contrast to the way in which events unfolded in Medina is still of immense contemporary interest.[39] The matter is hugely complex. On the one hand, it may be argued that Islam, as the return to a pristine, ethically rigorous monotheism could not have survived in the maelstrom of Meccan socio-religious life. It can be further argued that history cannot be re-run. Moreover, it will be said that Islam is a faith that, because it encompasses the whole of life, must be expressed in terms of socio-political ends. The alleged separation of spheres of rule between God and Caesar just is not possible to contemplate within the parameters of the Qur'anic message.

On the other hand, it could be argued that no human decision is historically determined in advance of its being taken. It may be strongly conditioned by the circumstances within which it has to be taken; but it is not so controlled that no other course of action would have been possible. It might further be argued that Muhammad could have adopted a different policy in Mecca in seeking to communicate his message, or that, having decided to emigrate to Medina, he and his followers could have lived as a minority community, without having to take hold of the reins of power. These questions are difficult to resolve for those who live at such a distance from the original situation. Nevertheless, in the light of the damage inflicted on Islam by those Muslims who insist that it has a particular political role as a religion, perhaps a major rethink of the nature and impact of the *hijrah* could lead to an unimaginable renewal of the faith.

[38] See, Cragg, *The House of Islam* (Belmont, CA: Wadsworth, 1975), 23.

[39] A number of Muslim leaders of recent times (among them Ali Shari'ati, Ghulam Ahmad Parwez, Hassan Turabi, and Mahmud Muhammad Taha), even though hotly contested, have urged that contemporary Islam identify itself anew with its Meccan phase. Further on we will explore the implications of such a move.

One thing is certain the fateful events of 622 still cast a long shadow over current interpretations of Islam.

We will need to return to these and similar questions in later chapters. Meanwhile, in order to gain another perspective on these matters, we will turn to the early history of Christianity. The main purpose of the exercise will be to explore the similarities in the history of the origins of both faiths, whilst not neglecting the divergences. We will note, for further reflection at a later stage, how the two faiths reacted in contrasting ways to similar pressures.

Chapter 6

Another Tale of Two Cities: Jerusalem and Rome

On April 7th, in the year 30 AD,[1] a man from the small village of Nazareth in the north of Israel was crucified alongside two others just outside the city limits of Jerusalem. His name was Jesus ben Joseph, the son of Mary and the brother of James and Jude. Three days later a few of his companions, even though they had witnessed his burial, claimed to have seen him alive again. During the next forty days, many others alleged that they had met with him at different times of the day in various locations. Then, suddenly, these encounters ceased. Nevertheless, the companions formed themselves into a community and started proclaiming a message that this man was Israel's Messiah, or specially anointed envoy from God, whose death should be understood as a sacrifice that brings salvation from sin and evil for all who believe in him. Moreover, this man, though no longer visible to the naked eye, was alive and in close touch with his friends.

Approximately two hundred and eighty years later, the successors of this community were given a privileged position within the Roman Empire, and the faith that they espoused gradually became the one and only official religion of the state. The purpose of this chapter is to trace in outline the main events that led from the gathering of 120 followers of Jesus in Jerusalem, 50 days after the Passover in the year 30 AD, to the momentous events surrounding the accession of Constantine to the imperial purple in the year 312. This is the story of the origin of what has come to be called the Christian faith.

As one of the main reasons for telling this story here is to compare it to the story of the origin of Islam, particular attention will be made to the way in which this Christian community responded to the political, social and cultural milieu in which it arose and grew. In other words, this historical study assumes that one of the major keys to understanding its core beliefs and practices is to consider its relationship to the powers that dominated the Graeco-Roman world at the time of its birth and early development.

---

[1] See Ben Witherington III, *New Testament History: A Narrative Account* (Carlisle: Paternoster Press, 2001), 134. This date (14 Nisan in the Jewish calendar) is a conjecture. Others believe that Jesus death occurred at Passover time in the year 33 AD: so, for example, Paul Barnett, *Jesus and the Rise of Early Christianity: A History of New Testament Times* (Downers Grove: IVP, 1999), 229.

This account is limited in its scope. There is no pretence that the whole history of the expansion of the church, South and East as well as North and West, will be told. The interest is to see what kind of a community originally arose in the wake of the life and teaching of Jesus and how, in response to its surroundings, it gradually grew into an institution significantly different from the one that had started out on the first Pentecost of its life, a few weeks after the death of its central figure. The ways in which it interrelated with the dominant power of its day are crucial to understanding what sort of community it is called to be in the present and what kind of message it is commissioned to share with all.

This particular focus is not intended to neglect or minimize other essential factors that contributed to the new community's self-understanding, the main one being, of course, how it saw itself in relation to its Jewish heritage. The way in which it conducted itself, in the light of the severe tensions it experienced with the Jewish people caused by its interpretation of the meaning of Jesus, is also a key to appreciating its self-awareness as a distinct body. Indeed, its relationship to Judaism was part of the way in which Roman officials viewed it, from Gallio in Corinth (Acts 18.12-17) to Pliny in Asia Minor in his famous letter to the emperor Trajan.[2]

Historical Reliability

As was the case with the origin of Islam, it is not possible to enter into the intricacies of the debate about the reliability of historical documents. Here, I take what I believe to be the mainstream view that the major sources of our knowledge of the origin and development of Christianity (the New Testament, Josephus, assorted Roman historians, the so-called 'Fathers' of the church, writing in Greek and Latin from the late first century onwards) are sufficiently reliable to be able to reconstruct a plausible history with some confidence.

The Gospel narratives of the ministry of Jesus, for example, though not to be compared with a biography in the modern sense, nevertheless present a selective set of short stories that focus on the teaching or actions of Jesus in particular settings. They follow the ancient biographical convention of using indirect portraits to reveal the nature of the central figure. The goal was to reveal who the person was, not to recount all the detailed events of his life. So, we are presented with a representative sampling of a person's life activities that are sufficient to reveal that person's character and life's work.[3] It is more than likely that they were working with oral and written traditions about Jesus that

---

[2] See Paul McKechnie, *The First Christian Centuries: Perspectives on the Early Church* (Leicester: IVP, 2001), 113-115.

[3] Here I am following the account of the Gospel writers' historiographical interests as set out in *New Testament History*, 20-25.

had been faithfully handed down from eye-witnesses. After an exhaustive study of the multiple evidence of the first century, Richard Bauckham concludes:

> (I am) arguing that the Gospels, though in some ways a very distinctive form of historiography, share broadly in the attitude to eyewitness testimony that was common among historians in the Greco- Roman period. These historians valued above all reports of first-hand experience of the events they recounted. Best of all was for the historian to have been himself a participant in the events.... Failing that..., they sought informants who could speak from firsthand knowledge and whom they could interview. This, at least, was historiographic best practice, represented and theorised by such generally admired historians as Thucydides and Polybius.[4]

Christopher Rowland, after a survey of the complexities involved in determining the origin of the sayings and deeds of Jesus, concludes that there are two good reasons for considering that the Gospels present by and large a faithful representation of Jesus in his historical context:

> First of all, the more one looks at related Jewish texts, the more plausible a case can be made for the authenticity of much of what is contained in the Gospels. Second, this approach is based on the assumption of authenticity of evidence unless there are strong reasons to doubt it.[5]

In the case of the Acts of the Apostles (the second volume of Luke's story of the birth and expansion of the new Christian movement), once one understands that the author's purpose in writing was not to give a disinterested account of the facts, the historical reliability of what is reported can be judged fairly. Luke selects events in accordance with his aim to chronicle the most significant incidents in the life of the early Christian community. As well as showing how the message of Jesus Christ reached and grew among the Gentiles, he records numerous summaries of critical speeches given at key moments in the chequered progress of the faith from Jerusalem to Rome.

There are numerous questions to which curiosity would love to have an answer. Why, for example, does the Apostle Peter disappear from the narrative half way through (after chapter 15)? Why does the narrative stop tantalisingly with Paul in Rome (presumably) waiting for a judicial review of his case? What was the outcome? Did he continue on his missionary journeys, eventually even reaching Spain? Why does Luke dedicate one quarter of his manuscript to the events leading up to Paul's journey to Rome? These are imponderables about

---

[4] Richard Bauckham, *Jesus and the Eyewitnesses: The Gospels as Eyewitness Testimony* (Grand Rapids: Eerdmans, 2006), 479.

[5] Christopher Rowland, *Christian Origins: The Setting of the Character of the Most Important Messianic Sect of Judaism* (London: SPCK, 2002/2), 129.

which one may speculate, but have no certain explanation. Nevertheless, the reasonable presumption that Luke was writing with his own agenda in view does not automatically invalidate the accuracy of what he was describing. All of history is written selectively according to the interests of the narrator. However, to suggest that selectivity equals inaccuracy is to beg the question. Only, if a historian reports an event in a way that totally contradicts other reliable accounts would one have the right to question the veracity of his record. The latter has not been demonstrated in the case of the Book of Acts.

The Public Life of Jesus

John the Baptist

In the only major accounts that we have of Jesus itinerant ministry (begun round about 28 CE), he is portrayed initially as representing a prophetic renewal movement among his own people. He identifies himself closely with the preaching and baptismal practise of his cousin John, which called for a clear ethical revival among the Jewish people, in order to 'bear fruits worthy of repentance' (Lk. 3.8). John spelt out acceptable practice, in the case of the affluent, collectors of taxes and the armed forces (Lk. 3.11-14), in view of the reality of God's rule over his people (the kingdom). John's uncompromising preaching and expectation of an imminent climactic event drew around him many people. Although the content of his message was not directly political, in that he was not lobbying for power, it had political consequences, for it focused people's discontent with the present regimes by calling for a new kind of world.[6]

Josephus states that Herod Antipas, the Tetrarch of Galilee and Perea, feared John's popularity, alarmed that he might be able to persuade the common people to rise up against this client king of the Romans. So, he had him imprisoned and eventually executed at the behest of his wife. However, John's intention was not to stir up a political movement of protest, but to prepare the Jewish nation for God's special involvement in the life of his people through a special envoy about to appear on the scene. Baptism, which was the initiatory rite for Gentiles who wished to follow the religion of Israel, was intended to show that no-one was exempt from God's judgement on the faithlessness of the people.

Soon after John had been arrested and thrown into prison, Jesus began his public preaching. He chose both the synagogues of the Galilean region and also the open air to make known his message. The main burden of his exhortation

[6] See, Ian Hazlett, *Early Christianity: Origins and Evolution to AD 600* (London: SPCK, 1991), 31-32.

was that people should prepare themselves for a new manifestation of God's saving power by repenting of unworthy lives, believing that this fresh activity was good news and by following him (Mk. 1.14-20).

Herod Antipas

Although John still exercised a considerable authority from prison (see, Mt. 11.2-6; Mk. 6.29), many of his disciples must have been bewildered, wondering perhaps whether the shadowy figure, said by John to be 'more powerful than me', (Mt. 3.11) would continue the movement in the desert:

> The people have looked to John for deliverance. Now he is in prison, and the question is whether Jesus will take up the role of national deliverer and also free John.[7]

If he were to have followed John's lead, he would have given evidence of his credentials as the messiah whom the nation was eagerly awaiting. So, Jesus could have capitalised on this situation, particularly the sense of frustration at the arbitrary removal of John, and re-initiated his work in the desert. He could have built upon a rising tide of opposition to Herod Antipas. Many would have agreed with John's denunciation of Antipas for stealing his half-brother Philip's wife and for 'all the evil things Herod had done' (Lk. 3.19).

Herod was a kind of war-lord, possessing a sizeable personal army. As long as he regularly paid tribute to Rome, maintained borders against the threat of Syrian invasion from the North and did not attempt to become independent of imperial rule, he was allowed freedom to control his territory as he wished. He was only superficially religious, thus incurring the anger of the Pharisees. He was loyal to Rome, thus provoking opposition from the various groups of 'freedom-fighters'. He heavily taxed ordinary citizens to fund his extravagant building projects and lifestyle, thus creating resentment among the self-employed artisans and labouring classes. The time might well have been right for an attempted uprising.

Galilee of the Nations

It appears, however, that Jesus, despite the opportunity to organise the disaffected masses into a political movement, deliberately turned his back on the desert with its false messianic associations, rejecting it as a sphere of legitimate ministry. He actually chose to begin it in Galilee (Mt. 3.12). The importance of this decision, which is geographical in its outcome, but

---

[7] Alan Storkey, *Jesus and Politics: Confronting the Powers* (Grand Rapids: Baker Academic, 2005), 71.

'theological' in its intent, cannot be over-estimated. Both the desert and Galilee, as specific geographical locations, had their own special significance. The desert was for ever associated with testing and purification. It was the place that Israel had to learn obedience to all God's laws and precepts or perish. There they had to learn to trust God to remove all their enemies and give them possession of the promised-land (Deut. 9.1-3). Galilee, on the other hand, was characterised by its mixed population. There had been a steady influx of Greeks and Romans, bringing with them a pagan culture. Herod Antipas had built alien cities like Sepphoris (CE 10) and Tiberias (CE 25). He persuaded people to move into these 'impure' cities by offering free houses and land and exempting the inhabitants from taxes for the first few years.

From the beginning of his public life, then, Jesus refused to interpret his ministry in the narrow sense of a national liberator, founded on an outmoded theocratic ideal. Rather, he construed his role in universal terms, to bring salvation to the nations.[8] This interpretation of the messianic role, backed by concrete action, was a great scandal to his own people. They rejected Jesus, precisely because he saw his ministry inclusively, extending beyond the bounds of only one ethnic group (see, Lk. 4.25-30).

It has been pointed out that Galilee, just because of the admixture of different peoples, religions and cultures, would have been a focus for the kind of strict torah observance promoted by the Pharisees:

> Surrounded and permeated as it was by paganism, Galilean Jewry naturally looked...to the symbols of distinctiveness which mattered in the local setting. The Torah assumed new importance in border territory...And the features of Torah which loomed largest were those which functioned specifically and obviously as cultural, social and religious boundary markers, i.e. Sabbath, food-laws and circumcision.[9]

This social setting helps to explain the vehemence with which the Pharisees opposed Jesus, when he reinterpreted the meaning of the Sabbath (Mk. 2.23-28; 3.1-6) and the laws concerning fasting (Mk. 2.18-20) and purification (Mk. 2.15-17; 7.1-8, 14-15). In each case he loosened considerably the boundaries between a strict, orthodox practise of the faith and the needs of the ordinary people. The kingdom of God in the preaching and action of Jesus was not

---

[8] This is, perhaps, more accentuated in Luke's Gospel than, say, in Matthew's. The sympathetic treatment of the Samaritans in both Luke and John's account of Jesus, the references to the widow of Zarephath, Naaman the Syrian (Lk. 4. 24-27), those who will come from the four corners of the world to eat in the kingdom (Lk. 13. 29) and the Greeks who wished to meet Jesus (Jn. 12.21) are some of the indications of the universal intent of Jesus message and ministry.

[9] See, N.T. Wright, *The New Testament and the People of God* (London: SPCK, 1992), 168.

captive either to the insurrectionists of the time or to the narrow legalistic fanaticism of the self-appointed guardians of the law.

The coming Messianic Age

Jesus was treading a new path. He refused, beginning with the temptations in the desert, to interpret his life's work in terms of the expectations of his day. He needed to affirm that he saw himself as the Messiah, and yet at the same time to reject current interpretations of what this would have meant. So, he refused the opportunity to call the nation back to a strict, legalistic understanding of Torah, and he disassociated himself from those who believed that faithfulness to God implied armed resistance to the foreign forces of occupation. Rather, he taught his disciples a more profound and challenging ethic that confronted the superficial external observance of rules and regulations (Mt. 5.17-48.; Lk. 6.27-38). Above all, he taught his disciples to welcome and associate with those deemed by the orthodox religion of the day to have been condemned by God: the physically and mentally disabled, the poor, enemy collaborators, women, and traditional adversaries (like the Samaritans).

He proclaimed the dawn of a new messianic age that would be inaugurated, not by rigorous adherence to the letter of the law and the traditions of the elders, even less by force of arms, but through a compassionate serving of the needs of the people. Above all, he taught that ultimately only through suffering could the world order become radically changed (Mt. 5.10-16, 38-48; Mk. 8.31-37; 10.42-45; Lk. 22.49-53). His preaching, teaching and ministry of healing implied a rebuke of those who wielded power in the public domain, particularly those who, for reasons of personal gain, colluded with the Roman Empire. These are described as the courtiers and officers of Herod's personal fiefdom and the leaders of Galilee (Mk. 6.21). However, his opposition to the ruling authorities of the day did not issue in a call for a regime-change in the conventional sense. Jesus was not interested in replacing the Roman system with another one. There is nothing in the Gospel narrative that sets Jesus apart from the prophetic ministry of a Nathan, Jeremiah, Isaiah, Amos or Micah. His words and works do not indicate the slightest interest in changing the forms of temporal power, replacing one system of government with another, or whether those who ruled were believers or pagans.[10]

A new style of community

Jesus strategy was altogether different. It was to call out and prepare a community that would understand its place in society in radically different

---

[10] See, Christopher Bryan, *Render to Caesar: Jesus, The Early Church, and the Roman Superpower* (Oxford: OUP, 2005), 50.

political terms. In the context of the question about who the disciples thought Jesus was (Mt. 16.13-17), he lays down the absolute requirements of discipleship: 'if any want to become my disciples, they must expect to follow me (and not lead), forego their own political and religious inclinations and ambitions and be willing to be crucified on false charges, as misunderstood pretenders to power'.[11] Just as Jesus is the suffering, servant Messiah, his followers will have to come to terms with that kind of leader. They will have to deny themselves, deny all ambition for worldly power based on human strategies, take up their crosses (daily according to Lk. 9.23), that symbol of the death of the most servile criminal,[12] and be willing to face, in the future, the disgrace of following a crucified Messiah (Lk. 21.12). If it is true that the cross is inevitably a scandal for human beings because they tend to think in terms of the pragmatic advantages of strategic power, the avoidance of it may be called a scandal to God.

So, the new community was, by following Jesus, to model a different kind of presence in the world. It was to be a life of non-violence. When Jesus said that his 'kingdom was not from this world' (Jn. 18.36), he did not mean that its location was somewhere else (either beyond the world or beyond the present). It is clear from the conversation with Pilate that Jesus is referring to the nature and implementation of the kingdom here and now. So, he continues, 'if my kingdom were from this world my followers would be fighting to keep me from being handed over to the Jews' (Jn. 18.36). In other words, he was affirming that a strategy of resisting violence with violence betrays the nature of the present kingdom of God.

---

[11] This is my paraphrase of the likely meaning of Mt. 16.24 in the context of the concrete historical choice facing Jesus at that time. The principle is laid down of accepting Jesus on his own terms, involving loss of life (or loss of face) and the abandoning of alternative schemes designed to advance self or group aggrandisement.

[12] Writing much later, Peter illustrates what the cross came to mean for him using two significant words. The word 'wounds' (1 Pet. 2.24) translates a word commonly used in the context of the punishment of slaves: for example the weal produced by the whip employed in the galley ships. The word 'tree' (or 'wood') was the instrument used in the event of slaves being killed. Peter emphasises, in the context of a passage devoted to the manner in which slaves ought to behave towards their owners, the fact that the Messiah died for them as a slave, he suffered the cruellest and most humiliating death possible. In all the references to the suffering of Jesus Christ in 1 Peter, the absolute term, 'Christ' (Messiah) is always used. When Peter speaks of the resurrection or ascension he uses the more normal title Jesus Christ or Christ Jesus. From this observation we conclude that Peter deliberately wished to emphasise the fact that the Messiah did indeed suffer for the sins of the people to bring them back to God and to re-establish true righteousness on the earth (1 Pet. 2.24; 3.18; 4.1, 13). It is also in this sense that Paul adds the words, 'even the death of a cross' (Phil. 2.8) to what is otherwise generally considered a hymn or creed borrowed by Paul and dedicated to the servant Messiah.

One can imagine what might have happened. Jesus sanctions a violent response to his arrest. There is a skirmish at the foot of the Mount of Olives. One or two of the disciples are killed. Jesus is arrested and tried for sedition. This time, however, it is for real. In terms of the political reality of the day, his crucifixion would have been the result of his own folly. There is little doubt that no more would have been heard of him. If the kingdom of God represents a new order of living it is inconceivable that it functions on the basis of the old order of forced compliance. Hence the sequence of commands, 'love your enemies, do good to those who hate you, bless those who curse you, pray for those who abuse you' (Lk. 6.27-28), is the only possible way of living in this kingdom.

The community was to practice the right use of money. If the temptation to repay violence with violence is exceedingly strong, even for those who know that it is forbidden in the sphere of God's reign, the temptation to seek security and well-being through wealth is probably even stronger. Jesus is quite clear in his teaching on the right use of money. One might summarise this teaching by saying that Jesus is seeking to liberate his disciples from the illusions that financial well-being brings a satisfied and contented life. So much of the teaching has to do with warnings about the corrupting power of wealth. The rich fool (Lk.12. 16-21) was never satisfied with what he had. He also believed that wealth was the secret of a life of comfort and happiness. The lost son (Lk. 15.11-19) believed that he was owed a life of self-indulgence. Nothing that he wanted should be refused. The Pharisees allowed money ultimately to dictate their relationship to God. When faced with the choice of a life of security in God or in riches, they chose the latter (Lk. 16.14-15). The rich man ignored the injunctions of the law and the prophets to share his wealth with the disadvantaged (Lk. 16.19-31). Zacchaeus, on the other hand, demonstrated the reality of his salvation in following Jesus by an act of restitution for the fraudulent use of his position as tax collector and by dispossessing himself of a large percentage of his accumulated wealth (Lk. 19.1-9). It would be difficult to misinterpret the meaning of Jesus' teaching. His disciples are to be unconcerned about the means they need to support life (Mt. 6. 25-34) and they are to be generous in giving to others (Lk. 21.1-4). In both cases the principle at work is one of trust. Financial matters test the disciple's relationship to God as a caring father as perhaps nothing else does.

The community was to care for victims. In the teaching of Jesus, the judgement of the sheep and the goats brings out the nature of victimhood and the call to respond in spontaneous compassion. The victims may suffer from hunger, thirst, lack of clothing, lack of shelter, sickness or false imprisonment. The list can be extended. In some way these people are identified with Jesus himself who was the victim: the lamb 'looking as if it had been slain' (Rev. 5.6). Following in the way of Jesus unmistakably implies care for victims. This is a major facet of Jesus' community's mission in the world.

The community was to take care of the vulnerable. The community is also bidden to care for those who, whilst not necessarily victims of some natural disaster or the evil or folly of others, nevertheless are much more vulnerable than others to the threat of various kinds of abuse. These are people who do not have adequate resources to fend for themselves against threats and exploitation. One may think especially of children, who are deprived of one or more parent or who are the subjects of neglect, forced-labour, trafficking or others forms of violence. Another group prone to ill-treatment and exploitation are the elderly when they are physically or mentally unable to cope with the normal conditions of living, or who are easy targets for unscrupulous fraudsters. Other categories of vulnerable people are young lone-parent mothers, released prisoners attempting to reintegrate into society and people with mental health challenges. All these, and more besides, cry out for advocacy and compassionate service.

The community was to bear witness to Jesus and God's reign of justice and peace. Logically, response to the good news of Jesus and the kingdom of God through repentance, faith and the reception of the gift of God's Spirit is the necessary process for a transformed life that issues instinctively in a life of non-violence, generosity and the compassionate care of victims and vulnerable people. Love is exacting and costly. Thus, for example, in a drug-rehabilitation programme, the most immediate priority may be to supply secure accommodation and the required medical and therapeutic treatment to start the process of detoxification and healing. However, trust in the forgiving and healing power of Jesus is a fundamental ingredient of a long-term cure. Through a constant, secure relationship with the living God, addicts are able to address not only the symptoms but the underlying causes of their destructive habit and recreate their lives as beloved children of a caring Father.

Death and New Life

At a still comparatively young age, Jesus was arrested, tried before the Jewish Sanhedrin and the Roman governor, Pontius Pilate, and condemned to death by crucifixion. There were two main charges: blasphemy, because he claimed to be equal with God (Jn. 19.7; Mt. 26.63-66), and the threat of sedition (Jn. 19.12; Lk. 23.2). He was accused of crimes against both God and Caesar. There are few historical events of the first century that are better attested than the execution of Jesus of Nazareth. There are no evidential grounds for denying that he died and was buried in a tomb supplied by the prominent Jewish leader Joseph of Arimathea (Jn. 19.38-42).[13]

[13] The claim made by Islam, based on a particular interpretation of one Qur'anic verse (Q. 4.157), that Jesus only appeared to die, but actually recovered, or that someone else was crucified in his place, is not based on any known reliable sources. It is grounded on a particular understanding of what God would, or would not allow his prophets to

The execution of Jesus is fully explicable within the context of his place and time. The Roman authorities were trying to maintain a semblance of order in a most troublesome outpost of their empire, whose geopolitical strategic value was immense because of the threat of the Parthian empire to the East. Unlike other parts of the empire, it was impossible to co-opt the Jewish people into acquiescing to Roman domination through the well developed system of patronage and the emperor cult; more direct means of control had to be applied. The Roman military presence was, therefore, proportionately much greater in Judea than elsewhere. If, therefore, the Roman governor could be persuaded that Jesus might pose a threat to the political modus vivendi of the province – 'he stirs up the people all over Judea by his teaching' -, even though Pilate seemed to discount this (Jn. 18.38; Lk. 23.4), he was quite dispensable. As in many decisions that involve a potential threat to political power the ends justified the means.

In the normal course of events one might assume that the movement that had sprung up around Jesus would have come to an end. Although the disciples of John the Baptist continued as a distinctive community for a few years after his execution (Acts 19.1-3), eventually they ceased to exist as such. Meanwhile the disciples of Jesus not only continued as a close knit group, but grew and spread throughout and beyond the entire Mediterranean region. Given that their leader, teacher and inspirer had died, that they appeared as a result to be a demoralised and confused band of people, how does one account for this unlikely historical event? The explanation that Jesus' followers gave was that he was raised from the dead and had appeared over a period of forty days to many assorted groups of people, at various times and in different places (1 Cor. 15.4-8).

The historical evidence for the resurrection is complex.[14] It is not possible to survey the data in detail. Suffice it to say that the persuasive force of the standard account, namely that three days after Jesus death the tomb was found empty and that during the following forty days Jesus re-appeared to many of his followers, is the result of its explanatory power in comparison with any possible alternative explanations. In other words, it constitutes the best explanation of the events in terms of plausible historical causes and effects.

---

experience. The task of attempting to explain to Muslims why in God's plan of salvation it was necessary for Jesus, God's servant, to offer his life as a sacrifice for sin is extremely difficult, given the different understandings of God and human imperfection. A notable attempt has been made in David Emmanuel Singh (ed.), *Jesus and the Cross: Reflections of Christians from Islamic Contexts* (Oxford: Regnum Books International, 2008). The Qur'anic verse in question does not have to bear the weight that Muslims have traditionally put upon it. There are legitimate interpretations that avoid the embarrassment of having to deny, on dogmatic grounds, a clear historic fact.

[14] Tom Wright sets out the case towards the end of his near exhaustive study of the resurrection, *The Resurrection of the Son of God* (Minneapolis: Fortress Press, 2003), 686ff.

One fact is the transformation of Jesus' disciples from despondent and disillusioned men and women into people who proclaimed a message that, if it were not true, would have seemed utterly ludicrous. Another is the failure of the authorities, who opposed the preaching of the resurrection, to produce the body of Jesus, even though they had placed guards outside the tomb. It is inconceivable that the disciples would have removed the body, reburied it somewhere else and then suffered imprisonment, torture and death for proclaiming the fiction that Jesus had risen from the dead. The fairly common practice of grave-robbery can, therefore, be discounted. There is little evidence that they were expecting some extraordinary, indeed unique, event to take place, which they then fabricated by inventing stories about an empty tomb and physical appearances of the one who had died a few days earlier. Even more extraordinary, if the whole episode was concocted, and given the cultural assumptions of the time, would have been to cast women as the first witnesses of the events.

As Tom Wright argues so cogently, what we find when we look carefully at all the evidence is that the only sufficient and necessary explanation for the existence of the early Christian community is the resurrection as told soberly in the Gospel accounts. What began to happen a few weeks after the death of Jesus of Nazareth presupposes precisely the event that is recounted:

> All that is required to demonstrate that the tomb-plus-appearances combination is not a necessary condition for the rise of early Christian belief is the possibility that some other circumstance, or combination of circumstances, was equally capable of generating this belief.[15]

In spite of many ingenious suggestions, no other sufficient and necessary conditions have ever been demonstrated with any degree of plausibility. Without the historical reality as presented in the New Testament, the birth of the Christian community is an intrinsically inexplicable conundrum.[16] Therefore,

> We may insist...that whatever else happened, if the body of Jesus of Nazareth had remained in the tomb there would have been no early Christian belief of the sort we have discovered.... The specific faith of the earliest Christians could not have been generated by a set of circumstances in which an empty tomb did not play a part.[17]

---

[15] Wright, *The Resurrection of the Son of God*, 694.

[16] On the necessity of actual historical facts for Christian belief, see the discussion in Roger Trigg, *Rationality and Religion: Does Faith need Reason?* (Oxford: Blackwell, 1998), 93-97, 103-109.

[17] Wright, *The Resurrection of the Son of God*, 695.

The expansion of the Christian community

The first disciples of Jesus, beginning in Jerusalem, began to spread the message that Jesus of Nazareth, though killed by crucifixion, was raised to life again and freed from death and is the Messiah, promised in the Jewish Scriptures as 'servant of God' and 'son of man'. Through his death, as atonement for sin and evil, forgiveness of sin, a restoration to fellowship with God and the gift of new life is made possible. Moreover, he has been named as the one Lord over all creation, meaning that in due time 'at the name of Jesus every knee should bend…and every tongue should confess that Jesus Christ is Lord' (Phil. 2.10-11).

Now, this message contradicted the core beliefs of Jew, Greek and Roman alike. The Jewish leaders in Jerusalem tried to silence the disciples (Acts 5.17-33). Synagogue leaders in the Jewish Diaspora in Asia Minor and Greece opposed and harassed Paul and his companions. Greek philosophers and debaters in Athens ridiculed his message about Jesus and the resurrection (Acts 17.18-21). Felix, the Roman governor of Judea, became unsettled and alarmed, when he 'heard (Paul) speak concerning faith in Jesus Christ and…justice, self-control and the coming judgement' (Acts 24.24-25).

In spite of persecution for their beliefs (many were imprisoned for refusing to keep silent), the group in Jerusalem grew rapidly in numbers and new ones soon appeared as far away as Damascus and Antioch. After a time, Gentiles also joined them and the movement spread to Cyprus, Asia Minor, Greece, Rome and North Africa. For a time, at least, they shared their belongings and met principally in each others' homes. They had a deep sense of belonging together. So much so that, when there was a famine in Judea, groups who identified themselves as also belonging to the Way[18] sent aid from the Greek provinces of Macedonia and Achaia.

The communities were quite often caught up in disturbances. However, these appeared to be caused by people who found their teaching threatening. They were further oppressed for refusing to offer worship to the emperor. Despite major persecutions by Nero, Domitian and, later, Decius and Diocletian, they resolutely refused to join in the imperial cult. As a result they were declared to be atheists. They also refused to enlist in the armed forces. By the year 70 CE, when the Roman army under Titus captured Jerusalem, they had become separated from the Jews and refused to join in defending the city or in any way being involved in the national war against Roman occupation.

For approximately 280 years (CE 30-310) they survived as a persecuted minority, sometimes allowed to exist in peace, but often harassed. They had no distinctive places of worship. They continued to grow as people accepted their invitation to believe. There was no coercion or compulsion. They did not

---

[18] 'The Way' was an early name given to the new Christian movement (see, Acts 9.2; 19.9, 23; 22.4; 24.14).

exercise political power. Their reverence for life marked them out as a highly distinctive community. By the time of the emperor Constantine, about 10% of the population of the empire belonged to the church.

A clash of civilisations? (Many lords, one Lord)

The community of Christian believers proved to be an irritant to the various authorities spread across the Roman Empire. They simply did not fit into the religious *modus operandi* by which the Empire sought to legitimate its power and control its far-flung conquests. As we shall see, there was bound to be a major conflict at the heart of the way the Roman Empire and the young Christian movement understood their respective missions in life.

The empire was born in 31 BCE, when Octavian (given the title Augustus in 27 BCE) defeated Mark Anthony at the naval battle of Actium off the coast of Greece, and thus consolidated his power over the numerous territories conquered by the Roman armies. The empire was built on the ideology, sustained by Stoic philosophy, that Rome had been destined by the gods to subdue the barbarian hordes that always threatened civilisation as represented by the Roman and Greek ways of life. Rome spread abroad the dogma that its hegemony

> ...was ordained by the gods, whose favour Rome had deserved by piety and justice.... (The gods implanted in the Roman people) a love of peace and tranquillity which enable justice and good faith most easily to flourish.[19]

Expanding the frontiers outwards was intended to keep the savage tribes further away from the assumed refined sophistication and moral superiority of the new commonwealth. This was to be achieved by the famous pax romana, based on military campaigns, conquest and the subsequent settlement made with the defeated peoples. Continuing Roman control over the conquered territories was maintained by a combination of military force, institutionalised in the slave system, patronage, the emperor cult and the rhetoric of gratitude and unity. Antoinette Clark Wire calls these the four legs that upheld the imperial throne. [20]

What held the empire together was not so much a visible military presence, nor an extended administrative network, as a shrewd system of patron-client relations. Social control was implemented through the distribution of beneficia as personal favours to patrons who would reciprocate by keeping order,

---

[19] Cicero: quoted in Neil Elliott, 'Paul and the Politics of Empire' in Richard A. Horsley (ed), *Paul and Politics: Ekklesia, Israel, Imperium, Interpretation* (Harrisburg, PA: Trinity Press International, 2000), 30.

[20] 'The Politics of the Assembly in Corinth' in Horsley, *Paul and Politics*, 128.

collecting taxes, sustaining the emperor cult and organising spectacles for the local populaces. A central feature of the ideology of Roman imperialism was fides/pistis: Romans showed their constancy by helping and protecting their 'friends'; the friends showed their loyalty to Rome by being compliant citizens. Thus, patronage served to integrate the empire within subject cities through the gradual consolidation of economic resources under the control of a few wealthy families.[21] These operated a certain amount of self-government in the cities as magistrates and members of local city councils. They controlled the primary resources of land and labour in their locality. They ingratiated themselves both with Rome and the local population by sponsoring civic buildings, amenities (like bath houses), trade, religious gatherings, festivals and entertainment.[22]

The most effective instrument of control was, undoubtedly, the emperor cult. Caesar was reverenced as the great benefactor, bringing the blessings of justice, peace and the development of infrastructures (such as harbours, water supplies and road systems). The cities of Greece and Asia Minor established shrines, festivals, games and temples to honour their 'saviour' and 'lord'. In Ephesus, for example, the temple of Augustus was built in a prominent position in the centre of the upper square. Almost the entire population participated in the annual festivals honouring the emperor. These were modelled on the traditional Greek ceremonies that were held to honour the gods with a view to ensuring through sacrifices their good favour in bringing well-being and stability to the people.[23]

Divinization of the emperor was a more secure way of legitimising political rule than the use of naked force. Religion and politics are both ways of constructing power. However, the former is more effective over the long-term in guaranteeing submission, stability and solidarity, for it establishes an ultimate rationale and explanation for the status quo in the mystery of divine-human relations. It is not surprising then that statues of the emperor were sometimes cast in the guise of Jupiter, the leader of the gods, or that the figure of Augustus, as the archetypal patron, was displayed in a prominent colonnade directly behind the stage in the public theatres, a position also occupied by the gods.[24] Commenting on this reality, the first century Jewish writer, Philo said:

---

[21] See, Richard Horsley, 'Patronage, Priesthood and Power: An Introduction' in Horsley, *Paul and Politics*, 90-94.

[22] Warren Carter, *The Roman Empire and the New Testament: An Essential Guide* (Nashville: Abingdon Press, 2006), 3-6.

[23] See, Tom Wright, 'Paul's Gospel and Caesar's Empire' in Horsley, *Paul and Politics*, 161; Richard Horsley, 'The Gospel of Imperial Salvation: Introduction' in Richard A. Horsley (ed), *Paul and Empire: Religion and Power in Roman Imperial Society* (Harrisburg, PA: Trinity Press International, 1997), 12.

[24] See, S.R.F. Price, 'Rituals and Power' and Paul Zanker, 'The Power of Images' in Horsley, *Paul and Empire*, 10-13, 14-24.

> The whole inhabited world voted him (the emperor) the honours usually accorded the Olympian gods. These are so well attested by temples, gateways, vestibules and colonnades that every city that contains magnificent works new and old is surpassed in these by the beauty and magnitude of those appropriated to Caesar.[25]

By the end of the first century, the emperor Domitian demanded to be addressed as dominus et deus ('lord' and 'god'). The worship of the emperor was the supreme test of loyalty.[26] The empire may have institutionalised the claim that the gods had chosen Rome to be a blessing to the nations. The Christians, however, declared that the gods did not exist and Jesus alone was God's chosen one to bring blessings to all peoples!

> Indeed, even though there may be so-called gods in heaven and on earth – as in fact there are many gods and many lords – yet for us there is one God, the Father, from whom are all things and for whom we exist, and one Lord, Jesus Christ, through whom are all things and through whom we exist. [27]

Now here is a recipe for a major clash of perspectives. In the following chapters, we will review some of the consequences of these irreconcilable viewpoints and how the first Christian communities responded to the political environment in which they found themselves. We will seek to show how this response differed from that adopted by Muhammad and the first Muslim communities and how these contrasting visions of God's purpose for his people in respect of political power affect contemporary views of religion and political life.

---

[25] *Legatio ad Gaium,* 149-150.

[26] See, Suetonius, *Domitian,* 13.2; Dio Cassius, *Roman History*, 67.4.7.

[27] 1 Cor. 8.5-6.

Chapter 7

The Impact of the Formative Years, Part I

The Purpose of Studying Origins

Crucial to the main thesis of this book is the ability to make sound connections between the founding features of a religion – in this case Islam and Christianity – and the beliefs and practices of its adherents many centuries later. In considering the most significant historical events and the way in which they are interpreted and applied in contemporary life, we need to identify those aspects that are particularly relevant to the question of an alleged clash of civilisations. This chapter and the next, therefore, will endeavour to draw out from the material, gathered in the previous two chapters, facets that bear directly or indirectly on current religious approaches to political life. The issues most often cited have to do with the exercise of political power and the use of force or violence to achieve religious ends. We will examine, therefore, the early history in each case, with a view to detecting how the original main actors contemplated the questions of power, physical compulsion and moral constraint.

Problems of Procedure

In seeking to achieve the purpose, two main difficulties have to be recognised and dealt with. First, there is the dilemma of trying to compare the origins of two quite distinct religions that emerged in notably dissimilar historical circumstances. It might be objected that the two cases are so far removed from one another that attempts to make comparisons are not of much value. At the same time, from a contemporary perspective, there can be no doubt that followers of both religions derive considerable guidance for belief and action from their respective foundation documents and early history and traditions. Moreover, both Muslims and Christians are dealing with a similar set of actual events. If, then, it is possible to discover how different groups go about deriving their current attitudes and actions from the initial story of their founding, it should also be possible to perceive legitimate analogies and correspondences.

The second difficulty has to do with the temptation to preselect historical events in order that they may fit into pre-arranged ideas and schemes. Obviously, there is a danger of approaching the historical data with set questions already determined by the nature of the inquiry. This may mean that material which could be relevant will get overlooked. However, this risk is inherent in the very method of all historical study. Accounts of events are written from some point of view. This is plainly evident in the case of the sirahs or life narratives of Muhammad as recounted in the biographies of people like Ibn Ishaq, Ibn Hisham, al-Waqidi and Al Tabari and in the *sunnah* or actions and sayings of Muhammad not found in the Qur'an. It is also discernible in the Gospel narratives of the life of Jesus, in the account of the expansion of the early Christian communities recorded in the Acts of the Apostles and in the occasional letters written by leading figures in the early Church.

Clearly, the accounts of origins are dependent on the sources available. A pre-selection has already been made, either deliberately or fortuitously, which is beyond the contemporary historian's control. There are, however, reliable historical and literary methods which can help to minimize obvious anachronisms and which offer a variety of different interpretations of the events portrayed. Nevertheless, even when full account is taken of the vagaries of historical study a substantially coherent picture of the beginnings of each faith emerges. Even were it not the case that a reliable reconstruction of the early history could be made, the outlook of contemporary members of the two faiths is based on the supposition that it is the case.

Common Themes and Contexts

God alone is sovereign; Jesus is his emissary

Jesus and Muhammad both preached a message that challenged and threatened the status quo of their respective societies. Central to Jesus' preaching was the coming of God's reign of justice and healing. 'The good news of God' is that 'the kingdom of God has come near'. (Mark 1.14-15). This is the Gospel as Jesus understood it. Everything else is an unfolding of that reality.

In the Old Testament the m*alkuth* Yahweh expresses God's sovereignty over all things: for example, his complete control over the natural order (Psalm 103.19); his governance of his people (Ex. 19.6) (this was later threatened by the coming of the monarchy, 1 Sam. 10.19), and his ordering of the life of all the nations (Amos 1-2; Isa. 19.24-25). God's kingdom is both a present reality and a future reference: God's intervention in his creation makes all things new, beginning now and coming to completion in the transformation of all things (Isa. 65.17-25; 66.1, 12-14, 22). The kingdom is God's final and complete salvation, when the righteous will be vindicated, the wicked destroyed, justice established among the nations and a new created order inaugurated. Then, God will be fully recognised as the sovereign Lord of the universe:

> How beautiful upon the mountains are the feet of the messenger who announces peace, who brings good news, who announces salvation, who says to Zion, 'Your God reigns' (Isa. 52.7).

In this message we see peace (*shalom* – welfare) fully restored, through salvation as a gift of restored relationships, and God's authority finally vindicated and upheld. All this will be accomplished through God's special representative, a righteous servant king. He will establish justice and peace through suffering. This is the Messianic age.

Jesus first public act, after his baptism and temptation, is to announce that 'the kingdom has come near'. He then calls his first disciples to be a nucleus of the new community of the kingdom (Mt. 4.18-22), demonstrates the power of the kingdom (Mt. 4.23) and teaches the standards of the kingdom (the Sermon on the Mount, Mt. 5-7). The kingdom in the teaching of Jesus is dependent on the Old Testament expectations.

However, there are at least two wholly new elements. First, the kingdom is now here. A Jewish scholar, David Flusser, makes the startling assertion that: 'Jesus is the only Jew who is known from ancient times to have proclaimed that the new age of salvation had already begun'.[1]

He proclaimed this because he knew himself to be the Messiah. The coming of the Holy Spirit in his baptism (Mt. 3.16) and in the mighty works (Mt. 12.28) was evidence of the dawning of a new age. The good news of the kingdom is that God's kingly rule, in which the entire created universe is reclaimed and will be remade, is operating in and through Jesus. In his ministry Jesus reversed all the consequences of sin (i.e. of rebellion against God's kingly rule): disease, demon-possession and guilt (Mk. 1.21-26; 32-34; 2.10-11); the caste system of ritual purity and impurity (Mk. 7.1-15); religious oppression (Mt. 23.4); a hostile nature (Mk. 4.35-41); scarcity of food (Mk. 6.35-44; 8.1-9); commercial exploitation (in the cleansing of the temple) (Mk. 11.15-17), and death (Mk. 5.35-42). The kingdom marks the end of all that destroys or disfigures God's good and beautiful creation.

Secondly, individuals are called to enter the kingdom. Christ, in his public ministry, called people to repent, believe the good news of God's salvation and follow his teaching and example. Belonging to the Jewish people was no guarantee of receiving the blessings of the new age (Mt. 8.11-12). In other words, from now on, obedience to God meant becoming a disciple of this itinerant preacher and healer. The way of Jesus represented the will of God. People would be judged on the basis of whether, or not, they had received Jesus as the fulcrum of their lives. The challenge of the kingdom is summed up in Jesus' invitation: 'Come to me...Take my yoke upon you...Learn from me' (Mt. 11.28-30).

---

[1] David Flusser, *Jesus* (New York: Herder and Herder, 1969), 87.

The religious and political leaders of Jesus' time were infuriated to think that this self-proclaimed prophet had the audacity to pronounce himself the authentic interpreter of God's law and his will and to claim that he was God's final representative on earth through whom God would establish his promised new order of peace and justice. It is not surprising, therefore, that from the beginning of his public ministry, having challenged many of the set ideas and customs of the leaders, the latter (Pharisees and Herodians) should conspire to destroy him (Mk. 3.6).

God alone is God: Muhammad is his herald

Muhammad also incurred substantial and persistent opposition to his preaching. He insisted that he had been chosen to call the people of Mecca (and by implication the whole of humankind) back to the pristine purity of faith in one sovereign Lord, creator, law-giver and judge as proclaimed from time to time by prophets sent by God. He denounced the religious observances of the Meccan population as a travesty of the way of life demanded by Allah:

> The message…required a clear-cut distinction between *tawhid*, faith in one God, and the polytheism of the Quraysh…Muhammad's message threatened the age-old balance in their society. Both their gods and their power could be challenged, and the danger was serious….The first Muslims were called to a profound and radical spiritual conversion, and this had been well understood by opponents within their own clans, who feared the considerable upheavals the new religion was bound to bring about in the beliefs and organization of their society.[2]

Implicit in the message were a number of serious challenges to the people of Mecca. First, to have a sacred text 'was to constitute a people'[3] and therefore to confront tribal rivalries, which caused the disunity of the Arab people. Secondly, to proclaim that the Meccans were engaged in idolatry, abhorrent to the one and only true God, jeopardized the financial gain to be had from being the guardians of the sacred shrine dedicated to a panoply of gods. Thirdly, the Qur'an sanctioned a move from tribal solidarity to individual responsibility: God would judge each person according to their beliefs and deeds. No longer would loyalty to one's kinsfolk be the main criterion for what would be considered right and wrong.[4] The individual could no longer find refuge in the collective will of the clan, nor could the clan impose its will against the conscience of the individual. Adherence to Muhammad's band of followers now became the overriding mark of identity. Fourthly, Muhammad's claim to prophetic authority and leadership and the constitution of one single, universal

---

[2] Ramadan, *The Messenger*, 39-40.
[3] Cragg, *The House of Islam*, 22.
[4] Montgomery Watt, *Islam and the Integration of Society*, 21.

community undermined Meccan political authority based on inter-tribal arrangements. Fifthly, Muhammad's message directly denounced the socio-economic inequities that prevailed in Meccan society. These were based on false contracts and excessive usury, and led to the exploitation of the weak and vulnerable, such as orphans and widows.[5]

As a result of their preaching, both Jesus and Muhammad suffered considerable opposition. In the former's case, this led eventually to death; in the latter's case to numerous threats, the death of some of his followers, to ostracism, banishment and exile from the city. Similarly, the early Christians were persecuted for their alleged blasphemy in proclaiming that Jesus of Nazareth was both the Messiah foretold in the Jewish Scriptures and the Lord over all lords and gods. They suffered various forms of punishment and martyrdom for refusing to adhere to Jewish laws and customs, to pay homage to the gods of the Greco-Roman world or to acknowledge the divine status of the emperor.

Examples to follow

A MODEL OF SACRIFICIAL AND SUFFERING SERVANTHOOD

The lives of both Jesus and Muhammad were taken by their early followers to be supreme examples to follow. In the case of Jesus, his life is seen as a pattern of service, suffering and sacrifice. Thus, Jesus informed James and John, two of the closest disciples, that he could not offer them positions of authority and power, but he could promise them a share in his suffering. When the rest of the disciples objected to the fact that the two brothers had stolen a march on them, Jesus deliberately distanced his kind of ministry from that of the political rulers of the time (Caesar, Herod and their deputies). So, Jesus gave his disciples a visual lesson in proper humble ministry by performing the duty of the household slave in washing their soiled feet: 'I have set you an example that you also should do as I have done to you' (Jn. 13.3-16). He showed that true leadership is measured, not by demonstrating a greater capacity to rule by force, but by a willingness in all circumstances to serve others, even to sacrifice one's life for them (Mk. 10.35-45). Jesus promised his disciples continuing persecution (Mk. 10.30), and in all circumstances a life which springs from the death of self-aggrandizement and self-assertion (Mk. 8.34-37; Lk. 14.11).

This example of self-sacrificing ministry was used by the early Church as a powerful motivation for life in the Christian community and in the non-Christian world. Paul uses Jesus' willingness to exchange the glory and majesty of the divine being for the vulnerability of life on earth as a motive for exemplary Christian living:

[5] See, John L. Esposito, *Islam: The Straight Path* (Oxford: OUP 1991/2), 10.

> Do nothing from selfish ambition or conceit, but in humility regard others as better than yourselves. Let each of you look not to your own interests, but to the interests of others. Let the same mind be in you that was in Christ Jesus.[6]

Peter also used Jesus' reaction to the totally unjust treatment he suffered at the hands of power-crazed rulers as an example to follow, whenever Christians, being innocent, were abused and handled violently:

> If you endure when you do right and suffer for it, you have God's approval. For to this you have been called, because Christ also suffered for you, leaving you an example, so that you should follow in his steps.[7]

The writer of the letter to the Hebrews expressed himself in a similar vein:

> Consider him who endured such hostility against himself from sinners, so that you may not grow weary or lose heart.[8]

Later, we will need to explore further the significance of suffering servanthood in the following of Jesus as an example.

A MODEL OF VIRTUE AND LEADERSHIP

In the case of Muhammad, there can be little doubt that Muslims hold him in the highest possible regard, so much so that to speak detrimentally of Muhammad is sometimes taken as a more serious offence than that of disparaging the Qur'an.[9] Muslims use the most elevated language to describe the prophet's role:

> The Prophet...is both the Universal Man and the primordial Man (al-insan al-qadim). As the Universal Man he is the totality of which we are the part and in which we participate; as the Primordial Man he is that original perfection with respect to which we are a decadence and a falling away.[10]

Muhammad is chosen as a model for Muslims to embrace:

> The Messenger of God is an excellent model for those of you who put your hope in God and the Last Day and remember Him often.[11]

---

[6] Phil. 2.3-8

[7] 1 Pet. 2.20-23

[8] Heb. 12.3

[9] Geaves, *Aspects of Islam*, 144.

[10] Seyyed Hossein Nasr, *Ideals and Realities of Islam* (ABC International group, 2000), 82.

[11] Q. 33.21

It is often pointed out that the dual clauses of the central confession of Islam (the *shahadah*)[12] – *la illah il' Allah, Muhammadun rasul Allah* (there is no God but Allah and Muhammad is his Messenger) – run together. For Muslims Muhammad is the very intermediary between the ultimate, divine word and humanity, without which humans would remain in ignorance about the real meaning of life and the requirements for abundant living:

> Within the Muslim world there is no character who is his equal or so well known, for he possesses all the human values: the mine of all virtues and manners. He is the last of those special beings who have been chosen to bring the word of God to men and women throughout history.[13]

Thus his life is taken as exemplary in all its aspects, a model of perfection to which all Muslims should aspire:

> For Muslims, the Prophet is the perfect model of total humility before God and neighbour; nobility and magnanimity of soul, which means to be strict to oneself but generous, charitable and forgiving to others; and finally, perfect sincerity, which means to be totally truthful to oneself and to God.[14]

Muslims believe that his life is a model to inspire, not only in the essential qualities of his character, nor only in the interpersonal relationships he maintained with his family, his companions and even his enemies,[15] but also as a prophet, a leader of the Muslim community, a political leader and warrior:

> The armed prophet of Madina would remain the perfect exemplar for Muslims of all ages, his career a model of moral and political action that would be consciously imitated by those seeking to create a juster social order in this world.[16]

Thus, and this is absolutely crucial for understanding Islam, it is the consensus of Muslim scholars to regard the life and times of the prophet (understood principally as his governorship in Medina) as the normative summit to which all Muslims must aspire:[17]

---

[12] The first of the five pillars of Islam.

[13] Geaves, *Aspects of Islam*, 143.

[14] Nasr, *The Heart of Islam*, 35.

[15] See, Akbar S. Ahmed, *Discovering Islam: Making Sense of Muslim History and Society* (London: Routledge and Kegan Paul, 1988), 22-29.

[16] Malise Ruthven, *Islam in the World* (London: Granta Books, 2006/3), 77.

[17] See, Abu-Rabi, *The Blackwell Companion to Contemporary Islamic Thought*, 149.

> The Prophet offers a paradigm and the basis for an ideology for the fusion of religion and state in Muslim experience. The early Islamic worldview provides a model both for the formation of a state and for protest and revolution.[18]

The Way of Jesus and the Way of Muhammad

For the purpose of this study it is clearly important to be able to show that, although living in appreciably different historical moments, there are similarities in the situations of Jesus and Muhammad that make a comparison of their respective reactions to their circumstances valid and illuminating. There can be little question, for good or ill, that these reactions and those of their immediate followers, are as divergent as it is possible to be. They began in a similar way by the public preaching of a message that each claimed to have received from God and calling their own people to believe the message, repent of a life that displeased God and amend their ways. However, they responded to the provocation and resistance that the message caused in entirely different ways.

Attitudes to the use of political power, force and violence

In Early Islam

The most controversial matter associated with the origin of Islam is the religious defence of the use of violence. The verses in the Qur'an that manifest intolerance and justify violence against non-Muslims, including the followers of other faiths, are too numerous to ignore. There are many verses, particularly in *surah*s 3, 4, 5, 8 and 9, that enjoin violence against idolaters and unbelievers. Significantly they all come from revelations received in Medina. The use of force was sanctioned to protect the integrity of the Islamic faith once it was accepted that Muhammad was to invest time and energy into ruling a civic community. Compliance with the rules of the state have to be enforceable, otherwise chaos ensues. In Medina, opposition to Islam could easily be interpreted as political treason. This conclusion will always be arrived at where political power and social cohesion are made the central issues. Thus, it became almost inevitable that sooner or later polytheism would no longer be tolerated as a legitimate religious commitment.[19] So, for polytheistic worshippers, conversion to Islam became a political necessity for survival, once the Islamic forces demonstrated their military superiority:

---

[18] Esposito, *Islam, the Straight Path*, 15.

[19] It is intriguing to note that the Roman Empire dealt with polytheism in a different way: the peoples under Roman jurisdiction were free to follow whatever gods and religions they chose, as long as they recognised formally the deities that upheld the right of Rome to rule.

When the [four] forbidden months are over, wherever you encounter the idolaters, kill them, seize them, besiege them, wait for them at every lookout post; but if they turn [to God], maintain the prayer, and pay the prescribed alms, let them go on their way, for God is most forgiving and merciful.[20]

The decision to ally faith in Allah with political power in a city-state has brought with it many consequences for the whole history of Islam. From a non-Muslim perspective some of them appear to be noticeably ill-fated. For example, Islam is saddled with two exceptionally controversial events, which we have already mentioned, from its earliest years: the slaughter of some 7-900 male members of the Jewish Banu Qurayza clan, and the unprovoked attack on the city of Khaybar. Such actions may be justified pragmatically according to the conventional concepts of self-defence, exemplary punishment or preventative first strike. However, even by the amoral standards by which warfare has usually been conducted, they are dubious. To use religion to sanction them is, to say the least, to make it a hostage to fortune. Conventionally Muslims have defended the resort to force as the lesser of two evils, in circumstances where the community that is protecting and disseminating the fresh revelations from Allah was in danger of being annihilated:

(The Muslims) were no longer required to resist passively (as in Mecca); rather they were to defend themselves against enemy aggression...A new possible form of *jihad* was now added: al-qital, necessary armed resistance in the face of armed aggression, self-defense against oppressors.[21]

There can be no doubt that the Qur'an sanctioned the use of force to defend the interests of faith:

Those who have been attacked are permitted to take up arms because they have been wronged – God has the power to help them – those who have been unjustly driven from their homes only for saying, 'Our Lord is God'. If God did not repel some people by means of others, many monasteries, churches, synagogues, and mosques, where God's name is much invoked, would have been destroyed. God is sure to help those who help His cause – God is strong and mighty.[22]

However, even from a Muslim standpoint, there are serious problems with this new policy adopted after the *hijrah*. In the first place, it appears to express the view that Allah could not have protected his people in Mecca. In fact, one might say that Allah was never given the chance, seeing that Muhammad and his followers themselves came to the conclusion that emigration was the only

[20] Q. 9.5 (emphasis added); see also Q. 47.4.

[21] Ramadan, *The Messenger*, 98 (emphasis added).

[22] Q. 22.39-40

recourse left to them in the face of the severe persecution they suffered - the Meccan revelations do not suggest that the Muslims should leave the city, let alone command them to do so.

In the second place, it assumes that, once they had arrived in Medina, it was necessary for Muhammad and his companions to take over the running of the city. Was this the only condition on which the *hijrah* could have been contemplated? Could not the Muslim community, as a distinct group with a powerful message to proclaim, but without the ambition to rule, have settled in Medina as a place of sanctuary from oppression? Even if, at the time, the course that Muhammad followed appeared to be the only one open to him and his followers, should this set a precedent for all time? Why has a historically contingent event become normative for all subsequent history? In the third place, the alliance of religion with political power means that, more often than not, the latter has to be justified at all costs in order to be able to defend the former; whilst the former's sanction of state coercion also has to be upheld.

Few people doubt that the move to Medina was fateful for the future of Islam. The religion developed in a way that, when the initial revelations were received in Mecca, could not have been foreseen. The tone of the revelations in Medina now changed: justification for war, the taking of hostages and booty and the imposition of severe taxes now appeared for the first time: 'There is a dimension of harsh belligerence in the Qur'an, a strong pugnacity on behalf of faith'.[23]

The legitimacy of armed struggle as a way of defending and furthering the religion of Allah now became embedded in the foundation Scriptures. Muslims of all generations inherit this legacy, and are obliged by critical voices to explain, interpret, defend or reconstitute their beliefs in the light of the origins of their faith as founded on their sacred book.

IN EARLY CHRISTIANITY

The case of the early Christians is entirely different. They too were persecuted, by the Jews, because they were claiming that a crucified itinerant preacher from Galilee was the Messiah promised by God in the Jewish Scriptures and that God's way of salvation now passed irrevocably through Jesus Christ, who had instituted a new covenant with his people (that included the Gentiles) and had risen from the dead. They were harassed by Roman officials for being an 'underground' religion (not an officially recognised one), which proclaimed that the Jewish trouble-maker executed on the orders of the Roman governor of Judea was actually the ultimate ruler of the universe, to whom earthly rulers would have to give an account. Moreover, this new religion categorically refused to join in the ceremonies that marked a proper deference to the

[23] Cragg, *The Qur'an and the West*, 9.

emperor, thereby threatening one of the most effective ways, dreamed up by the Romans, of keeping the peace and security of the empire.

Christians also experienced exile. In the build-up to the Jewish War against the Romans (66-70CE), the Christian inhabitants of Jerusalem fled from the city (Mk. 13.14). In the persecutions unleashed by Saul of Tarsus, the Christians were driven from their homes and forced to go elsewhere, or they were imprisoned (Ac.8.1-4; 9.1-2; 11.19). However, they did not envisage settling in one place and taking over the reigns of power there. Rather, as the story narrates, they travelled in those early days 'as far as Phoenicia, Cyprus, and Antioch' (Ac.11.19), bearing witness to Jesus Christ. It might well be argued that, given the circumstances of the tight control exercised over the provinces and city-states by the Roman administration, any attempt to set up an independent city with the Christians in charge would have been ruthlessly suppressed. In other words, the historical circumstances of the time simply ruled out the possibility of a Christian city-state. This is no doubt true, but actually irrelevant: the early Christians would not have envisaged such a prospect, not on the pragmatic grounds of such a project being unattainable but on the basis of the conviction that this was not their calling.

How the early Christians envisaged themselves as a community, in the light of their experience of Jesus, determined both their strategy towards the political forces of the day and their consistent attitude to the use of force in the interests of propagating or defending their faith. Although the evidence is scattered, and somewhat circumstantial, there are sufficient grounds for believing that the Church of the first century consciously organised itself as an alternative class of community to the civic assemblies of the Greco-Roman world. Rather than understanding their task to be that of founding a more perfect model of what already existed, they saw themselves as distinct communities, called to be a foretaste of the quite special, coming rule of Christ throughout the world.

For example, in his first letter to the Christians in Corinth (chapter 7), Paul deals with three sets of human relationships that would have been highly significant in the culture of the day: Jews and Gentiles; slaves and free; men and women. He advises the Christians to consider how their new status in Christ, through faith and baptism, fundamentally altered their view of all conventionally interpreted social standings. Thus, he counsels the Christians to leave their former situation and live out the new radical freedom they possess in Christ within the socio-cultural context in which they are placed. Those who were formerly Jews or pagans should not remain in that state. Slaves should seek to become free, whenever the opportunity came (1 Cor. 7.23). Husbands and wives should recognise a full equality and mutuality in their marital relationships. Widows should remain free of the marriage bond for fear of marrying a non-Christian and thereby being forced to revert to a pre-Christian, patriarchal relationship. It is probable that Paul had in mind what might be called 'the baptismal declaration' of Galatians (Gal. 3.28), when addressing these current issues of human relationships.

Christians understood themselves as a new family, called into the one fellowship of Jesus Christ (1 Cor. 1.9), and they expressed this self-understanding institutionally in the creation of house-churches. As a result, 'the religious ethos of equality was transferred to and came into conflict with the patriarchal ethos of the household'. [24] For example, to advise women to remain unmarried was an infringement of the right of paterfamilias, since in Roman law women remained under the tutorship of father and family, even after marrying.[25]

It is quite evident from Paul's first letter to the Corinthian Christians that current cultural and social practices continued to intrude into the life of the new family in Christ, with painful and harmful consequences. There is plenty of evidence to suggest that elite members of the church saw the communities as another place to exert their influence and gain honour through the traditional patron-client relations. In particular, the place of meals in the culture was crucial to social standing. Meals were part of the daily life of honouring the imperial cult, celebrating the Isthmian games in Corinth, or seeking the favour of a god or goddess. Meals commonly reinforced social hierarchy with the quality of the food, the table settings and the service offered. In other words, believers were importing cultural practices into the church, continuing to behave as if Christ had not transformed the whole apparatus of superior and inferior standings among people (1 Cor. 10.14-11.1; 11.17-34). However, 'the Gospel requires moral and ethical standards that override cultural accommodations'.[26]

Those outside the church also noticed the different ways in which Christians behaved. As they did not participate in the normal recreational activities, associations and festivals, did not belong to the trade guilds or social clubs, for this would have involved them in participating in religious festivals that honoured the patron deities, they were seen as anti-social, cultural non-conformists and even subversives. Their behaviour violated the conventions of society, and as a result they were labelled as dangerous deviants. [27]

Their attitude had implicit political implications. By refusing to make offerings to the emperor and the usual deities they were seen as jeopardising political stability by risking the divine wrath. Rejecting the common practice of participating in the imperial cult meant that Christians disqualified themselves from military service, which required an oath of allegiance to the divine

---

[24] See, 'The Praxis of Coequal Discipleship' in *Paul and Empire,* 234. I am indebted to this article for the material on 1 Corinthians 7.

[25] Horsley, *Paul and Empire*, 233.

[26] See the whole section on 'Paul's Communities' in *The Roman Empire and the New Testament*, 57ff.

[27] See, Ivor J. Davidson, *The Birth of the Church: From Jesus to Constantine (AD 30-312)* (Grand Rapids: Baker Books, 2004), 197, 200.

emperor and a regular presence at polytheistic rites. [28] Their behaviour was easily interpreted as disloyalty to and betrayal of the society into which they were born. Their refusal to compromise the new reality ('the age to come' which they had entered through turning to Christ and being baptised, meant that they would have been viewed as a deeply disturbing, anomalous, sectarian sect:

> The followers of Jesus inherited from Judaism their sense of being a distinct community, a kind of nation of their own. The singular history of their confrontation with Graeco-Roman society is not likely to be explained simply in terms of its systems of rank and status. Their aim was not to find their place in the world as it was. They brought with them ideas and practices which undercut the classical order.[29]

Hierarchical and homogeneous societies find it almost impossible to cope with such groups. It is not surprising, therefore, that they were reviled and persecuted as a-theists.

Their confession of Jesus as Messiah and Lord caused the early Christians to re-evaluate the nature and position of the political powers of the day. Speaking in general terms, it would seem that the early church adopted a dual attitude towards the governing authorities. On the one hand, it taught that governance in civil society was an institution ordained by God (Rom. 13.1-7). Those called to rule could count on possessing the authority of God. Therefore, Christians must submit themselves to this authority and respect those who rightfully exercise it. They must live good lives, avoid doing wrong and pay their taxes. The New Testament does not consider how the particular authorities of the time come to exercise their power – whether there rule is self-appointed, dynastic or through the will of the people. As far as the secular power was concerned, the first Christians did not discuss whether its actual legitimacy came from above (from the gods) or from below (from the people), or perhaps from both. Their concern was with the institution of government itself.

At the same time, they were fully aware of the kind of authority that, as a matter of fact, held the reigns of power. So, Jesus, Paul, Peter, Luke and John, all of whom made mention of Roman rule, had to come to terms with the existing 'powers that be'. The need simultaneously both to refer to political authority as such and also to deal with the current exercise of it in imperial Rome has caused much confusion in the mind of interpreters of the New Testament down the ages. The context in which the teaching comes is crucial. Jesus' response to those who tried to trap him, by questioning him about paying taxes, into opting either for Roman occupation of the Promised Land or for

---

[28] Davidson, *The Birth of the Church*, 197.

[29] E.A. Judge, 'Rank and Status in the World of the Caesars and St Paul' in David M. Scholer (ed.), *Social Distinctive of the Christians in the First Century: Pivotal essays by E. A. Judge* (Peabody, MA: Hendrickson, 2008), 155-156.

(armed) resistance, addresses both issues. The fact that his answer – 'give to the emperor the things that are the emperor's, and to God the things that are God's' (Lk. 20.25) – silenced them demonstrated that he had not only avoided having to choose between two false options, but had also set the matter of political authority in its proper frame of reference. 'What belongs to Caesar and what belongs to God' are not separate, autonomous spheres, in which each has absolute jurisdiction over a portion of life that pertains to its independent jurisdiction. Caesar and God are not symmetrical entities. On the contrary, in Jewish thinking God is the owner of and ruler over all things, including Caesar. Therefore, although Caesar's rule is legitimate, in every respect it is accountable to God.

Paul seems to be saying the same thing, using different words, in his admonition to the Christians in Rome: 'there is no authority except from God' (compare Jn. 19.10-11). Three times in this passage, Paul reiterates that the authority is God's servant.[30] It has been appointed to reward the good and to punish evil doing. In other words, the authority has been given an ethical mandate to distinguish between right and wrong and to ensure that civil society operates on the basis of this distinction. In so far as it does this, it is God's servant. Now, the implication has to be that, whenever the authorities reverse this process, rewarding evil and penalizing virtue, they cease to be God's servants; they have set themselves up against God's rule. There are plenty of precedents of both kinds of rulers in the history of Israel.

So much can be said for the institution of governance as such. Paul and other New Testament writers also deal with the actual exercise of authority, only too apparent in every corner of the Mediterranean world known to them. Paul's teaching in Romans is, therefore, also context specific. It refers to some kind of persecution that the Christians were undergoing (Rom. 12.14). The instruction is quite explicit: they are to respond to those who would harm them by invoking God's blessing on them rather than seeking revenge, living in peace with their neighbours and serving the needs of those who have made themselves their enemies (Rom. 12.14-21). Within this context, the Christians are also to submit themselves to the governing authorities (Rom. 13.1). In other words, they are not to take matters into their own hands. They are not to resort to force (Rom. 13.4). If the Roman state is acting as God's servant, it will exercise the appropriate judgement on those who persecute innocent people.[31] The model response to persecution and suffering is that of Christ (1 Pet. 2.20-21).

---

[30] Twice in the singular using the word *diakonos*; once in the plural using the word *leitourgos*.

[31] Compare 'the wrath of God' (Rom. 12.19) with 'it is the servant of God to execute wrath on the wrongdoer' (Rom. 13.4).

However, the writers of the New Testament did not conclude their understanding of the Roman Empire at this point. There is sufficient evidence that they saw, in its actual operation, a marked contrast to the empire of Jesus, the crucified Messiah.[32] The evidence can be summarised in the following way:

> The various assumptions about the pervasive imperial cult in the Roman East, Paul's apocalyptic thinking, and his gospel of the crucified Jesus as the Lord and Savior, as well as the parallelism of important terms (e.g., kyrios, *soter*/*soter*ia, euangelion, dikaiosune, pistis, eirene, eleutheria, elpis, parousia, apantesis) between the Roman imperial ideology and Paul's preaching of the gospel of Jesus Christ, all seem to invite an anti-imperial reading of the Pauline epistles. It appears natural to suppose that in the Roman world Paul's proclamation of Jesus as the messianic king, Lord (kyrios), and Son of God, and as the Savior (*soter*) who would come to destroy the rulers of this age/world and establish the kingdom of God, could have been understood as proclaiming a rival king to Caesar and subverting the Roman imperial order. At least some of Paul's several imprisonments (2 Cor. 11.23) must have been due to this political charge.[33]

So, Paul's message was a summons to total loyalty to another king (Acts 17.7). Jesus, not Caesar, was the true Son of God and Lord (Rom. 1.3-4). It has to be remembered that Jesus was crucified by order of the Roman governor, according to the much vaunted lex romana (Acts 3.13; 4.25-27). But this voluntary sacrifice was a subversive act by which the 'rulers of this age' (1 Cor. 2.8) were unmasked and the 'present form of this world' (1 Cor. 7.31) was already judged.

The debate among historians of the New Testament concerning the extent to which the documents portray an 'implicit and explicit subversion of the new ideology which was sweeping the Mediterranean world – that of the Roman Empire'[34] will continue. There is probably a consensus that the early church taught that political governance has been instituted by God for the sake of maintaining a social regime that upholds justice and punishes evil, that the Roman authorities would be held accountable for exercising this responsibility, and that they would be held to account whenever they claimed too much for themselves or betrayed the trust they had been given. As servants of God they are to be respected, but not given the honour which is due to God alone.[35] In

[32] 'In Greek cities, such as Corinth, *euangelion* was the 'gospel' of the 'salvation' and 'peace and security' established by the imperial saviour Augustus and successors...Paul was proclaiming an alternative gospel of an alternative emperor as well as building an alternative assembly in the city of Corinth,' Richard A. Horsley, 'Rhetoric and Empire and 1 Corinthians' in Horsley, *Paul and Politics*, 91, 92

[33] Syyon Kim, *Christ and Caesar: The Gospel and the Roman Empire in the Writings of Paul and Luke* (Grand Rapids: Eerdmans, 2008), 65.

[34] N.T. Wright, *Paul: Fresh Perspectives* (London: SPCK, 2005), 59.

[35] See, Christopher Bryan, *Render to Caesar*, 78-93.

other words, in general terms, the early Church, as one might expect, articulated an essentially Jewish political theology in line with the prophets.[36] The prophet does not wield direct political power, but does speak from God, and ultimately will not be silenced.

There remains a difference of opinion about how far the early Church might have been prepared to go in withdrawing its support from the institutions and general ethos of imperial rule. There can be little doubt that the ecclesia that belongs to Christ and that sought to be his presence in the world clashed at various points with the social expectations and culture of the ecclesias under the jurisdiction of Rome. Being a Christian meant living according to the new order of life in community brought by the Spirit of Christ. Roman rule represented the old order:

> The Roman Empire is another embodiment of the reign of Satan, and therefore the pax Augusta/Romana achieved through military conquest and political suppression is no real peace.... Luke makes it clear that the Empire of Rome and the lordship of Caesar are to be replaced by the Kingdom of God and the Lordship of Christ.[37]

Nevertheless, there is simply no evidence to suggest that the first Christians ever thought of organising themselves into a political force that might have had ambitions one day of taking over the reigns of power. They were guided not simply by pragmatic considerations – the total impossibility of any force opposed to Rome being able to overcome its power – but by deeply held theological convictions: they were called to be an alternative community, which through example and prophetic preaching constantly held an unredeemed community to account to live by the precepts of God. This stance implied a rejection of violence as a way of bringing about a society of justice and peace. It pointed to another interpretation of the exercise of power.

Conclusion

We have begun to assess some of the implications for the current practise of both Islam and Christianity of their respective origins. We have considered in particular the pivotal role played by both Jesus and Muhammad in the formation of the subsequent histories of the corresponding communities. We have also looked at the question of a public stance towards the exercise of political authority.

In continuing to compare the origins of Islam and Christianity as a guide to how each faith tradition views the relationship between religion and the state,

---

[36] Wright, *Paul: Fresh Perspectives*, 70.
[37] Kim, *Christ and Caesar*, 191.

we need to examine next the way in which each understands the meaning both of the prophetic office and of community. As we shall see, these also are two fundamental issues that both unite and divide the two faiths.

Chapter 8

The Impact of the Formative Years (Part II)

The Nature of Prophethood

It is a truism that both Islam and Christianity claim to be prophetic religions. Although prophecy of a kind can be found in most religions, including in shamanism and other popular forms, and 'was also known in the religion of the Greeks, Romans, Celts, Germans and North American Indians',[1] it becomes much more prominent in the monotheistic religions, particularly those associated with Abraham. In religions with a strong Scriptural tradition, prophets are those people 'who proclaimed the word (of God) under compulsion from God', who communicated 'what God wants to say'.[2] They see themselves as spokespeople, conduits for the living message that comes directly from God. The prophetic word often encompasses three main elements: a warning to the people of the consequences of a life conducted contrary to the will of God; a call to repentance, which involves returning from idolatry to the worship of the one true God and making restitution for injustices committed against weak and vulnerable people, and promises of blessings to those who continue in the ways of God.[3]

Prophets have often been isolated figures, despised and rejected by their communities for bringing a message of 'gloom and doom'. They consider themselves to have been chosen for the difficult task of speaking the truth about God's requirements for authentic worship and right living, even though these cut across the prevailing beliefs and practices of their respective communities. They are often portrayed, for this reason, as reluctant messengers, knowing the

---

[1] Walter J. Hollenweger, 'Prophecy' in Karl Muller, Theo Sundermeier, Stephen B. Bevans, Richard H. Bliese (eds), *Dictionary of Mission: Theology, History, Perspectives* (Maryknoll: Orbis Books, 1998), 368. Guidance from prophets is cited as one example of similarities between the primal heritage of the people of Melanesia and the biblical world; see, Hinnells, *A Handbook of Living Religions*, 422.

[2] K. Asamoah-Gyadu, 'Prophecy' in John Corrie (ed), *Dictionary of Mission Theology* (Nottingham: IVP, 2007), 319, 320.

[3] See, J. Andrew Kirk, 'Mission as prophecy: a voice from Latin America' in J. Andrew Kirk, *Mission under Scrutiny: Confronting Current Challenges* (London: Darton, Longman and Todd, 2006), 157-160.

cost of conveying unpopular statements.[4] However, the prophetic message is not just one of judgement and condemnation; it often contains words of great comfort and hope for the future.

Prophecy in Islam

Islam may rightly be called a religion of prophecy. Indeed, one of its main claims is that Muhammad, who is reputed to have received revelations directly from God, is the seal of the prophets. Islam is based on the assumption that people are born into the world innocent of evil, but that through temptation and desire they often go astray from the will of God. In order to return to the right path, they need to be instructed in the ways of God. For this purpose, God sent prophets at various times and in diverse places.[5] The first prophet was Adam, the father of the human race. Subsequently, other prophets were called and sent by God to bring people back to himself in a relationship of trust and obedience. Of these, the most renowned were Noah, Abraham, Isaac, Ishmael, Jacob, Moses, Job, David, Solomon. Elisha, Jonah, Dhu'l-Kifl (possibly Ezekiel [6]) and Zachariah (the father of John the Baptist). Then Jesus (Isa) is also included among the long line of prophets.

Muhammad has now had conferred upon him the status of being the very last of the prophets. The revelation that he received claims to reiterate the same message that all the prophets proclaimed, confirming the original, pure faith in God and authenticating all that is true in other expressions of religion. It is not surprising that 'the second basic postulate of Islam is to believe in the Prophethood of Muhammad'.[7]

> Every prophet of God, according to the Qur'an, strove to build man's relationship with God on the principle of God's sovereignty and the acknowledgement of the authority of the prophet as source of divine guidance.... The Guidance is revealed through the prophets. It is part of their mission to translate that into practice, in their own lives and in the society they try to reform.[8]

---

[4] For Jeremiah, see Jer. 1.6, 17-19; for Amos, see Amos 7.14-15; for Muhammad, see Q. 36.2-18. A *hadith* reported by Aisha and authenticated by al-Bukhari says, 'No man has ever brought what you have brought and not been treated as an enemy!' quoted in Ramadan, *The Messenger*, 30.

[5] According to tradition, there were 124,000 of them; see, Nasr, *The Heart of Islam*, 17.

[6] See, *The Qur'an: A new translation* by M.A.S. Abdel Haleem (Oxford, OUP, 2004), 207, note b.

[7] Khurshid Ahmad (ed), *Islam: its meaning and message* (Leicester: The Islamic Foundation, 1980), 31.

[8] Ahmad, *Islam: its meaning and message*, 31.

So, for Muslims, prophecy is inseparable from the person of Muhammad, and Muhammad is inseparable from the accounts about him. Prophecy is not only the word of God, but also the word of God put into practice. Thus, Muhammad as a prophet is inseparable from being a full example of what it means to be obedient to that word.[9] Hence, the vital importance assumed by the *hadith* (the sayings and actions of the prophet transmitted outside the Qur'an). It is crucial to the self-identity of Islam and its future direction that the pattern of social and political life in Medina, instigated by Muhammad, be considered as part of the revelation. In this regard, Muhammad in a sense takes on the mantle of (the prophet) Moses, the giver of divine laws and the leader of a theocratic community that, when necessary, had to defend itself by military means.[10]

The date of the birth of Islam is celebrated by Muslims as the moment when the first companions of Muhammad left Mecca and emigrated to Medina. However, given the essential integration in Islamic thinking of belief and practice, and practice and corporate life in society, the birth of Islam could possibly be considered also as the time of the Muslims' first armed engagement in January 624 in the raid on Meccan caravans at Nakhla; or, it might be regarded as the moment when 300 Muslim soldiers defeated a Meccan army three times their size at the Battle of Badr:

> Badr, the first major battle of Islam, is the most critical. Indeed historians rank Badr as one of the most decisive engagements in history. If the Muslims had lost, Islam might well have perished...The tide had turned in favour of Islam.[11]

> As a result, Muhammad managed to secure his first major victory which also became a turning point in his career.... The battle itself is portrayed as a sign of God's support and the eventual triumph of the prophet's mission.[12]

These two events indicate that the nature of Islam as a prophetic community could include, when necessary, the defence of religious faith by the use of force. The reality of fighting for the cause of God was legitimated for all time; it is enshrined unmistakeably in the Qur'an:

> Remember how God promised you [believers] that one of the two enemy groups[13] would fall to you: you wanted the unarmed group to be yours, but it was God's will to establish the truth according to His Word and to finish off the disbelievers

---

[9] See, Rippin, *Muslims: Their Religious Beliefs and Practices*, 216.

[10] See, Richard Bell, *The Origin of Islam in its Christian Environment* (London: Macmillan, 1926), 125.

[11] Ahmed, *Discovering Islam*, 20.

[12] Nanji, *Dictionary of Islam*, 25-26 (emphasis added).

[13] The Meccan trade caravan or their army.

> – to prove the Truth to be true, and the false to be false, much as the guilty might dislike it.... Your Lord revealed to the angels: 'I am with you: give the believers firmness; I shall put terror into the hearts of the disbelievers – strike above their necks and strike all their fingertips'. That was because they opposed God and His messenger, and if anyone opposes God and his Messenger, God punishes them severely.[14]

The Truth, referred to in this passage, is that finishing off disbelievers by force, when they attack the believers, is divinely sanctioned. In this passage the concrete event of Badr seems to be expanded into a general principle of divine punishment. Anyone who actively opposes God, which is the same thing as opposing his messenger, may legitimately be struck down by human means.

Prophecy for Islam is understood, then, primarily in terms of the life and mission of Muhammad. The triumph of prophecy is measured, at least in part, by the conquests achieved through the use of superior force, even if used only as a last resort.

> Islam is the least 'other-worldly' of the great religious systems, the one which, above all others, seeks to realize its aims in this world.... Thus the armed prophet of Madina would remain the perfect exemplar for Muslims of all ages, his career a model of moral and political action that would be consciously imitated by those seeking to create a juster social order in this world.[15]

From henceforth, the divine revelation is replete with rules and regulations for the conduct of social life that, through a long tradition of Qur'anic interpretation and the addition of authenticated *hadith* of the Prophet, have been assembled into elaborate legal codes:

> This organisation of action in this world implies the organization of all facets of human existence, individual and collective, hence educational, economic, political and social. *Shari'ah* provides the guidelines, the rules of external conduct.[16]

Prophecy in Christianity

For the Christian faith, prophecy, whilst sharing some of the same characteristics as those that are prominent in Islam, also begs to differ at certain crucial points. The nature of prophecy for the writers of the New Testament is determined largely by the life and witness of the literary prophets of Israel, i.e. the corpus of writings from Isaiah to Malachi, stretching over several

---

[14] Q. 8.7-13

[15] Ruthven, *Islam in the World*, 77.

[16] Ahmad, *Islam: its meaning and message*, 24.

centuries.[17] It is a curious, though significant, fact that these prophets are not mentioned in the Qur'an, with the one exception of Jonah. Those that are mentioned, though figures of great stature and authority in the history of Israel, are not usually considered to be prophets in the strict sense, although figures like Moses and David (presumed writer of a number of Psalms) do exercise prophet-like traits.

On the whole, the prophets mentioned in the Qur'an were also political leaders, called to direct and guide the Israelite nation. However, the prophets, whose writings have been recorded in the Old Testament, did not exercise public power in the state. On the contrary, it is quite clear that their message of warning, judgement, the call to repentance and the promise of new beginnings was directed mainly towards the rulers of the people. In other words, they stood apart from the power structures as an alternative voice, sent by God to hold the monarchs and their court (including the false prophets, paid to support the regime) to account.

In terms of a possible comparison, their situation was more like that of Muhammad in Mecca. They were opposed, vilified, persecuted, marginalised and sometimes killed (Rom. 11.3; I Thess. 2.15; Matt. 23.29-31, 37). However, their role could never have been fulfilled had they sought to wield political power themselves. Their God-given task was to recall the leaders to their responsibilities under the covenant to maintain an order of justice, compassion and peaceful welfare (*shalom*) for all the people, and especially for the poor and vulnerable (Mic. 6.8). This was part of their true worship of the one and only God, sovereign ruler of the nations (Isa. 1. 11-17; 58. 1-10; Amos 5.11-15).

In many ways the faith of Jesus and the early Christian church was built on a rediscovery of this prophetic tradition over against an excessive dependence on religion as observance of the law. It is to the prophets (including some of the Psalms) that the first Christians turn to find the initial announcement of the good news of a coming saviour and king who would give his life to create a righteous people, making atonement for sin. The law, by itself, had shown its inability to produce a society that lived up to God's standards. God was now making a new covenant with the whole world, through which the law of God would become a habit of the heart (Jer. 31.31-34).

So, in marked contrast to the notion of prophetic 'success' in Islam, the prophets of Israel might have seemed to have been failures. Their message led sometimes to periods of renewal, as under Josiah, Hezekiah, Ezra and Nehemiah, but on the whole Israel continued to flout God's demands for justice and compassion, go after false gods, align themselves with untrustworthy allies, oppress the weak, and base political life on deceit, lies and corruption. This

[17] Other prophets, prominent in the history of Israel, but who did not leave a written legacy, such as Elijah and Elisha, are also significant.

continued to be the situation right down to the time of Jesus. As we shall see, God's strategy of bringing blessings to the nations was fulfilled in a new and original way through Jesus and his followers.

Different understandings of prophecy

There is a dispute, then, between Islam and Christianity with regard to the true nature of prophecy. For the former, persecution, suffering and a meagre response to the message cannot be a long-standing situation for a prophet of God. This is illustrated by the reception that Muhammad experienced when he went to the town of Taif (619CE). He was looking for support and sanctuary for his new community of believers in Allah. It was not given:

> He met with a very cold reception, however, and the chiefs mocked his claim to be a prophet. If he was, they asked, how could God allow His Messenger to beg for the support of strange tribes?[18]

So, he was sent packing. The inference seems to be that a true prophet would be protected and would gain some fame and eminence among his people. However, one might ask why suffering should be considered a failure? Why is it not a sign of the truth of the message and of faithfulness?

According to Andrew Rippin, the idea of success in the world was central to Islamic ideology from the beginning:

> Islam would not have been revealed to the world, as God's last statement, if it were not divinely pre-ordained to succeed. God's word cannot be frustrated by human obstinacy.[19]

The corollary is that, whenever Islam has failed to live up to the high standards demanded by Allah, it is a sign of corruption and a return to the pre-revelatory age of jahiliyya (the period of ignorance and godlessness). The success of faith is measured ultimately by the ability to sustain a society obedient to the commands of God as received in the Qur'an and the *sunnah.* The significance of this belief is that the religion of Islam must regulate and direct all the affairs of state:

> When Muhammad failed to dissuade what was, in the Quraish, a local political hegemony from its strongly sanctioned idolatrous religion, he attained to dislodge and dispossess it of its pagan religion by dint of its martial/political surrender to

[18] Ramadan, *The Messenger*, 68-69.

[19] *Muslims: Their Religious Beliefs and Practices,* 174.

> his force. That 'manifest victory' emphatically sealed a religio-political pattern as the very theme of Islam.[20]

The consequence is that other non-Islamic peoples, under Muslim rule, cannot possess an equality of political rights, as they have refused to acknowledge that Muhammad is the final prophet, the faithful transmitter of God's last will and testament.

So, the divergence between Islam and Christianity in their respective interpretations of the prophetic vocation is at the heart of their dispute over the meaning of faith in God. The emigration from Mecca entailed a radical new understanding of the prophetic experience.[21] Whilst in Mecca, Muhammad had been commissioned to no other task than that of preaching. After the *hijrah*, Muhammad remained a prophet, but combined this role with that of the governor of a city and the commander of an army. The prophetic message, therefore, now had to include the divine sanction for violence and war and instructions about how to handle the results of conquest, such as the taking of prisoners.

Jesus, the Kingdom of God and the use of violence

In the life of Jesus, the prophetic message disallowed recourse to violence. In fact the proclamation of God's rule (the kingdom) denied the possibility that it could be accomplished by the use of coercive force. This is the gist of the famous, and frequently misunderstood, saying of Jesus at his trial before the Roman governor,

> My kingdom is not from (*ek*) this world. If my kingdom were from (*ek*) this world, my followers would be fighting to keep me from being handed over to the Jews. But, as it is, my kingdom is not from here (*enteuthen*).[22]

Both the context and the use of the preposition 'from' show that Jesus is affirming that his reign does not have its origin in the way this world habitually thinks about the exercise of power. So, the first statement is explained by the second. Were the kingdom of Jesus to be from this world, that is governed by the normal procedures of human reasoning, he would have organised his followers into a military force to defy the authorities and defend his cause. In an equivalent saying, recorded in Matthew's Gospel, Jesus rebukes his followers for using violence:

[20] *The Qur'an and the West*, 158.
[21] See, *Muhammad in the Qur'an*, 90.
[22] Jn. 18.36

'All who take the sword will perish by the sword. Do you think that I cannot appeal to my Father, and he will at once send me more than twelve legions of angels?'[23] (The figure is more than enough to deal with the High Priest's guards and probably the entire Roman occupying forces).[24]

Many, both within and outside the Christian church have misinterpreted the saying about the kingdom, understanding it to be claiming that Jesus' kingdom does not belong here, but exists in some mystical, spiritual sphere, removed from normal earthly existence. No Jew of the first century could possibly have misunderstood the meaning of the m*alkuth* YHWH in this way:

> It is essential that Jesus' statement should not be misconstrued as meaning that his kingdom is not active in this world, or has nothing to do with this world.[25]

At issue is the question of origins:

> Both expressions mean that Jesus' reign does not have its source or origin in this world (cf. Jn. 8.23) – this world which is both created by God through the agency of the pre-incarnate Word (Jn. 1.2, 3) and locked in persistent rebellion against its creator (Jn. 1.10, 11). The kingships of this world preserve themselves by force and violence.[26]

In other words, the kingdom of God is a powerful presence within the world, but in a different way from that normally associated with human rule. Many people, including many Muslims, have assumed that Christianity preaches a message of private, individual, inward, spiritual and future-oriented salvation. Such a view, however, has little to do with a careful reading of the New Testament. An interpretation like this may, in fact, be politically or ideologically motivated: either to marginalise Christians from public affairs or to protect them from the accusation that their faith may motivate them to act as subversive elements in the state.

The situation has been confused further by a common misunderstanding of Martin Luther's doctrine of two kingdoms – the kingdom of God's right hand, and of his left. It might seem that he taught a dualistic separation of the kingdom of God from the kingdoms of this world, in such a way that the latter remained autonomous within its own sphere, not accountable to the higher authority of God's sovereign rule. Such an interpretation has given rise to the belief that Christians must in all things obey the injunctions of the state.

---

[23] Mt. 26.52-53

[24] In the first century a legion, at full strength, consisted of 5,280 fighting men. 12 legions, therefore, would have made an army of 63,360 men.

[25] George R. Beasley-Murray, *John* (Word Biblical Commentary, Volume 36: Dallas: Word Incorporated, 1991), 331.

[26] D.A.Carson, *The Gospel according to John* (Leicester: IVP, 1991), 594.

Behind the formulation of the two kingdoms, there is a genuine and proper concern that the two kingdoms do not become so intertwined that the church seeks to control the affairs of state or that the state seeks to regulate the life of the church. The relationship between the two kingdoms is much more subtle, one might say dialectical. For one thing, the kingdom of God cannot be identified with the church.[27] This means that the state has a certain amount of freedom from the church's putative claim to know and represent authoritatively and finally the divine will for the ordering of society. It also means that the governing powers exercise their authority only under the ultimate rule of God, which has to be discovered through a critical process of community discernment.

At this point in the discussion, it is enough to affirm that nowhere in the New Testament is there even the slightest hint that the message of Christ could be used to justify or endorse the use of force, in any circumstances, as an imperative of the Gospel. The Christian community in the first century was to live literally at peace with its neighbours. It was to give testimony to the reality of Christ's rule by adopting a strict policy of non-retaliation (see, Lk. 6.27-36; Rom. 12.14-21). As this was the path trodden by the servant Messiah, so it was to be the path of his servant disciples: 'As the Father has sent me (into the world), so I send you'. [28]

Rediscovering the true nature of prophecy

What is at stake in this discussion is not only the nature of prophecy, according to the two religions, but how does the religion itself maintain its prophetic constitution. Christians when they study the Islamic tale of two cities are likely to ask whether the respective messages given in Mecca and Medina belong to the same essence. The emigration from one city to the other was fortuitous. There is no reference in the Qur'an to it being commanded by God. The problem is that, once prophecy is identified with the office of ruler, it is almost inevitable that any other claim to prophecy will be denied and suppressed. Once the reigns of power are assumed, the prophet has to defend his purposes and projects. And, even if he associates these with divine revelation, there is no-one to challenge, for either the prophetic office has been restricted to one person or that one person acts as the final measure of all true prophecy. Dissent must be repressed.

Christians ask the same question of their own history. In what sense is the religion that came to dominate, after the establishment of Christianity as the official religion of the Roman state, the same as that proclaimed and lived out

---

[27] This relationship will be explored in the following section on the nature of community.

[28] John 20.21; 17.18

by the scattered communities of the followers of the Way during the first couple of centuries after Christ? Do we not, perhaps, find here a parallel capitulation, however understandable in the circumstances, to an inappropriate relation between faith and power? It is, surely, significant that in the Christian church, following its formal alliance with the state, prophecy was regarded with some suspicion and the prophetic office deprecated.

The early *surahs* of the Qur'an insisted that Muhammad had no political function. He was simply a nadhir (one who warns, Q. 22.49).[29] But in Medina faith and the campaign for governance became the same thing. If Islam was to survive in its chosen new surroundings as the authoritative guide for the new society, as was supposed, then there has to be a divine sanction for coercion against what came to be seen as sedition and treachery.[30] There is a sense in which Muhammad played a role similar to that of Constantine in using the powerful universe of a monotheistic faith to promote the good of the nation in ways that he saw fit: The profound difference, however, between the two stories is that

> ...the pivotal decision ('to abrogate the Meccan "innocence"') had the sanction of his own doing and came to be embedded – as Constantine has never been – in the founding Scripture of the faith.[31]

In other words, for the Christian faith the effect of the Constantine move first to tolerate and then favour the church represents a fatal compromise of its original calling. In a sense, the Emperor became its patron, thus provoking the danger that he would usurp the place that only its crucified and risen Lord could legitimately occupy. For Muslims, however, the Medina venture represents the ideal combination of faith and practical life, itself an interpretation of religion as being the perfect way for humans to live on earth.

In the substantial difference of origins and in the mainstream interpretation of their significance lies, I believe, the clue to contemporary attitudes to political power and social life. Some crucial questions, still to be addressed, remain: is there more than one way of being political? Is the Medina story really a model for all time? Does not a prophetic faith actually demand a different approach to realpolitik? These questions will be explored further in Part III of this study.

---

[29] Armstrong, *Islam: A Short History*,

[30] See, Kenneth Cragg, *Muhammad and the Christian: A Question of Response* (London: Darton, Longman and Todd, 1984), 25-34.

[31] Cragg, *The Qur'an and the West*, 10.

The Nature of Community

Community in early Islam

The *hijrah* not only transformed the nature of Prophethood in Islam, but also that of community. In Mecca, the Muslims numbered a few hundred. They were a well-defined body, who believed in the message brought by Muhammad, joined in the discipline of prayers five times per day, having first performed a ritual washing, and began to invite others to embrace Islam. The first to believe was Muhammad's wife, Khadija, then his cousin, Ali, followed by Zayd (Muhammad's freed slave) and Abu Bakr, a prominent merchant and highly respected citizen of Mecca. After three years of clandestine meetings, Muhammad began to proclaim his message openly.

In spite of persecution, the companions of Muhammad gradually grew in number. Opposition was due to the Muslims proclaiming a religion at odds with that of the Qurayshi people. They would have been marked out as those who refused to join in the idolatrous practices centred on the *Kaaba*. Their community life is summed up in the words of the 'twelve men of the Helpers' (from Medina):

> We paid homage to the apostle of Allah after the unmilitant manner of women – this happened before war was made incumbent upon us. We pledged that we should not associate other gods with Allah, nor steal, nor commit fornication, nor kill our female children, nor tell lies, nor disobey what was right.[32]

It is highly significant, and truly momentous, that the whole direction of the community changed once armed defense of the faith became warranted [33]:

> When Allah gave his apostle permission to wage war, the promise to fight immediately became a condition of allegiance to Islam. This had not been so at the first meeting on the hillside (between Muhammad and the delegation from Medina), when homage was paid 'in the manner of women'; Allah had not then given his apostle permission to fight. He had given permission neither to wage war nor to shed blood, but only to call men to Allah, to endure insults patiently, and to pardon the ignorant.[34]

---

[32] *The Life of Muhammad*, 55.

[33] See, Qur'an 22.39-40.

[34] *The Life of Muhammad*, 65. The italicised words emphasise the distinguishing marks of the Muslim community in Mecca.

Immediately following the verses that permitted war, the Qur'an goes on to say, 'Those who, when We establish them in the land, keep up the prayer, pay the prescribed alms, command what is right, and forbid what is wrong'.[35]

This suggests some of the principal activities that the community practised, whilst still in Mecca. Two of them – prayers and the giving of alms – became two of the 'pillars of Islam'.

So, whilst in Mecca, the small group of Muslims formed a viable community,

> whose particular feature was that it gathered, without distinction, women and men of all clans and all social categories (although the bulk were young and poor).... The prophet had gathered around him a solid core of trustworthy women and men; some were his relatives, but many came from different social categories and tribes, and he had been providing them spiritual and religious education for the previous three years...The first Muslims were called to a profound and radical spiritual conversion...[36]

Even admitting the ferocity of the persecution that they subsequently underwent, would it not have been possible to have remained a discreet, if irritating minority in Mecca, dedicated to win the compatriots to Islam by the power of the message and the quality of the community's life? And, even admitting that emigration was a legitimate option, why was it necessary for the community to assume the reins of political power? Would it not have been possible to have remained in Medina as a protected minority (as in Abyssinia), contributing to the welfare of the city, but not seeking political control?

It is the latter option, once embarked upon, that changed the Muslim community irrevocably and apparently for ever. Now, as has frequently been noted, the tone of the revelations changed. The use of violence was not only permitted to the community, but in certain circumstances enjoined upon it. Now also, rules to regulate the life of the whole community as a public, civil body began to appear:

> The Qur'anic material revealed to the prophet in Mecca is distinguished by scholars from the material that came after the Migration (Hijra) to Medina. In the Meccan period, the Qur'an was concerned mainly with the basic beliefs in Islam...In the Medinan *surah*s, by which time the Muslims were no longer the persecuted minority but an established community with the Prophet as its leader, the Qur'an began to introduce laws to govern the Muslim community with regard to marriage, commerce and finance, international relations, war and peace.[37]

---

[35] Q. 22.41

[36] Ramadan, *The Messenger*, 38, 39, 40.

[37] Haleem, *The Qur'an: A new translation*, xviii.

As the community expanded through conquest and conversion, there was a pressing need for further laws and regulations. These developed over the course of the next two to three centuries. Islam became identified supremely as a religion of law. In terms of the comparison we are making with the origins of the Christian community, the leaders of the Islamic community took the place occupied by the Roman authorities according to the New Testament (Rom. 13.1-7; 1 Pet. 2. 14): to punish wrong-doing and uphold justice. Islam was transmuted from an independent community within a wider community into an empire (caliphate), in which ideally, as in medieval Christendom, the civic community entirely coincided with the religious community.

Community in early Christianity

The early Christian communities, though also beginning as small, persecuted minorities, took a different path. Unlike early Islam, there was no one leader. Two of the inner circle of Jesus' disciples, Peter and John, were prominent in the life of the movement in its early years in Jerusalem and Judea. However, as theirs became an itinerant ministry, leadership in the first church in Jerusalem devolved to James, a half-brother of Jesus, and a group of elders. Later, significant communities sprang up in Damascus and Antioch, and these became centres for the spread of the message of the Christ to surrounding areas. Subsequently, Saul of Tarsus, an infamous persecutor of the church, but who came to acknowledge Jesus as the Messiah alive in the midst of his followers, became a leading figure in the spread of the message into Asia Minor and Greece.

At the time of the first 'council' of the church (in Jerusalem, sometime between 48-50 CE), there were several influential people occupying positions of leadership. The account in Acts 15 mentions Peter, Paul, Barnabas, James, Judas and Silas in that order. However, the decisions taken by the council were the conclusions of the whole body, apostles and elders acting in unanimity, under the leading of the Holy Spirit (Acts 15.22-28). In the church in Antioch, there appeared to be a collective leadership, exercised by prophets and teachers (Acts 13.1). Later the leadership of the churches founded by Paul was invested in a group of elders (*presbuteroi*) (Acts 20.17).

So, what we find in these early years is a fairly loose-knit group of communities of believers in Jesus, known as 'the Way'. They were scattered throughout Judea, Samaria, Syria, Asia Minor, Greece, along the Adriatic coast, Italy, North Africa, and probably even further afield. They were held together by a common pattern of teaching (*tupos didakes*, Rom. 6.17; 2 Tim. 1.13), a common ethical life (Eph. 4.17-5.21), a mutual concern for the welfare of one another (Gal. 2.10; 6.2,10; 2 Cor. 8-9) and by periodic visits from people with apostolic credentials (apostles, the companions of the apostles and others with special authorisation).

How did these communities see themselves? They would probably have laid hold of familiar language that described corporate bodies:

> It was not possible for new religions to set up novel institutions in the Roman Empire. They required a license. The emergence of the Christian church was made possible and its growth and continuance were made secure by the way in which it used existing social institutions and adapted them to its own ends.[38]

The three institutions most immediately apposite were the Jewish synagogue, the household and voluntary associations. The early Christian communities resembled all of these in some aspects of their common life, whilst being distinguished from them in others.[39] Another well-known institution, particularly in the Greek city-states was the assembly (*ekklesia*), where people would have come together to perform specific functions, probably in the name of a famous person, god or patron. The Christians assembled in the name of the Christ, to celebrate their salvation, listen to teachers and prophets, engage in worship (sometimes with ecstatic manifestations), share a meal together, distribute financial aid to vulnerable members of the community, such as widows and the unemployed, listen to reports of new converts, welcome them into the community and take counsel about aspects of the community's life and witness.[40]

They would have interpreted their life together as the attempt to be models of a new kind of society, in terms of how they conducted inter-human relationships. So, to describe their mission in the world, they would most probably have used metaphors like light, salt, seed and leaven, used by Jesus in his account of the impact of God's kingdom within human history (Eph. 5.8-14; Acts 26.18; Gal. 5.9). They saw themselves as alternative assemblies or societies, with different forms of government, gender relationships, and attitudes to slavery. The message of Christ was seen as a radically new beginning (2 Cor. 5.17; Rom. 6.4; Gal. 6.15), a permission to break with the customs and ethos of an oppressive society, under the tyrannical rule of capricious gods, a violent empire, self-serving patrons and hierarchically ordered families.

Now it might be argued, and this is certainly part of the burden of the Islamic critique of Christianity, that these initial Christian communities were wholly apolitical, uninterested in the daily life of the polis. Their 'citizenship (*politeuma* – social belonging) is in heaven' (Phil. 3.20), and therefore they

---

[38] D.J. Tidball, 'Social Setting of Mission Churches' in Gerald F. Hawthorne, Ralph P. Martin, Daniel G. Reid (eds), *Dictionary of Paul and His Letters* (Leicester: IVP, 1993), 887.

[39] See, Tidball, 'Social Setting of Mission Churches', 887-888.

[40] See, Eckhard Schnabel, *Paul the Missionary: Realities, Strategies and Methods* (Downers Grove: IVP, 2008), 231-236.

could disregard 'earthly things' and simply concentrate on preparing themselves for the coming again of Jesus, who would then transform the whole of existence 'by the power that enables him to make all things subject to himself'.[41]

On the other hand, it might be argued that these Christian communities were thoroughly political, but in a different sense. They were small societies seeking to live out, in the circumstances of daily life, a sense of liberation and freedom brought about by the activity of God in their midst. In terms of the social norms of the time, their way of life was deeply subversive. By being an alternative to the dominant culture, they would have been seen as threatening. It is true that they were 'expecting from heaven a Saviour (*soter*), the Lord Jesus Christ'.[42] Therefore, they did not need to invest all their hopes in the continuation of life in this world as it is. However, it is also true that this Saviour was already working in their midst to bring about the transformation of the normal, unjust, unequal, discriminatory, violent and arbitrary patterns of social existence, as a foretaste of what could be, were people to embrace the reality of God's kingdom.

So, even if it might have been possible for the small band of Christians to have exerted actual political power in the cities of the time, they would not have done so. Had they been invited, as was Muhammad, to take over the governance of a city-state, in order to rule it according to the laws of God, they would have refused. And the reason is that this would immediately have compromised their ability to act as a prophetic witness within society. If the religious body is identified with the reins of power, then the prophetic ministry is likely to be seen as treacherous, for, in so far as it is critical of governance, it will be accused of deviating from the official religious line.[43]

Conclusion

Power tends to create a situation were opposition is seen not only as anti-social and disloyal but also heretical. A theocratic society cannot entertain the existence of groups whose ultimate allegiance is not to the divine-human state. Here we can appreciate a fundamental divide between Islam and Christianity in their relationship to political and social life, arising from the different ways in which they originated and have understood their divine calling. The respective understandings of the nature of prophecy and being a community of faith are keys to appreciating the differences between the two religions.

---

[41] Phil. 3.21

[42] Phil. 3.20

[43] Examples in the history of Christianity would be the John Wyclif, the Lollards, the Waldenses, John Huss, Girolamo Savonarola, Erasmus and the Anabaptists.

There is, however, a caveat: were it possible for Muslims to reinterpret their early history by rediscovering the prophetic nature of their faith as a minority community and locating it at the heart of their beliefs and practice, they might find an unexpected source for reinvigorating their role in contemporary societies. After all, since about one quarter of all Muslims live as minorities in non-Muslim states, where the reality of a Muslim political system is out of the question, it would seem logical that Muslims would work out a way of being faithful to the revelation they have inherited without having to pursue an Islamic state as the only ideal. To this possibility we now turn in the third part of our study.

Chapter 9

Islam and the West

The Argument so Far

Not long after the collapse of Communism in the Soviet Union and the states of Central and Eastern Europe, Samuel Huntington, a professor of political science at Harvard University, discussed the prospect of a clash of civilisations involving the West and other sectors of the globe. In particular, he thought it likely that Islam, as a total way of life, would become a dominant factor in world politics, challenging the hitherto assertive power of Western nations.

Since the advent of serious terrorist atrocities in East Africa, Bali, New York, Washington, Madrid, Istanbul and London, linked to a network of radical Islamist groups, opposed to the political, economic and military stratagems of the USA and its allies, Huntington's prediction seems to be coming true. The book was written, I believe, not to forecast a pending disaster, but to take stock of a potentially dangerous situation. The object was to discuss ways of building different relationships between peoples with seriously divergent visions of what is good for humanity.

Huntington's proposal has been keenly debated. Both Muslims and non-Muslims are divided over his arguments. Probably the majority who have commented have found his claims unconvincing, not least because they reason that it is not justifiable to talk about Islam as if it were one, undifferentiated body:

> We are not dealing with an entity called 'Islam'; we are dealing with Muslims of many different kinds and countries of many different kinds in which...the majority happen to be Muslims.[1]

Nevertheless, in so far as conflicts are still taking place in politically unstable nations like Afghanistan, Iraq, Iran, Pakistan, Somalia, and the Yemen and plots to cause widespread, indiscriminate death in these and other nations continue to be uncovered, it is not wholly disingenuous to maintain that the issue of a possible clash of civilisations is still on the agenda. As has been pointed out in numerous writings, speeches and broadcasts, for many centuries Islam (originally in the form of different Caliphates) and the West (in the shape

[1] Colin Chapman in a personal communication to the author.

of the emerging nations of Europe and also subsequently its various extensions in North America and Australasia) have lived in tension. The main reasons for this state of affairs were given in chapters 3 and 4. Would it not, therefore, be somewhat credulous to minimize the evidence that testifies to a serious problem regarding the ability of two distinct ways of interpreting human life to find the means of living together with a degree of mutual respect and concord?

My particular interest in this book is to explore the alleged 'clash of civilisations' between Islam and the West by examining how the origins of Islam and Christianity may have contributed to contemporary dominant political systems and ideologies and to the exercise of political power in a globalised world. Is it possible to discern a way of understanding how human societies should be organised already embedded in the original histories of the two faith communities? And, if it is, how may this understanding help to bridge the apparently divisive perceptions that Muslim and Western communities have of one another, in order to promote the desire implicit in the sub-title of Huntington's book – 'The Remaking of World Order'?

Islam and the West in the Twentieth Century

Certain events that followed the First World War have irrevocably shaped the existence of Islam as a socio-political force on the world stage. The collapse of the Ottoman Empire, followed by the conversion of modern Turkey into a secular state, has deprived Islam of any kind of unifying focus-point. The geo-political rearrangement of the Middle East by the nations that triumphed in 1918 has caused understandable resentment throughout the region.

In 1921 the seizure of power in Iran by an Iranian army officer, Reza Khan, who declared himself Shah, backed by the British government, led eventually to great animosity among the people. Relationships with some Western nations worsened, when they intervened to support the overthrow in 1953 of the democratically elected prime minister, Dr. Mohammed Mossadegh. The coup, orchestrated by Great Britain and the USA, was the first time the latter had openly helped to overthrow an elected, civil government. The modernising reforms of Muhammad Reza Shah, called the 'White Revolution' (1963-71), an increasing secularization of the state and a campaign of repression against the people led eventually to a popular revolt, orchestrated from exile in Paris by the Ayatollah Khomenei. He returned to Iran in 1979 as the head of a new Islamic Republic. Since that time, relations between Iran and Western nations have become increasingly tense, due to the support given by the latter to Saddam Hussein during the Iran-Iraq war (1980-1988), the accusation that Iran was involved in international terrorism and its alleged development of a nuclear weapons programme.

Present day Iraq was (since 1534) part of the Ottoman Empire until the outbreak of the First World War, when British forces drove the Turks out of the region. After the war Britain was granted a mandate to run the country under the League of Nations. It recognised Ahd Allah Faisal, son of the sharif of Mecca, as king. Until the fall of the monarchy in 1958, British influence remained strong. Since that time, and up to the overthrow of Saddam Hussein in 2003, Iraq was ruled by the Ba'ath Socialist Party. From the time of the accession of Khomenei in Iran in 1979 until the first Gulf War in 1990, Saddam Hussein received the backing of the West. However, from that time onwards relations broke down because of the internal repression of Kurds in the North and Shia populations in the South of the country, and because of disputes over the international monitoring of the development of suspected weapons of mass destruction. The second Gulf War, a massive invasion of Iraq by a coalition of forces led by the USA, ensued in 2003.

Space does not allow a significant trawl through the history of other Middle Eastern countries, such as Egypt, Jordan, Lebanon and Syria. However, in each case either the British or the French were deeply involved in the past as semi-colonial powers. They were seen as foreign intruders, unwelcome meddlers in the affairs of other peoples. The question of Israel has already been considered. In this case, the almost undiscriminating support given to the new nation, since its inception, by the USA has deeply alienated the Arab nations of the region.

By the end of the first decade of the new millennium, the Middle East still remains volatile. Israel and the Palestinian state appear to be no nearer concluding a permanent settlement of their intractable disputes. Iraq is still the scene of intermittent, internal violence and a continuing failure to rebuild the nation's infrastructure. Iran's regime is unstable, following supposedly fraudulent elections in 2009. Its alleged development of a nuclear weapons' capability, its exaggerated hostility to Israel and its well-documented abuse of human rights against its own citizens have put it on a collision course with Western nations. The strategic location in the region of the world's largest operating oil reserves contributes to an acute nervousness among importing nations about a long-term, guaranteed supply.

Added to the geo-political unpredictability, all these nations, not to mention others in Africa and Asia also going through turbulent times (Sudan, Somalia, Pakistan and Afghanistan) are Muslim-majority countries, proud of their long association with the faith of Islam. There is the added question of the considerable immigration into the West of Muslim populations from SE and East Asia, North Africa and Turkey. Huge efforts are being made by Western governments to see that they are well integrated into what initially will have been seen as alien cultures.

However, points of tension remain, and from time to time flair up, such as dress-codes, anger towards what Muslims see as the dishonouring of their religion, alleged preferential treatment given to Muslims, the question of self-government and the limited use of *shari'ah* in domestic affairs, arranged marriages, honour-killings and the incitement to indiscriminate violence by a small, radical minority. Is it possible, then, for Muslims to take a long, fresh look at their early history and come to an agreement on the interpretation of their foundations documents – the Qur'an and the *sunnah* – that will enable the undoubted conflict between their truth claims and the current value-systems of the West to be handled peaceably? To this question we now turn.

Approaching the Past

Islam is irrevocably based on a series of revelations alleged to have been received by Muhammad from God during his public life (610-632) and collected after his death into one volume – the Qur'an:

> The Qur'an is the supreme authority in Islam. It is the fundamental and paramount source of the creed, rituals, ethics, and laws of the Islamic religion. It is the book that 'differentiates' between right and wrong, so that nowadays, when the Muslim world is dealing with such universal issues as globalization, the environment, combating terrorism and drugs, issues of medical ethics, and feminism, evidence to support the various arguments is sought in the Qur'an…The entire religious life of the Muslim world is built around the text of the Qur'an.[2]

Unless one understands that Muslims invest the whole of their lives in the veracity and validity of the whole text, they understand nothing about Islam. Having duly emphasised this cardinal point, it is also clear that no living Muslim scholar or ordinary reader of the book has direct access to the original meaning. Interpretation of the text is unavoidable, using all the necessary linguistic and historical tools available. Indeed, the quotation given above implicitly highlights this fact, for none of the universal issues cited occurs as such in the various *surahs* of the Qur'an. Nobody would expect them to be present, for the Qur'an is a revelation given at particular moments in the history of one person. That was fourteen centuries ago. History has moved on. The shape of the world has changed immeasurably.

Now, as soon as one recognises the inevitability of interpretation, it is obvious that in a number of instances careful readers of the text will give different explanations and come to a variety of understandings of how the original should be applied in the circumstances of the twenty-first century. This is exactly what has happened throughout the centuries and continues to take place today. Exactly how the Qur'an forms the beliefs of Muslims and guides their conduct has to be deduced from the text. There is no parallel, infallible handbook that dictates in every aspect both the exact original meaning and how it refers to contemporary existence. So, what one envisages in theory turns out to be reality in practice. Contemporary Muslims, like contemporary Christians with regard to the Bible, quite often come to disparate understandings of how the text relates to current affairs.

---

[2] Haleem, *The Qur'an: a new translation*, ix.

Addressing the context

We are speaking here of what technically has been called 'contextualisation', namely the process of relating the original message(s) of revelation to the totality of human experience as this arises out of family background, ethnicity, geographical location, the traditions and values of one's community, education, social engagement, economic circumstances and political realities. This practice may be seen as one of translation, i.e. conveying in contemporary language and thought-forms what was intended by the original writings. More loosely, it entails reformulating the message in such a way that it makes sense to modern listeners. However precisely understood, the object of the exercise is simultaneously to remain faithful to the original meaning and to demonstrate its significance and relevance to actual real-life situations. How this is to be done is a matter of great debate and not a little friction among those who come to divergent conclusions.

Contemporary Muslim thinkers acknowledge that the process must go on. Consciously or unconsciously, it already has for the past fourteen centuries. Different philosophical and law schools are based upon different interpretations of the Qur'an and the sayings of Muhammad. This being the case, the struggle (could one call it a *jihad*?) for an accurate and appropriate interpretation of revelation is a constant challenge. The following quotations give a flavour of the enduring task:

> The task of interpretation today must consider time, location and understanding of how the tenets and directives respond to the contemporary context. They also share a commitment to the inner unity of the Qur'an and a rejection of random and selective citation.[3]

> For Parvez, Islam has an unchanging core, but in application it is adaptable and fluid. If the underlying reasons for ethico-legal instruction are associated with specific circumstances and these no longer exist, then the practice of that ethico-legal instruction becomes suspended.[4]

> We are here confronting the fundamental distinction that should be established between timeless principles and contingent models, a distinction that is the direct consequence of a normative reading of the sources and, as such, is in itself fundamental.[5]

---

[3] Farid Esack, *Qur'an, liberation and pluralism: An Islamic perspective of interreligious solidarity against oppression* (Oxford: One World, 1997), 60.
[4] Saeed, *Interpreting the Qur'an*, 21.
[5] Ramadan, *Western Muslims*, 35.

> For Zayd,[6] the careful interpreter, who examines both the original context of the Qur'an and their own context, can identify those messages that have significance across both contexts from 'the historical and temporal, which carry no significance in the present context.[7]

Interpreting the text in context

One of the fullest treatments of the intricacies of contemporary approaches to the Quranic text is given by Abdullah Saeed.[8] His concern is to rescue the vitality and intrinsic authority of the revelatory message from the over-scrupulous, literalist, traditional interpretation of past jurists, handed down in an unreflective set of conventions. Unless the interpretation of the Qur'an can be refocused on contemporary life, there is a real danger that the content will gradually be ignored or become irrelevant and Muslims will lose connection with their sacred Scripture.

Saeed argues that there are basically three broad approaches to interpretation. First, there are the textualists. They believe that the meaning of the Qur'an is universal and has been fixed for all time. The significance is the same for all peoples in every generation. In this sense, the work of interpretation has already been largely done. Secondly, there are the semi-textualists. They too believe that the ethical and legal injunctions remain constant in all ages. However, there is a need to present them in more modern idioms, so that at least they appear to be addressing the live issues of contemporary societies. Thirdly, there are the contextualists. They differ from the other two categories in two ways: they stress the importance of reading the Quranic directives within their original context, and they argue that the modern scholar should have a degree of freedom in distinguishing between the mutable and immutable in what was originally given.

After the first three centuries of Islam, the Quranic text and the *hadith* were used to construct laws. In effect the jurists of the time made the Qur'an into a legal 'manual'. In Islamic law both sources enjoy almost equal authority in ethico-legal matters. In many ways the 'textualist' and 'semi-textualist' positions arise from the fear that unqualified people may distort the sense of the original, taking it upon themselves to find meanings that suit their own circumstances. This could result in a kind of hermeneutical free-for-all, which would split the Muslim community into many different camps. However, the insistence that there should be no change from the tradition assumes that the

---

[6] Nasr Hamid Abu Zayd, 'Divine Attributes in the Qur'an: Some Poetic Aspects' in John Cooper, Ronald Nettler and Mohamed Mahmoud (eds), *Islam and Modernity: Muslim Intellectuals Respond* (London: I.B.Taurus, 1998).

[7] Bennett, *Muslims and Modernity*, 102.

[8] Saeed, *Interpreting the Qur'an.*

tradition can never be questioned, on the supposition that it is the one correct and immutable understanding of what God requires for his creation. The problem with this line of reasoning is that in Islam there never has been a centralised, uniform, universally acknowledged authority that can pronounce on the validity, or otherwise, of any particular understanding of the original documents. No-one is able to speak 'ex-cathedra'; there is no magisterium.

This being the case, there are in the real world many disputes between Muslims about the true significance of some verses, especially where these raise controversial issues in the light of contemporary sensibilities about human rights. In a sense, this is how it should be for the Qur'an itself instructs the faithful to think about and reflect on its meaning (Q. 4.82; 38.29; 47.24). Even Muhammad, to a certain degree, allowed a free discussion on the meaning of the revelations he received. He invited his companions to express their opinions about the most appropriate understanding of the recitations.[9]

There are a number of good reasons why Quranic interpretation should remain open. First, the Qur'an itself witnesses to a variety of verses that have different standings - those that are absolute (*mutlaq*), qualified (*muqayyad*), abrogating (*nasikh*) and abrogated (*mansukh*).

Secondly, in the early years after the death of Muhammad, some of the initial rulings of the Qur'an changed several times to meet the evolving needs of the community. The practice of abrogation (*naskh*), meaning annul or supersede (see Q. 2.106; 13.39; 16.101) was carried out. For example, the original punishment for adultery was home confinement (Q. 4.15). This was abrogated in favour of laws related to flogging (Q. 24.2).

Thirdly, a significant difference can be detected in the rulings given to Muhammad whilst still in Mecca and those given subsequently in Medina, after the *hijrah*. When the Muslim community was weak, the Qur'an urged them to be patient and to tolerate the hostility of the Meccans (Q. 16.126-127). When, from Medina, they were able to resist the Meccans, they were urged to fight in self-defence (Q. 9.5).

Fourthly, the interpretation of the Qur'an down the ages has by no means been static. There has been a long tradition of exegesis (*tafsir*) based on reason. The word is related to either *fasr*, meaning to expound and make intelligible, or *safara*, meaning to uncover or unveil. '*Tafsir* is the area of knowledge by which one understands, explains and derives rulings and wisdom from God's book'.[10] The philosopher Ibn Rushd (died 1198) argued that *tafsir* based on reason (*ta'wil*) was essential for communicating the message of the Qur'an to each succeeding generation.

Fifthly, and perhaps most importantly, the Qur'an is not intended to be a legal text. There are relatively few verses that are strictly legal. It is not

---

[9] Saeed, *Interpreting the Qur'an*, 47, 73.

[10] Saeed, *Interpreting the Qur'an*, 57-58.

interested in minutiae. Therefore, there is a need to distinguish between the outward forms of ethico-legal rulings and the moral purpose that lies behind them.

These are weighty arguments in favour of a more flexible approach to discovering how the message of God becomes a contemporary word for the Muslim community and the world. Rahman suggests a methodology for eliciting sound general principles via a double movement. First, the text of the Qur'an is to be understood within its original historical setting, in order to discern general ethical principles like justice and fairness, repentance and mercy. In a second movement these principles are to be used as the basis for formulating rules and laws relevant to the modern period. The ethical value of 'right action' is the main guiding principle.[11]

Looking at the issues that seem to set Muslim societies somewhat apart, and observing the situations that have led people like Huntington to propose a possible clash of civilisations, it would seem that keeping the meaning of the Qur'an open to fresh understandings will make a vital contribution to lessening tensions. Such an approach is also the only way of bringing Muslims and non-Muslims closer together in their perceptions of what is needed for human communities to flourish. There are fortunately a number of signs that this approach is gaining some momentum among those Muslims who wish to live out the basic elements of their faith without compromise and yet also without unnecessarily antagonising those who do not share their fundamental beliefs.

Medina Cannot be Repeated

It would seem obvious to most observers that history cannot be repeated. The situation of the Arabian peninsular in the 7th century will not occur again. What Muhammad achieved in subduing hostile forces assembled against the new community of Islam, bringing some unity to the perpetually warring tribes, seeking to implement justice and compassion in a severely divided city cannot be re-enacted fourteen centuries later. Circumstances have changed dramatically. The world is entirely different. Rightly or wrongly an Islamic state modelled on that of the first administration of Muhammad is not a possibility. These are some of the reasons why aspiring to recreate such a model is likely to be frustrated and why other ideals should be pursued.

First, there is no direct access to the prophet of Islam. Revelation has long since ceased. No authority can say with the certainty of the first generation what kind of society should be implemented. Access to the primary events is always mediated: by the way the Qur'an is read and how the authenticity of the

[11] This principle appears to be employed as a 'middle axiom', a technical term used by ethicists to describe a means of moving from universal statements about right and good to concrete policies and legal enactments.

historical records is judged. Therefore, it is dubious to pretend that a social and political blueprint, allegedly laid down as a prototype for all generations, can be reconstructed.

Secondly, no nation today is entirely free to go its own way and set up a system of government entirely of its own choosing. Convictions about the pre-eminence of human rights, individual conscience, freedom of religion, speech and assembly, and democracy entailing genuine opposition and fair elections will always contest the imposition of rule by an elite minority in the name of an unchallengeable interpretation of the law of God. These convictions, though sometimes stimulated from outside an autocratic regime will also arise from within, creating an unstable society.

So, thirdly, those who advocate an Islamic republic will be driven by modern circumstances to establish a repressive rule, which denies some of the fundamentals of the Islamic faith, such as *shura* (the concept of consultation in legal and political decision-making) and *'ijma* (the required consensus of the Muslim community). Indeed, it is suggested by a number of Islamic scholars that the true guardian of the implementation of the law of God (*shari'ah)* is not a self-appointed clerical body, but the community, for the latter is primordial and precedes the state: 'The state is only the political dimension of the collective endeavour of the Muslims'.[12]

> The implications of this understanding are far-reaching. Shari'a is designed to constitute a comprehensive defence mechanism against oppression and arbitrary rule...It was never intended to be an instrument of authority in the hands of any particular government, because it exists independently of the state. The citizen is granted the freedom to question and monitor government activity by constructive criticism and ultimately by refusal to obey a government which transgresses the law (as is suggested in Q. 9.71; 3.104, 110; 22.41).[13]

According to this principle of the accountability of government to the people, a state seeking to be authentically Islamic would not be far removed from a democracy understood in modern terms. In other words, there is no justification either in the Qur'an, the *sunnah* or early Islamic history for a government and legal system imposed by a self-perpetuating, unelected, religio-political establishment.[14]

---

[12] H. Turabi, 'Principles of Governance, Freedom and Responsibility in Islam', *The American Journal of Islamic Social Sciences*, 4.1, 1987, 3.

[13] J. Andrew Kirk, *The Meaning of Freedom*, 172, based on the reasoning of M.H. Kamali, 'The Limits of Power in an Islamic State', *Islamic Studies*, 28.4, 1989, p 323-352.

[14] For further discussion on differing views of democracy among Muslims, see 'Muslims and Democracy' in Clinton Bennett, *Muslims and Modernity*, 40-62.

Fourthly, at least one quarter of all Muslims are living out their faith in non-Islamic nations. If it is true, as Tariq Ramadan and others argue persuasively, that Muslims can still be faithful to the essentials of their faith, even within a society that does not privilege any particular religious interpretation of the common good, then this point of view must be allowed to stand as a legitimate interpretation of the core beliefs of the faith. In recent times, some commentators have revived the notion of *Dar al-Suhl*, meaning the territory of treaty, where non-Islamic nations agree to protect Muslim communities, allowing them all the rights of full citizenship. This situation, where Muslims are free to practice their faith and witness without hindrance to their convictions, is interpreted as an authentic option in the modern world. No longer do Muslims have to view the concourse of nations divided between *Dar al-Islam* (the dwelling of Islam), the territory where Muslims are in control, and *Dar al-Harb* (the dwelling of combat), territories under the rule of non-believers. They are liberated from the Manichean dualism of regarding reality always in terms of a complete contrast between light and darkness.

If the type of governance established in Medina cannot any longer be considered a realistic (or even legitimate) pattern to follow, it follows that Muslims are free to reassess the importance of Muhammad's prophetic ministry in Mecca. It is certainly true that history cannot be rewritten, but it can be re-evaluated. Kenneth Cragg has pointed out that Muslims living in diaspora (outside of Muslim nations) are in a situation much more akin to that of Mecca than that of Medina. Emigration to Western nations may be likened to a *hijrah* in reverse, or perhaps to the first exodus from Mecca to Abyssinia. In the diaspora, 'These Muslims, as it were, are back in the original Mecca, without benefit of power and identified as 'Muslim' by their faith alone'. He goes on to raise a salient point: 'If their security is seen as precarious, the present factors lie in the suspicions engendered by the 'other' Islam we have reviewed (i.e. the Islam of Medina)'.[15]

The conclusion seems obvious, although emotively very tough to admit: Muslims, if they wish to be citizens of the world as it is, have to substitute the dream of re-establishing a form of state like that of Medina at the time of the 'rightly-guided caliphs' for a fresh ideal. The challenge they confront in the twenty-first century is to use the universally applicable precepts of their faith to help rebuild a world order in which just relations between and among peoples prevail and peaceful collaboration has a chance of succeeding.

---

[15] Cragg, *The Qur'an and the West*, 160.

'Manifest Success'[16]

The apparent reluctance of some Muslims to live peaceably alongside their non-Muslim neighbours may be traced to the belief that the Muslim community as a whole has been called to a special destiny by God.

> The idea of success in the world was central to Islamic ideology from the very beginning.... Islam would not have been revealed to the world, as God's last statement, if it were not divinely pre-ordained to succeed. God's word cannot be frustrated by human obstinacy.[17]

This belief in the ultimate triumph of Islam, as the only true interpretation of human existence, divinely appointed to shape the future of the nations, has its origin in the life of Muhammad and in the subsequent rapid spread of an Islamic empire:

> Muhammad never lost hope of success nor, indeed, the dire and stark realization that he was duty bound to succeed. It is part the Qur'an's doctrine that simply to deliver the message, to suffer frustration, and not to succeed, is immature spirituality.[18]

There exists, within mainstream Islam, a kind of inner logic that feeds upon itself: the very idea of God carries with it the notion that what God wills must ultimately prosper; so, when what God is reputed to have commanded, namely the subjection of forces mustered against the companions of his prophet, is achieved, the thesis of 'manifest success' is vindicated. As Cragg puts it, Muhammad's manifest victory over the Quraysh sealed a religious-political pattern as the very theme of Islam. Only Muslims must rule. The only authentic Islam is the one that saw the Quraysh both physically subdued and converted to the faith of the prophet.[19] The rapidity of the early military successes is certainly taken by some Muslim writers as evidence of Islam's divine origin.[20]

There are many problems with this view of history. In the first place, it is a highly selective reading of the events. Although Muhammad was ultimately able to defeat his Meccan enemies, his struggle against them was not without its set-backs: he won two major battles and lost one; even on the verge of an ultimate victory over the Quraysh, he was obliged to sign a treaty

---

[16] A fuller treatment of the next two sections is to be published in the journal *Transformation* in 2010, under the title, 'God is on our side: the anatomy of an ideology.'

[17] Rippin, *Muslims: Their Religious Beliefs and Practices*, 174.

[18] Fazlur Rahman, *Islam* (London: 1961), 15, quoted in Cragg, *Muhammad and the Christian*, 43.

[19] Cragg, *The Qur'an and the West*, 159.

[20] Ruthven, *Islam in the World*, 70.

(*Hudaibiyyah*) in which the significant words *rasul-Allah* (the messenger of God) to describe him had been eliminated, a clear sign that the people of Mecca still repudiated his claims;[21] after his death, the Muslim community was riven by conflict and intrigue, leading to the assassination of three of the first four 'rightly-guided Caliphs;' lastly, following on the logic of war and violence, and perhaps the greatest tragedy for Islam, was the split between two major versions of the faith – the Sunni and the Shia –, the result of disputes over the legitimate heirs of Muhammad, leading to the death of Muhammad's grandson, Husayn ibn Ali, at the battle of Karbala in 681.

In the second place, a deeply existential and religious question is asked of Islam, when it manifestly is not in the ascendency. At least since the modern expansion of Western powers, those parts of the world dominated by Islam have been in decline. This might lead to one of two possible conclusions: either, the notion of 'manifest success' has to be abandoned, or at least greatly modified, as it appears to have been disproved by historical events, or the community needs to rediscover its true self, as the decline can be interpreted as God's punishment of a people that has lost its centre by no longer following God's clear instructions. For reasons that will be explored further on, the first of these two options has not seemingly been explored in any serious and systematic way. The second possibility has motivated different radical elements in contemporary Islam to propagate theories of mass apostasy from the true faith.[22]

There may be other conclusions that could be drawn: for example, the call for a reinterpretation of a long tradition, a thoroughgoing renewal of its inner life and a re-assessment of its outward political manifestations. It might be argued that, although Islam is not at present in the ascendency, it is only a matter of time before a rudderless Western civilisation will implode under the force of its manifold contradictions and lack of moral substance.[23] When this happens, Islam will again show its inherent qualities in being able to guide nations into authentic expressions of human well-being. Thus, Islamic commentators see the West as now divorced from the source of its 'Being', floating aimlessly on a sea of rational, material and secular interests that ultimately will prove fatefully and fatally destructive.[24] This situation, so the argument goes, is unsustainable. Like a building that has not been repaired, the West is crumbling. Moreover, although it may realise that something is

---

[21] Cragg, *Muhammad in the Qur'an*, 93.

[22] See, Northcliffe, *Islam: Faith and Practice*, 205.

[23] This would represent a kind of Islamic version of the Marxist belief in the historically inevitable collapse of the Capitalist system.

[24] See, for example, Taji-Farouki and Nafi, *Islamic Thought in the Twentieth Century*, 281; Rees, *Dining with Terrorists*, 235.

seriously amiss, it does not know where to find the proper materials to effect the restoration.

'Manifest Destiny'

From the perspective of anyone deeply concerned about the possibility of an escalating conflict between two historical civilisations in a nuclear age, to speak in grandiose terms about the ultimate, universal triumph of one creed is perilous talk. Unfortunately, it is somewhat the mirror image of the belief in some quarters of the USA that this nation has been entrusted with a 'manifest destiny', to be 'a light to the nations'.[25] Thus, it is reported that President George Bush in April 2004 (one year on from the invasion of Iraq) uttered the following highly significant words:

> I have this...strong belief that freedom is not this country's gift to the world. Freedom is the Almighty's gift to every man and woman in this world. And, as the greatest power on the face of the earth, we have an obligation to help the spread of freedom.[26]

Without wishing to over-analyse the sentiment expressed by these words, it is fairly obvious at first sight that there is a basic contradiction being expressed here. On the one hand, there is the notion of freedom, which, although it is by no means a self-evident concept, for it is easily turned into a political slogan or ideological weapon, nevertheless is usually interpreted to mean the absence of coercion and constraint. On the other hand, there is the notion that power, presumably interpreted in terms of military might and economic clout, can achieve the spread of freedom, presumably by superior compulsion.

Michael Northcott in a significant study[27] unveils the theory behind the idea of 'manifest destiny'. The term was used for the first time in the 1840s to describe the sense of a divine purpose being worked out in American history. America was a brand new nation, conceived of as a sacred space in which people were being called to be ' a special people' in implementing a new order of liberty from every kind of coercion, whether by colonial forces from the outside or internally by an excessively interventionist State.[28] From that time on there has existed, deeply embedded in the American collective psyche, a belief that its form of democracy, its model of economic emancipation, its rule of law

---

[25] This was the commission that God originally gave to his 'servant' – the remnant of his people that remained faithful to his cause – 'to open the eyes that are blind, to bring out prisoners from the dungeon, from the prison those who sit in darkness' (Isa. 42.6-7), 'that my salvation may reach the end of the earth' (Isa. 49.6).

[26] Quoted in Rees, *Dining with Terrorists*, 368-9 (emphasis added).

[27] *An Angel Directs the Storm: Apocalyptic Religion and American Empire*.

[28] Northcott, *An Angel*, 22.

is exemplary, and therefore should be an ideal to which all nations, irrespective of their history and culture, should aspire.

Hidden behind the concept of 'manifest destiny' is the notion of a double blessing: America has been blessed by God, therefore it has an obligation to share this blessing with others.[29] It is a kind of collective message of corporate prosperity: emulate our way of life and you too will progress and flourish. America interprets itself as 'a city set on a hill', in some sense a nation consecrated by its religious heritage and historical origins to draw all others to itself (as indeed it has done literally), so that they too may share in the dream. The immortal words etched on a plaque within the Statue of Liberty at the entrance to New York harbour sum up the mood of an extravagant claim to a renewal of the whole earth, beginning in the 'New World:'

> 'Keep, ancient lands, your storied pomp!' cries she
> With silent lips. 'Give me your tired, your poor,
> Your huddled masses yearning to breathe free,
> The wretched refuse of your teeming shore.
> Send these, the homeless, tempest-tossed to me,
> I lift my lamp beside the golden door!'[30]

Here, then, in the contemporary world, we encounter two visions of the future, inspired by two different religions, which tragically have a long history of inter-religious and inter-cultural strife and competition. It is not surprising that a thesis like Huntington's clash of civilisations should appear plausible. However, although there may still be many in the Islamic world and in the USA who hold passionately to a notion of manifest success or destiny, it is on both sides a dangerous illusion. This is the burden of Amartya Sen's monograph, *Identity and Violence*, whose subtitle is significantly, *The Illusion of Destiny*. The major problem that he identifies with this interpretation of global politics is that it asserts the wrong kind of identity. It is one of the unforeseen and paradoxical consequences of proclaiming a so-called 'war on terror' that an increasingly bellicose attitude is fomented by the imposition of singular and belligerent identities on gullible people by the very artisans of terror.[31]

People are, then, made to discover newly detected identities as the objects of a crusading spirit that wills to impose its vision of the world on the other by all means (including terror and counter-terror) possible. All other possible

---

[29] Michael Northcott gives a detailed account of the kind of religious reasoning upon which the notion of 'manifest destiny' appears to be founded (see 15-18 and 52-72). There is not space here to reproduce the thinking.

[30] The words come from the sonnet 'The New Colossus' by Emma Lazarus. One is tempted to ponder the symbolic nature of the author's name – the one brought back from the dead (John 11).

[31] Sen, *Identity and Violence*, 2.

identities, such as language groups, political preferences, occupations, economic position, cultural history, artistic predilections and above all a common humanity, are submerged under this primal way of seeing differences.[32] This is to use religion, or indeed an aggressive anti-religious philosophy, in a thoroughly ideological way. In the last resort, the twin ideas of 'manifest success' and 'manifest destiny', are created and manipulated in the interests of certain classes of people. They are both false and dangerous and should be repudiated.

Alternatives to Medina

By far and away the greatest challenge which Muslims face in the complex conjunction of events in the contemporary world is how to read their past history, and in particular that of the first generation, in order to receive opportune guidance for living in the present. Although it would seem to be making an immense claim, the only real hope for Islam both to renew itself and to be a force for renewal in a world dominated by the decadent and perverted values of current Western societies is to return to a form of the prophetic faith that it was at the beginning.

Whatever the justification for the *hijrah*, and as we have seen it was not commanded by God, it has to be viewed as only one possible response to opposition and persecution. The experiment of an imposed theocracy on the diverse groups that inhabited Yathrib cannot be repeated, for reasons already discussed. Muslims surely would rediscover the revitalising nature of faith, if they were content to work from the bottom up, rather than from the top down. Theocracy can only work, in a world which has tasted something of the ideals of democracy, by imposition and coercion.

An Islamic state in the modern world would tend to be authoritarian. It would probably have to work in a way not unlike that of the Communist states of the twentieth century: governed by a self-appointed 'vanguard' of the (religious) elite, who alone have a true understanding of right 'doctrine'. Power, then, would be invested in a hereditary class of religious authorities (as is the case of the Ayatollahs in Iran), who could not be challenged. They would be not so much theocratic regimes as ideological states. Opposition parties could not be allowed to flourish. Dissent would have to be suppressed, for in a theocracy someone (or some group) has to have indisputable access to the will of God.

Ultimately, then, the notion of *shura* (widespread consultation) and *'ijma* (consent) would not be taken seriously. In any case, the idea of an Islamic state

---

[32] Sen, *Identity and Violence*, 11-12.

is an invention of the twentieth century.[33] There is no such concept present in the Qur'an. The theory has been deduced from the concept of 'divine sovereignty' or 'divine governance' (al-hakimiyya), which first became current in the 12th century. In the Qur'an, the idea of 'divine sovereignty' has little to do with political or legal sovereignty, but means that 'God has bestowed a certain constitution on both the universe and man'.[34] The primary sources of Islam offer broad guidelines for righteous behaviour in the public sphere. There is no specific type of public administration that was understood by the earliest Muslims to have been mandated by the foundational texts.[35]

Moreover, and here is the rub, theocracy in practice actually subverts the true meaning and exercise of faith. Here there is an ongoing internal Muslim debate about the relationship between personal faith and the laws of the state. Muslim radicals argue that religion is too important to abandon it into private hands as merely a matter of private choice. Sound religion requires public enforcement, for otherwise gradually (as in the secular West) the public square is governed by those who have turned their back on God's laws and do what is right in their own eyes.

On the other hand, the Muslim opponents of *shari'ah* insist that state sponsorship of religion threatens the moral foundations of religion. Intervention by the state confirms secular suspicions that religious belief is too weak to stand alone. In the last resort, conscience cannot be coerced. This is a lesson that political authorities seem reluctant to learn, whether guided by religious or secular principles. Beliefs that are shaped by the sanction of the law are inauthentic; obedience that is obtained by external pressure alone is a sham:

> If the state must procure the allegiance of believers, then religion cannot pretend that its truth claims have intrinsic persuasive merit, and so religion must disingenuously yield right of way to behavioural norms dispensed by the State.[36]

Governance by God and governance by the people

If it is true that the genuine nature of religion is likely to be compromised, when identified entirely with one particular form of government, then in the context of this discussion two consequences follow. First, the yearning for a return to a caliphate of some description is ruled out as unrealistic and actually

[33] See, Fazlur Rahman, *Islam and Modernity: Transformation of an Intellectual Tradition* (Chicago: University of Chicago Press, 1982).

[34] Fazlur Rahman, 'The Islamic Concept of the State', in John J. Donohue and John L. Esposito (eds), *Islam in Transition: Muslim Perspectives* (New York: OUP, 1982), 264.

[35] See the discussion in Asma Afsaruddin, ' The Islamic State', 163-5, and Asghar Ali Engineer, 'Islam and Secularism' in Abu-Rabi, *The Blackwell Companion to Contemporary Islamic Thought*, 339-340.

[36] Sanneh, 'Shari'ah Sanctions', 161.

a betrayal of the deeper meaning of Islamic faith. Secondly, Muslims have to be part of the search for a political order in which every person is able to participate and which does not prejudice their faith. This is a difficult task, given the limited choice often offered to the Muslim world, of supporting either a reactionary traditionalism or some form of modernism.

Islam would commend itself greatly in the modern world, if it were able to reinterpret its own essential nature as a prophetic religion by participating critically in the endeavour to create societies that reflected the moral precepts revealed in its foundation document. This can only be achieved with integrity if the means that are chosen to fulfil this task match the desired ends. In other words, Muslims need to forego the temptation to seize power for themselves and work, rather, for the transformation of societies through advocacy and persuasion. Societies have never been changed for the better by those idealists who believe that if the 'righteous' are in control then they will be able to establish the good. Real transformation has come about through the tireless and selfless effort of people of faith working from the grass-roots for the real flourishing of human communities according to the blueprint that God has revealed.

Muslims are right to sense that the Western world in general is facing a crisis of legitimation. Legislators are increasingly producing laws that reflect the confusion of a people that has lost its moral bearings. Above all this can be seen in the creeping disregard for the sanctity of life as in the cases of the disposal of unwanted foetuses and of people who believe that their lives are no longer supportable. Giving legal status to same-gender couples on a par with those participating in a conventional marriage displays an immense ignorance of what makes a human being truly human. In each case, legislation has given a semblance of normality to practises that are aberrant and ultimately sacrilegious. Muslims are wrong, however, if they believe that these situations can only be put right by gaining control of legislation themselves and implementing laws, some of which have all the hallmarks of a cynical disregard for the unqualified dignity of all human beings.

It seems likely that Muslims will be truly free to campaign, alongside others who believe in the moral givenness of the universe, when they have left behind any nostalgia for the return of an Islamic society ruled according to laws formulated twelve centuries ago. With all its many defects democracy, understood as the active participation of a populace in the governing of itself, is preferable to any other form of government that has been tried in the course of human history. Islamic societies are not notorious for either having protected the value of every individual human being or creating the conditions for societies of excellence. It is a tragedy that, instead of just criticising the democracies of the West (with justification), Muslim societies do not themselves show a better form of democracy. Some Muslim thinkers are indeed engaging creatively with the principles of democracy, drawing on the resources of their own traditions of egalitarianism, justice, consultation, consensus and public interest (*al-maslaha*). There can be no question but that the form of democracy practised in the West needs over-hauling. So, Muslims can, if they are willing, contribute imaginatively to such an enterprise?[37]

It has been said famously that 'man's capacity for justice makes democracy possible; but man's inclination to injustice makes democracy necessary'.[38] Many Muslims have still to be persuaded that governance by the people is not necessarily contrary to governance by God. Even the latter notion implies mediation by human beings. Someone or some group has to decide the concrete details of a society governed according to the law of God. This, then, also implies a type of governance by the people. To be true to itself, by people Islam means the '*ummah*, the whole community that confesses the faith disclosed through Muhammad, not a self-selected body that purports to speak on behalf of all.

So, the abiding challenge to Muslims today, as it is to Christians, is to reflect carefully on how they should live their faith in the real world of the third millenium. For clear and obvious historical reasons for some considerable time they have been on the defensive in the face of the aggressive self-promotion by the West of its values. Now is the time for Muslims to take the initiative, not in trying to deconstruct all that the West represents, but in seeking ways of saving the West from itself by cogently contending for those moral principles, compatible with the highest values endorsed by Western societies, that spring from its own best heritage.

[37] See, for example, Abdullahi Ahmed An-Naim, *Toward an Islamic reformation: Civil liberties, human rights and international law* (Cairo: American University of Cairo Press, 1992), 40-45.

[38] Reinhold Niebuhr, *Children of Light and Children of Darkness* (London: Nisbet, 1945), vi.

Chapter 10

Christianity and the West

From Prophetic Community to Political Faith

From Mecca to Medina

In our study of the origins of both Christianity and Islam, we have noticed that the two faith communities took a fundamentally different direction. The most fateful event in the history of Islam appears to have been the decision of Muhammad and his companions to leave Mecca for a new life in the northern city of Yathrib (Medina). Although not commanded directly by God, and therefore not a divinely appointed change of strategy, the move soon received divine sanction. In the new set of circumstances the tone of the revelations changed:

> This was the period in which the revelations began to contain legislation on all aspects of individual and communal life, as for the first time the Muslims had their own state.[1]

From now on the Muslim community would be remodelled: leaving behind its experience of suffering as a defenceless minority community, on account of the message it proclaimed, it took up the reigns of power and sought to govern a city-state in the name of Allah, 'the Lord of Mercy, the Giver of Mercy…Master of the Day of Judgement' (Q.1.1-3). For good or ill, the new faith became inextricably linked to the messy business of exercising political power; just how messy can be seen in the events that unfolded in the years immediately after Muhammad's death. From then on, this turn of direction was interpreted as an essential aspect of submission to the will of Allah, not as a fortuitous happening that might have turned out quite differently. The message now changed, to spell out how the faith was to be implemented as a unitary whole that incorporated both personal devotion and corporate life in all its dimensions and on every level.

Today, looking back, the Medina *surahs* appear to have played the role of adjusting a whole set of beliefs to new circumstances. I argued in the last

[1] Haleem, *The Qur'an: A new translation*, xii (emphasis added).

chapter that Islam's position in the contemporary world as an authentically prophetic faith depends on being able to interpret its identity in a way that does not depend on the dream of repeating in modern circumstances the Medinan model of 'divinely-guided' rule. In other words, if potential or real conflicts between Islamic longings for restoration and the hope of peaceful co-operation between the nations are to be avoided, this tension in the tale of two cities has to be resolved.

From Jerusalem to Rome

The Christian faith took an entirely different route. For about the first three hundred years of its existence it remained more or less true to its initial prophetic vision. In a way, like Islam, it saw itself as the culmination of the prophetic message given to the people of Israel by Yahweh and recorded in the books of the law, the prophets and the writings (wisdom literature). When it too suffered on account of the message that it proclaimed, it was not tempted to resolve its adverse circumstances by becoming an independent polis in some corner of the Roman Empire. As we shall see, it understood its calling in quite different terms.

Nevertheless, its own relative success in terms of growth and influence, combined with a particular set of circumstances that transpired in the Roman Empire, brought about a radical change in its situation, status and self-perception. This was the Constantinian watershed. For reasons closely linked to the Emperor's bid for control of the Empire and the subsequent consolidation of his power, he decided firstly to concede to the Christian community proper legal status and then, subsequently, to make it into a favoured religion. Christendom was born. Ultimately it acted to guarantee and defend the legitimacy of state power.[2]

The situation was not equivalent to the city of Medina 300 years later. Representatives of the Christian church did not exercise power directly. Nevertheless, those that did govern claimed to do so in the name of the Christian God. There can be no doubt that a massive shift occurred in the way the Christian community carried on its life and work. Official persecution by the state, except for a brief period under the Emperor Julian (361-363), who attempted to restore paganism as the imperial religion,[3] came to a halt. As martyrdom in the cause of witnessing to Jesus Christ ended, so the practice of venerating the relics of the martyrs took its place.[4] So, the triumphant faith that

---

[2] See, Stuart Murray, 'The Coming of Christendom' (Chapter 2) in Murray, *Post-Christendom.*

[3] See Murray, *Post-Christendom*, 39.

[4] Stuart G. Hall, 'Ministry, Worship and Christian Life' in Hazlett, *Early* Christianity, 110.

persevered in the face of extreme provocation was transformed for many into mere superstition.

The state's demand for a unified Christianity, to underpin the unification of the Empire, led to the imposition of 'right belief' on the Empire's subjects. Potential schismatics, like the Donatists in North Africa, were suppressed. Interestingly, in the context of our discussion, the thinking of the Donatists was based on the ideal of a pure church, i.e. one that avoided having to compromise with a still semi-pagan authority.[5] (Perhaps this means that all Christian communities that see their vocation to be non-conformist and counter-cultural are heirs of the Donatists).

Alan Kreider portrays the transposition that occurred in the years following Constantine's change of perspective as a shift in the social significance of conversion from voluntarily becoming counter-cultural to compulsorily becoming like everybody else. This innovation implied a movement away from the social change required when new believers became members of a community of 'deviants'. From now on, new believers were assimilated into society's norms; baptism into the faith of Jesus Christ only required making superficial lifestyle changes.[6]

By the end of the 3rd century there were about 6 million converts to the Christian faith. Over the next 75 years a further 25 million were either baptised into the church or became catechumens. In 341 an imperial edict stigmatised pagan worship as a superstitio. In 392 Christianity had become the sole legal cult in the Empire, and in 529, at the time of the Emperor Justinian, conversion became compulsory. How should one interpret this massive transformation in the fortunes of the Christian faith from a persecuted minority sect to the status of a favoured and then the official religion of the state? What were the implications of this new relationship to political power?

As the 4th century progressed, one can imagine two diametrically opposed interpretations of the new situation that Christians found themselves in. On the one hand, it would be perfectly reasonable to understand Constantine's 'conversion' as a providential act of God. Perhaps, with reference to the history of Israel, Christians could have seen themselves as leaving a long period of exile, in which they had to cope as best they could in hostile surroundings. Now, their yearning for a situation where they could settle down in a comfortable environment, delivered from their enemies, was fulfilled. Constantine, then, might have been seen as a kind of Cyrus redivivus – 'He is my shepherd, and he shall carry out all my purpose'; 'His anointed, Cyrus, whose right hand I have grasped to subdue nations before him…to open doors

---

[5] See, Gerald Bonner, 'Schism and Church Unity', in Hazlett (ed), *Early Christianity*, 225.

[6] Alan Kreider, 'Introduction' in Kreider, *The Origins of Christendom in the West*, xi.

before him…'; 'I have aroused Cyrus in righteousness, and I will make all his paths straight; he shall build my city and set my exiles free…'[7]

Eusebius, the renowned historian of the early Church, though he may not have made this equation, certainly viewed Constantine in the most favourable light. He became his theological adviser, helping him to navigate through the Christological and Trinitarian controversies that erupted during his reign. The Church no longer had to struggle against the animosity showed it by officials. Its work of bringing the Gospel of Jesus Christ to the vast majority of the populace who were immersed in pagan thought and practice could now be supported. As Christianity became known as the Emperor's religion, so it became easier for many to adopt the same faith.[8] Constantine became a benefactor, restoring church property, making large gifts to the Church (including the Lateran Palace in Rome), subsidised its costs, built new churches, outlawed gladiator shows and made Sunday a public holiday.[9]

On the other hand, the tacit accommodation reached between the Church and the state, beginning with Constantine,[10] might have been deplored. One writer has described Constantine's career as 'the erratic boulder that diverted the stream of Christian history'.[11] A new pattern of life and mission had been set for the Christian faith. It had been an alternative community, attractive to those outside only because of its message of hope in a pagan order, driven by fate and ending in despair, and its unremitting practical concern for the poor and vulnerable. It became a religious pillar of the political establishment.

From now on adherence to orthodoxy became a matter of sanctions administered by the state.[12] The state offered powerful incentives for conversion to Christianity. Above all, it became much easier to become a Christian. The rite of baptism, for example, instead of being the outward expression of an inner conversion that had already taken place, became an emotional and psychological tool to bring about conversion. The rigorous requirements of an ethical life in conformity to the demands of the Gospel were lessened. Many gave up receiving communion rather than having to amend

[7] Isa. 44.28; 45.1; 45.13

[8] Alan Kreider, 'Changing Patterns of Conversion in the West' in Kreider, *The Origins of Christendom*, 23.

[9] See, McKechnie, *The First Christian Centuries*, 235-237; Ivor J. Davidson, *The Birth of the Church: From Jesus to Constantine (AD 30-312)*, 344.

[10] The Emperor's personal relationship to Christian faith remained ambiguous. At one and the same time he retained the pagan title of *Pontifex Maximus*, continued the imperial cult and at the very end of his life became a catechumen, was admitted to prayers and was eventually baptised.

[11] Noel King, 'Church-State Relations' in Hazlett, *Early Christianity*, 250.

[12] In 380, the Emperor Theodosius I promulgated an edict that penalised Christian groups that refused to accept the authority of the Bishops of Rome and Alexandria.

their lives.[13] This was the way that the Church coped with the enormous influx of new members from a pagan background, who wished to become Christian, but not too Christian! By the beginning of the 6th century it became compulsory to convert to Christianity.[14] From then on the Christian religion maintained a symbiotic relationship with the state for centuries to come.

Although the history differed in many ways from that current at the time of Muhammad, at least one substantial parallel may be drawn. In both cases the religious communities, which began by advocating an alternative way of living in the world to that predominant in the surrounding culture, were transformed into groups that upheld the prevailing social precepts of the dominant rulers of the time. They lost their prophetic cutting-edge. They no longer represented an original, distinctive option for life in community. Conformity and compliance, rather than contradiction, was a major factor in the development of both religions. It can be said that both, in different ways and for distinct reasons, had laid to one side the distinguishing message and practices that brought them into being.

'Manifest Failure'?

However, as we have reiterated a number of times, the parallels are not so exact. Most Christians today, especially those living in the West, who have inherited the consequences of the coming of Christendom, regard the Constantinian watershed as a failure.[15] It is a failure to recognise just how much Christian faith, when judged by the normal standards of an urbane and profane society, is a failure. For Muslims, on the other hand, the close alliance with political power is a natural and authorised development of the inner meaning of their core beliefs. There appears to be little appetite, except among a few atypical mavericks,[16] to question fundamentally the progression from Mecca to Medina. In the contemporary world, it behoves Christians, therefore, to explain,

---

[13] See, Paul Bradshaw, 'The Effects of the Coming of Christendom on Early Christian Worship' in Kreider, *The Origins of Christendom*, 276-278.

[14] This was a social reality a long way from the modern idea that faith is a purely personal and private matter.

[15] However, there are exceptions. Robert Forrest, for example, defends the Constantinian shift. His most powerful argument seems to be that it would have been inconceivable for the Roman state to have suddenly become secular. It either sought divine approval and protection through the pantheon of pagan gods or it became monotheist, acknowledging the God of the Christians as the true ruler of the universe. The fact that it did the latter brought considerable benefits, not only to Christians but to all inhabitants of the empire; above all in a more humane treatment of slaves and enemies. See, 'Love of Enemies in the Age of Constantine' in Craig A. Smith, *The Cross at the Crossroads: Loving our Enemies in the Twenty-first Century* (Manila: OMF, 2008), 96-133.

[16] Like Taha, see *Muslims and Modernity*, 56-57.

as carefully as they can, why Christianity, seen from the perspective of an interpretation of power as the ability to impose policies, laws and decisions from a position of authority and control, seems to be a flawed and inadequate faith.

At the very heart of the Christian faith is the claim that suffering is the means by which God brings about transformed lives and situations; not any kind of suffering, but that in which he himself was fully involved in the death of Jesus, the Christ. This is the point at which there is a major quarrel between Christians and Muslims. The latter have construed the ministry of the prophet in terms of the ultimate triumph of his mission judged by its political success. Perhaps, this is the reason why the prophets mentioned by name in the Qur'an (e.g., Q. 2.136; 3.84-85; 6.83-90; 42.13), although they may have suffered opposition, ultimately conquered adverse circumstances and prospered. In the case of the Jesus portrayed in the Bible, however, this is not the case. As we have seen, Jesus deliberately and resolutely resisted, on a number of occasions, the temptation to become the kind of political leader that needed to maintain his power through the use of coercive force.

It cannot be a coincidence, surely, that the Qur'an nowhere mentions the prophets of the 8th century BC onwards, many of whom did not achieve success in terms of changing the political landscape in the direction required by God: e.g. Isaiah, Jeremiah, Amos and Micah. The one exception is the prophet Jonah, who did persuade the people of Nineveh, including the rulers, to turn to God and amend their ways. As far as the New Testament is concerned, the supreme example of the faithful prophet is the 'suffering servant', portrayed in the servant songs of Isaiah (Isa. 42.1-4; 49.1-7; 50.4-9; 52. 13-53.12). He suffered relentlessly at the hands of hostile forces, without retaliating:

> 'To one deeply despised, abhorred by the nations, the slave of rulers;'[17]
>
> 'I gave my back to those who struck me, and my cheeks to those who pulled out the beard; I did not hide my face from insult and spitting;'[18]
>
> 'He was despised and rejected by others; a man of suffering and acquainted with infirmity; and as one from whom others hide their faces he was despised, and we held him of no account'.[19]

Now, the first disciples of Jesus saw in his ministry the fulfilment of the servant's vocation: 'Philip...starting with this Scripture (Isa. 53.7-8),

---

[17] Isa. 49.7
[18] Isa. 50.6
[19] Isa. 53.3

proclaimed to him (the Ethiopian 'Finance Minister') the good news about Jesus;'[20]

> To this you have been called, because Christ also suffered for you...'He committed no sin, and no deceit was found in his mouth' (Isa. 53.9)...by his wounds you have been healed' (Isa. 53.5).[21]

So, not only did God not rescue his servant-prophet from persecution and execution, he was the one who brought it about:

> We accounted him stricken, struck down by God, and afflicted...The Lord has laid on him the iniquity of us all...It was the will of the Lord to crush him with pain.[22]

> The redemption that is in Christ Jesus, whom God put forward as a sacrifice of atonement....[23]

Given their own understanding of the prophetic mission of Muhammad and all previous prophets, the public, humiliating death by crucifixion of Jesus seems to be incomprehensible to Muslims. It is no wonder that they are forced, by the logic of their own beliefs, to deny that Jesus ever died in this fashion, indeed that he died at all. Here, perhaps, more than in the controversies between Christians and Muslims about Jesus as the Son of God or about the Trinitarian nature of the one God, lies the most severe dispute between the two faiths. And yet, for Christians, the true character of God is most fully disclosed in the event of Golgotha.[24] Thus, Christians and Muslims disagree most profoundly, not so much about the metaphysical being of God, as about his moral character: how is it possible for God to be involved personally in an event in which, apparently, the enemies of God prevailed? And yet, it is precisely the reasons for this disagreement that bring profound consequences for the way in which the followers of the two faiths view the exercise of power and the legitimacy of violence.

In recent years, Kenneth Cragg has explored in depth the nature and consequences of the rupture at this point. One may begin, perhaps, with the contrast between Muhammad's triumphal entry into Mecca near the end of his life and Jesus 'triumphal' entry into Jerusalem at the beginning of Passover week.[25] In the first case, Muhammad came to receive the final submission of

---

[20] Acts 8.35

[21] 1 Pet. 2.21-22, 25

[22] Isa. 53.4, 6, 10

[23] Rom. 3.24-25

[24] The place outside Jerusalem, where Jesus was crucified (Mk. 15.22; Jn. 19.17).

[25] See, *Muhammad and the Christian*, 45.

his erstwhile enemies, over whom he had triumphed by virtue of having a superior military force. In the second case, Jesus allowed himself to be 'conquered' by his enemies. As he hung on the cross, the helpless victim of a gross miscarriage of justice, in the eyes of the world his whole ministry had ended in abject defeat and disaster. At that moment it would have been impossible for anyone to have believed that Jesus was fulfilling the healing and reconciling purposes of God for the whole of humankind. The mood of the two disciples on the road to Emmaus sums up the sense of defeat and despair: 'We had hoped that he was the one to set Israel free'.[26]

How could a man, crucified, dead and buried be God's Messiah? Everything pointed to a tragedy of grand proportions.

Well, he did not set Israel free in the way that was anticipated. The Romans remained in control of the land as an occupying power. The religious leaders maintained their tight grip on the privileges of their office. Active and passive resistance to the foreign presence smouldered for many more years, until it sparked into a major conflagration some thirty years later. Nothing seemed to have changed. And yet, in the conversation on the road to Emmaus, the two disciples reported another event (though met with a good deal of incredulity and scepticism):

> Some women of our group astounded us. They were at the tomb early this morning, and when they did not find his body there, they came back and told us that they had indeed seen a vision of angels who said that he was alive.[27]

The message that the women brought back was that the cruel suffering and agonising death by crucifixion was not the end of Jesus of Nazareth, a point confirmed to the two disciples by the companion who walked with them. Unmistakeably, this was Jesus, who had been dead, but was now alive. The regenerating power of God demonstrated that the very worst that evil people could inflict on an absolutely good man had been suffered and overcome.

The story that the followers of Jesus wish to tell the world is that hope for the future depends ultimately on the great events of the first Easter weekend having happened as recorded. First and foremost, suffering is not a failure, but a necessity if evil is to be defeated.[28] Though it may seem a curious paradox,

---

[26] Lk. 24.21 (NRSV margin)

[27] Lk. 24.22-23

[28] It is often pointed out that suffering takes on a different role in the Shi'a expression of Islam. Because of the early history of Islam, particularly the death of Hussayn, Muhammad's sole surviving grandson, Shi'a Muslims, who championed the leadership of the Islamic community through Muhammad's natural descendents, have developed a doctrine of suffering and martyrdom: 'The Shi'a embraced failure as their proof of being Allah's suffering remnant doomed to maintain the truth against overwhelming injustice until vindicated at the final days,' see Geaves, *Aspects of Islam*, 111, and the whole

deep, long-lasting change can only happen in the real world when people are willing to suffer for the sake of compassion, justice and genuinely new beginnings. Change that is brought about by inflicting suffering on others is superficial for it perpetuates the iron chain of reciprocal violence.

Islam and Christianity can both point to an Exodus story. For Islam it is the emigration from Mecca and the new beginning in Medina, where, as in the case of the inhabitants of the Promised Land, the enemies of God's people are subdued by force, so that a new community ruled by God's law can come into being. For Christianity it is the journey that is made from the power of evil through death to new life.[29] There is all the difference in the world between the two concepts. The exodus from Mecca and the entry into a new land tragically did not bring about any essential change. Life in the new city continued to be marked by violence, not the violence experienced by Muhammad and his companions in the 'Egypt' that they had left behind, but the violence they perpetrated on other groups in order to establish their rule in the new place. Since those days, Islam has acted and reacted as any state (and later empire) must, defending its institutions by force and taking pre-emptive action, when it sees itself threatened from outside.

So, what has changed? Can an impartial interpretation of history honestly claim that Islam, when in power, has produced some kind of model society? It has simply reproduced political situations where the basic consequences of human evil remain the same and have not been effectively dealt with. Like any other regime, it relies on instruction, law and some severe exemplary punishments to restrain its worst effects and, perhaps, alter people's worst habits. What, then, has Islam, when interpreted as an ideal alliance between divine revelation and political practice, brought to the world that is not already contained in the Torah of the Hebrew Scriptures and in the most enlightened of the regimes of the people of Israel (for example, under Josiah, Ezra and Nehemiah)? To triumph militarily, whatever the ideology, is, on its own, a

---

section, 97-115, and Cragg, *Muhammad and the Christian*, 143-145. However, the Shi'a, when in power, as in present-day Iran, do not appear to behave any differently from their Sunni cousins. Despite the rhetoric, an Islamic government in Iran has shown itself to be as ruthless in hanging on to power by all means, by engineering fraudulent elections, suppressing dissent and abusing human rights, as any non-Muslim autocracy. Nothing, tragically, has changed.

[29] See, Lk 9.31: 'They (Moses and Elijah) appeared in glory and were speaking of his departure (the original word is *exodos*), which he was about to accomplish at Jerusalem.' The two prophets who spoke with Jesus on the Mount of Transfiguration represented the sacrifice of death (the Exodus accompanied by the slaughter of the Passover lamb) and translation to new life (2 Kings 2.11). The first Exodus (from Egypt) itself symbolises death (in the Red Sea) and new life (a safe crossing).

hollow victory. It is particularly poignant, when the religion that supports the use of force also produces a society that looks remarkably like the norm.[30]

One of the main issues that arises in this discussion, and is at the heart of the burden that Christians have for Muslims, is the meaning of success and failure. If success is to be measured in terms of the expansion of the faith, by peaceful means where possible, but by coercion where necessary,[31] then the result may be failure, in that people may have converted to the religion of Islam, but without being converted to God! The profound difference in what constitutes success and failure between the two faiths is summed up by Cragg:

> Islam and Muslims instinctively recoil from the theme of the prophet's humiliation.... It implies some divine failure in due rescue, succour and deliverance.... They are in tune with much modern – and Jewish – disdain for a faith clustering round as dark and grim an image as a cross and thinking it might somehow belong to God;
>
> It is in line with its faith in divine 'self-giving'...that the New Testament has to be taken on its own terms, as quite contrasted with the Scripture of Islam;
>
> Is the world sufficiently comprehended as a 'school', or – more – a 'surgery', a haunt of ignorance only or a place of wounds?.... Is it seemly, one may ask, that two theisms should be at odds over whether humanity is more in need of a divine intervention that brought redemption and healing, rather than one which brought command, prohibition and inclusive education?[32]

If anything has been found to fail profoundly in the whole history of human endeavour, it is education, law and punishment as a means of bringing about a change of direction in the heart of humans. Perhaps, therefore, it is worthwhile to look again at what constitutes success and failure.

Different Ways of Being Political

In sharp contrast to the way Muslims often seem to portray the significance of the Biblical Jesus, his life, death and resurrection do have profound political implications. These may be less obvious and more subtle than the conventional

---

[30] The supreme example of the time, known to Muhammad, would have been Byzantium. We have already given reasons why this experiment in a religiously guided and sanctioned state does not commend the Christian faith.

[31] See the saying of the famous Muslim philosopher, Ibn Kaldun, 'In the Muslim community the holy war is a religious duty, because of the universalism of the Muslim mission and the obligation to convert everybody to Islam either by persuasion or by force,' *The Muqaddimah: An Introduction to History* (Princeton: Princeton University Press, 1967), I, 473, quoted in Zeitlin, *The Historical Muhammad*, 158.

[32] Cragg, *The Qur'an and the West*, 147, 148, 151.

way of looking at political life. On the other hand, they may also penetrate much deeper to the heart of the matter.

Seyyed Hossein Nasr is perhaps typical of those Muslims who misinterpret the mission of Jesus:

> To comprehend the significance of the prophet in Islam, it is necessary to remember that the great founders of religions are of two types. The first constitutes the category of those figures who preach detachment from the world and a spiritual life that does not become entangled with ordinary worldly matters with all their ambiguities and complexities. Supreme examples of this type are found in Christ...who founded what were originally small spiritual communities divorced from and not integrated into the political, social, and economic conditions of the larger society. Christ who said that his kingdom was not of this world did not marry and was not the leader and ruler of a whole human society.[33]

It is hard to know from where Nasr gained this portrait of Jesus. It seems to repeat a view that has been discarded by most commentators for a long time past. In the last fifty years, there have been innumerable well-researched, historical studies that show conclusively that Jesus of Nazareth was seen, even if indirectly, as a threat to the existing political order.[34] Why else would he have been crucified on orders of the Roman governor? But, then, perhaps Nasr does not accept the overwhelming historical evidence that Jesus was indeed crucified. He repeats the mistaken interpretation (already dealt with [35]) of the saying about the kingdom not being of this world, making it refer to an inner, personal reality separated from all 'ordinary worldly matters'. He wrongly imagines that verses like ' they (the disciples) do not belong to the world' (John 17.16) means that Jesus was teaching them to be detached from the world; whilst, in reality, he is clear that 'they are in the world' (John 17. 11), and he prays to God not 'to take them out of the world' (John 17.15).

We have also reviewed the evidence [36] for establishing that Paul and the other apostles understood the new Christian groups, not as private, voluntary, spiritual associations but as social communities that acted as alternatives to the dominant kind of society prevalent in the Greco-Roman world. To have

---

[33] Nasr, *The Heart of Islam*, 33.

[34] To mention but a few: Jurgen Moltmann, *The Way of Jesus Christ: Christology in Messianic Dimensions* (London: SCM Press, 1990); Jon Sobrino, *Christology at the Crossroads: A Latin American Approach* (London: SCM Press, 1978); Rowland, *Christian Origins*; Alan Storkey, *Jesus and Politic*; Oliver O'Donovan, *The Desire of the Nations: Rediscovering the Roots of Political Theology* (Cambridge: CUP, 1996); N.T. Wright, *Jesus and the Victory of God* (London: SPCK, 1996); John Howard Yoder, *The Politics of Jesus: Vicit Agnus Noster* (Grand Rapids: Eerdmans, 1972).

[35] See, 92-93.

[36] In chapter 6

interpreted their role in the terms put forward by Nasr would have implied a radical discontinuity with God's people of former times. It would have been inconceivable for a Jew of the intensity of Paul (see Rom. 3.1-2; 9. 1-5; 11.1; 2 Cor. 11.22) to have interpreted the message of Jesus as if he had taught his disciples to disengage wholly from life in the public realm. The Messiah always was, and remained, a political figure. His teaching and his actions impinge on the world of politics in all sorts of ways.[37]

Nasr, and those who write in a similar vein, commit the cardinal error of positing a false either-or. Either Jesus was fully immersed in the 'ambiguities and complexities' of the life of this world as it is, in which case he would have needed to have been 'a leader and ruler of a whole human society', or he was a heavenly-minded teacher of spiritual truths that would enable his followers to keep themselves 'unstained by the world'.[38] That this is a false dichotomy, an unacceptable dualism (or Manichaeism) is especially evident in James' letter to the churches in the diaspora. True religion is measured by how the vulnerable members of society (widows and orphans) are cared for, how the poor are treated, how conflicts and disputes are dealt with, and above all whether economic justice is administered.

The Muslim supposition seems to be that a religion can only be politically active, if it is able to shape society from the top down, as in the case of Muhammad. Islam traditionally authenticates the story of Medina and perpetuates its logic by holding that this expression of political power, religiously justified and directed, is the preeminent ideal for any society. It is the duty of the believer to submit to the ruler who acts in the name of and is guided by the prophet of Allah.[39] Christianity, on the other hand, when true to itself, believes that faith communities have a responsibility to engage with the world of politics from the grass-roots. It recalls Jesus' teaching about the 'seed growing secretly' and the 'yeast leavening the whole lump of dough'. [40]

If the ideal of Islam is to create a state governed in accordance with divine laws, the ideal of Christianity is to create a community of individually committed believers in accordance with the law of Christ. These contrasting ideals constitute one of the fundamental differences between the two visions of what it means to follow God's will. Christians accept that there always will be an essential distinction between the community of those who follow the way of Jesus Christ and the wider community of those indifferent or hostile to the meaning of his life. That this distinction was compromised by a policy of indiscriminate, universal baptism for a long period of the church's history does not invalidate the principle. The distinction does not, however, imply a

---

[37] As shown in chapters 6 and 7; see also, Storkey, *Jesus and Politics*, chapters 7 and 8.

[38] Jam. 1.27

[39] See, Cragg, *Muhammad in the Qur'an*, 100-101.

[40] Mt. 13.31-33

separation: the Christian community is still part of the wider community; Christians are also citizens, with attending rights and responsibilities.

It appears that for Islam the notion of a people belonging to God is coextensive with the people belonging to a particular jurisdiction: belonging to an Islamic state and belonging to God is one and the same thing. That is why the law on apostasy is so rigorous: falling away from the God of Muhammad is interpreted as treason against the state set up by God. Therefore, Islamic codes, based on sayings from the *hadith*, agree that adults who voluntarily renounce Islam, being in full possession of their faculties, deserve the death penalty. It is as if they no longer existed, and therefore, because there is no life outside of the '*ummah*, death is a fitting response to their denial of peoplehood.

From a Christian perspective, the problem for Islam is that it does not maintain the tension between distinction and separation. It has no concept of a church living with a distinct identity in the midst of a non-church community, like the people of Israel in exile in Babylon, commanded to pray for the peace of the city (Jer. 29. 7 and 1 Tim. 2.1-4). It lacks the tension between a realised and future eschatology.

The Christian concept of the kingdom of God allows this tension. A time will come, when God will create a new heaven and a new earth, in which his right to rule will be recognised by all and his purposes will be joyfully fulfilled. Then, and only then, will evil in the form of injustice, violence, oppression of all kinds, hate, exploitation, selfishness, greed, strife and much more, be eliminated. Meanwhile, Christians are called to work tirelessly for a society in which evil is lessened and goodness is promoted. They do this, not in order to force God's righteous rule on unwilling subjects, but in anticipation of God's final, decisive action to make all things new.

This perspective allows the state to be free from the duress of an authoritarian religion, and it allows the church to be free from the coercion of the state. There is a proper differentiation between sacred and secular activities. The church, then, is free from secular manipulation to fulfil its prophetic task of bearing witness to the justice and grace of God in Jesus Christ, and the state does not need to hold delusions of a god-like status. Though hard to accomplish in practice, the Christian community may fulfil its political calling by being a critical friend to the state, its institutions and its government. As it is not allied to the state, it does not expect any privileges (but does expect the guaranteed freedom to proclaim its message), and it has no wars to fight. [41] The good news of peace and reconciliation in Jesus Christ, the prince of peace, cannot be

[41] Whether or not Christians should support war in any circumstances has been a matter of controversy for centuries. For some of the main issues involved, see J. Andrew Kirk, 'Overcoming violence with violence: is it ever justified?' in Kirk, *Mission under Scrutiny*.

promoted by any coercive means whatsoever, for then ends and means would be in total contradiction.

It is not yet obvious that Islam as a whole has come to terms with the positive elements in the distinction between the sacred and the secular, or even that it fully understands the arguments. In commenting on the use of violence in a religious context, Zidane Meriboute comments on the dangers of 'sacralisation':

> More specific to the use of violence by Muslims...is the phenomenon that might be called sacralisation. Sacralisation, if it comes into play, leads to the intensification of conflicts when they take place in a religious context. The phenomenon of vengeance or reprisal for violence suffered intensifies when such a conflict has been sacralised by a spiritual leader or through an appeal to God.[42]

It is precisely this appeal to God which makes the sacred/secular divide of crucial importance, for it is the ability to distinguish that allows the body politic to enjoy a sphere of freedom from the dictates of self-appointed mouthpieces of the Almighty. It is one thing to proclaim the message of God to a people that may have wandered far from his best intentions, and to call them to a change of direction. It is quite another, to back up the message with an army or group of revolutionaries, ready to impose this message on a recalcitrant nation.

From a Christian perspective, the failure to acknowledge the legitimacy of a social realm where people are free from religious dictates to debate, agree or disagree about the common good is a failure ultimately to trust God. People of faith are right to be passionate about moral goodness and righteousness and to oppose the destructive forces that demean human dignity – like excessive alcohol, experimentation with character-changing drugs, casual sex, serial relationships, pornography, abuse of children and the elderly, the exploitation of workers, gambling, and others besides - ;[43] there are few things more unbecoming to a robust faith than an insipid liberalism that capitulates to the current culture of 'life-style choices'. At the same time, trying to make people righteous by imposing stringent rules, backed by heavy penalties, is to deny God's gift of freedom that allows people to make wrong, harmful choices. In the moral world created by God such damaging choices will inevitably end up in sorrow, grief and trouble. They bring their own, self-inflicted punishment. The correct attitude for people of faith to these tragic situations is, I believe, to help bind up the wounds, point out the principle that whatever is sown will be reaped (good as well as evil) and make known the good news that God's desire is to restore people to their full humanity in Christ.

---

[42] *Islam's Fateful Path*, 109 (emphasis added).

[43] These moral failures are not, of course, confined to secular Western nations.

The Christian Quarrel with the West

This whole discussion would not be complete, if the impression was given that the present alleged conflict of civilisations was only, or chiefly, between Islam and the West. Although the Christian faith spread, most significantly for future history, mainly into Europe, where it greatly influenced its whole cultural life and institutions for a millennium and a half, today it is truly a universal faith; its centre of gravity has shifted decisively to the non-Western nations. In gauging Christian reactions to the present-day standing of the West in global politics, it is necessary therefore to listen to the voices of Christians from outside the Western World.

In an intriguingly titled book,[44] Lamin Sanneh speaks about the resurgence of Christianity in the non-Western world and the increasing resistance to all things Christian in the West. He points out what to him is the peculiar blindness of many Western academics, analysts and politicians in believing that the West has achieved a level of civilisation that has surpassed that of all others, and in assuming that to be enlightened is to emulate and reproduce its achievements.

Such a tacit valuation of the direction of world history enormously irritates people living outside the West, because it ignores, or seeks to explain as an unnatural aberration, the many undesirable elements in the West's recent history (not least the hypocritical foreign policy of some Western nations). For example, the West proclaims the virtues and benefits of liberal democracies and then supports the overthrow of democratically elected regimes, because they do not support the West's policies and strategies.[45] It sends armed forces to help in peace-keeping operations in various parts of the globe, but also sells arms to odious, despotic regimes such as those of Saddam Hussein in Iraq, the Mujahidin in Afghanistan (in the 1980s) and the generals in Algeria.

> The latter's confidence in military solutions to complex problems, its reliance on foreign capital to fund its enterprises, and its insensitivity to the consequences of its action have made the United States a target of anger and resentment.[46]

In addition, non-Western Christians are exasperated by the paternalism shown to them by certain segments of the Western Church, when they seek to defend ordinary, orthodox Christian teaching against the not so subtle accommodation of its central beliefs to current cultural thinking:

> It is an accepted rule in the West that religion may be allowed within the bounds of reason alone, and so revelation, miracle stories, and notions of the supernatural

---

[44] Sanneh, *Whose Religion is Christianity? The Gospel Beyond the West* (Grand Rapids: Eerdmans, 2003).

[45] Most notably in Latin America in the 1960s and 1970s.

[46] Robert Schreiter, 'The Wrath of the Nations and the Gospel of Reconciliation'.

> must be sifted to mesh with the refined rules of reason...Accordingly they read the Bible with a specially designed minimalist tool to remove the naïve sediment of pious myth. Only the skill in dismantling the Bible as mythology makes it worth our attention at all.[47]

Behind this kind of attitude, implicitly critical of Christians in the global south lurks, unmentioned because 'political correctness' does not allow its articulation, notions of the primitive, the immature and the child. This approach to the faith of the majority of Christians is symptomatic of the West's implicit belief in the superiority of its education and moral values.

In an even more sinister move, doctrinally orthodox Christians in the West are finding their freedom of belief is being gradually curtailed. Laws are coming into existence, which prohibit people of faith criticising the beliefs and lifestyles of others. In particular, Christians are being dismissed from their jobs or having public funds withdrawn from their enterprises or charitable organisations, because they disagree with the state's formal recognition of same sex relationships. In the name of tolerance and anti-discrimination practices, Christian views are being suppressed and conscientious objections overruled. In the name of human rights, those of Christians to freedom of religion are being dismissed.

This trend could be interpreted as another step in the direction of the state arrogating to itself a kind of divine status, setting itself up as the final arbiter of what can and cannot be believed or openly expressed. Where there is a palpable moral vacuum at the heart of Western societies, the state steps in to decide moral virtue and moral vice. In the terrifying imagery of George Orwell, dismissed as absurdly alarmist when he originally wrote about it, [48] the 'thought-police' are on the march. Traditional Christian convictions can now be labelled as 'thoughtcrimes', for which it is perfectly possible to be prosecuted. This is a dangerous tendency in at least some Western societies.

There appear to be two major tendencies that are gathering momentum, both of which threaten the basic human freedoms of 'thought, conscience, religion, opinion and expression' and the accompanying rights 'to manifest religious belief in teaching, practice, worship and observance' and 'to hold opinions without interference' (Articles 18 and 19 of the Universal Declaration of Human Rights; Articles 9 and 10 of The European Convention on Human Rights). The first tendency is a particular interpretation of discrimination. There appears to be a cultural movement towards interpreting fundamental disagreements about issues of faith and morals as discrimination. So, when people make a truth-claim on behalf of their religion or belief, they are judged to be discriminatory, if this claim implies that another set of beliefs is wrong.

---

[47] *Whose Religion?* 61-62.

[48] In *Nineteen Eighty-Four* (London: Secker and Warburg, 1949 – original publication).

Or, if people criticise the beliefs, opinions and practices of others, they are held to be discriminating against those others. Thus, for example, if someone holding a public office as a civil servant criticises a particular lifestyle choice, she can be dismissed from her post for allegedly infringing laws safeguarding equality of opportunity.

The second tendency takes this contention one step further by adding the charge that disagreement is actually offensive to the other. So, if people dispute or oppose the beliefs and practices of others, they are considered to have offered them some kind of affront or insult. Even more, the language of harassment is now entering into common parlance to describe the supposed effect that sharp dissent may have on another person or group of people. The stakes may be raised even higher by the increasingly (mis)used term phobia, as in homophobia or Islamophobia, to describe serious dissent in particular cases. Following on from this line of thought, governments are now seeking to curb freedom of speech and opinion by law under the pretext that limitations are necessary 'for the protection of public order, health or morals, or for the protection of the rights and freedoms of others' (Article 10 of the European Convention).

Much confusion lies behind these increasing moves to prohibit certain opinions. Let us take the issue of discrimination first. The decision to take its meaning in a unilaterally negative sense constitutes a basic fallacy. It is usually interpreted to mean a policy that unfairly penalises a person or group on the basis of difference. Thus, for example, there are (justly) employment laws that prohibit prejudice against certain categories of people on the basis of the contingency of their birth (race, ethnicity, colour, gender, age). However, discrimination is also a positive value. To exercise discrimination is to be discerning about issues. It is to show that in life there are genuine differences, some of them enrich human life, some are completely neutral or insignificant, and some of the utmost consequence. To discriminate is to know which is which!

In point of fact, in the real world (rather than in some moral theory), everyone exercises discrimination in a right and proper sense, for they constantly make choices between alternatives. Parents, for example, may discriminate, by preferring one school for their children over another. Should they then be penalised by the law for the 'discriminatory practice' of rejecting the school judged to be less satisfactory? An employer may be said to discriminate, if he or she dismisses an employee from their job for repeated inefficiency or gross misconduct. Discrimination cannot become a blanket (one might say indiscriminate) term that can become a kind of ideological weapon to be used against beliefs and opinions that some people in society do not like.

Likewise with offence: there may be degrees that are permissible and degrees that are not. The fact that some opinion or remark is deemed offensive by another person does not mean that it should not have been expressed. This is a very subjective area and, therefore, a society should be extremely cautious before it puts any acts of offence on the statute book. To contest another person's staunchly held convictions may offend her, for it implies a judgement that her beliefs are mistaken or even damaging or dangerous. To restrict freedom of thought and speech on these grounds would be thoroughly detrimental to democratic processes. Even attempts to discredit another person's beliefs by seriously misrepresenting them, whilst morally and rationally inexcusable, does not constitute an offence in law. Where open debate is allowed, these distortions can be corrected against proper evidence.

There are, however, areas of personal or corporate abuse where some limits in law may have to be placed. Where one party deliberately sets out knowingly to wound the deepest feelings of another, with the express purpose of causing outrage and disgust, the law may have to intervene. The problem is that increasingly in the West the act of offence is being interpreted in ever broader terms. Where is the robust interchange of ideas and beliefs that allows for offence to be given and taken, without provoking the intervention of the state? Is not this trend towards the curtailment of tough argument and debate a sign of moral and intellectual flabbiness? If certain opinions have to be either defended or forbidden by the state they lack robustness.

Finally we come to the accusation of harassment. To charge someone with this wrong is a serious matter. Its nature, therefore, has to be most carefully defined. To criticise another or to dispute their views or values is not harassment per se. If anyone objects to another person's pursuits or habits (for example by stating that gambling is immoral), that does not constitute harassment. For harassment to be confirmed there has to be an element of persecution, i.e. the persistent molestation, annoyance, pestering or torment caused by one person or group on another, causing alarm or distress. Thus, for example, a neighbour's ('from hell') relentless interference in and disturbance of one's life or the repeated, unwanted and frequently spurned attentions of another could both be classed as harassment. However, in the realm of beliefs and values, when speaking of differences, it would seem inappropriate to use the term harassment, unless an organisation deliberately forbids someone from expressing their beliefs openly (as, for example, in the case of the wearing of religious symbols at school or in the workplace).

This discussion, using these examples, is intended to indicate that Christians are right to have genuine concerns about the direction in which Western societies appear to be heading. Perhaps, unlike Muslims, who may consider that the secular West is too permissive in what it allows, Christians fear that the 'open society' is becoming increasingly closed, at least in certain directions. Thus, whereas indiscriminate foul language, gratuitous violence and sexual obscenities are allowed in the public media, truth-claims about ultimate beliefs and moral values, and the right to propagate them, may be increasingly curtailed. Could it be that Western societies are being thoroughly inconsistent in legislating against some acts of discrimination, whilst at the same time discriminating in the personal and civil freedoms they allow?

It is perhaps a paradox that those who hold most persistently to a view that truth exists, that it exists absolutely, and that it can be known, also defend to the greatest degree the right of all to dispute the nature and content of truth. One of the first to defend the freedom of speech against state censorship was John Milton in his tract, Areopagitica (published in 1644). He argued that the most important goal of the body politic is to arrive at the truth of matters. This can only happen by allowing people, openly and without restriction, to hear many points of view and explore different ideas.

The suppression of certain views, therefore, because they do not please those entrusted to exercise power on behalf of others, is the beginning of the end of democracy. Democracy can only flourish where there is the greatest possible openness to a wide range of opinions on any subject. This means that even idiosyncratic, minority views that the majority of citizens have come to despise must be allowed free expression. The famous saying, 'I disapprove of what you say, but I will defend to the death your right to say it', [49] is often quoted in this connection. There is a certain pragmatism in this statement, for no-one knows where, in the future, the heavy hand of censorship may fall.

Are there any limits to freedom of speech? Many fewer than those in government would like to assume. There is often a willful confusion made between classified covert information of vital importance in ensuring the security of a population and information that merely embarrasses a government. Those in power, however, have a propensity to try to silence inconvenient material. There are, of course, grey areas. Should holocaust-deniers, for example, be allowed a public platform? Or, those who deliberately stir up racist hatred, or who promote violence from the platform, pulpit or in the media? On the one hand, such extreme views cause a huge amount of gratuitous offence (and possibly actual harm), and therefore should be considered beyond the limit of what can be tolerated. On the other hand, these views can only be countered when they are out in the open. There they can be made to look as ridiculous as they truly are. Even in the most fanatical attitudes, there may be something that those, whose first reaction is utter disgust, need to hear.

These then are some of the trends in contemporary Western societies with which Christians may have real difficulties. There are others, such as the cynical arms-trade, the exploitation of workers overseas, the incredible greed of many top executives in financial corporations, the breakdown of family life, the creeping assault on the right to live (through the legalisation of abortion and euthanasia), which make many Christians increasingly uncomfortable with the society and culture in which they live. These, too, could have been developed

---

[49] Often attributed to Voltaire (for example, in the *The Concise Oxford Dictionary of Quotations* (Oxford: OUP, 1981), 265), but actually coined by the writer Evelyn Beatrice Hall, writing under her pseudonym S.G. Tallentyre, in her biography of Voltaire, *The Friends of Voltaire* (first published in 1907).

as illustrations of the 'clash' between the West and Christian faith. If it is true, as Huntington maintains, that civilisations are closely linked, indeed dependent upon, religious beliefs, then the West is rapidly becoming the first in history to dissolve its two thousand year alliance with Christianity, the religion that has profoundly guided and shaped it. No-one can predict the future with certainty. However, where the moral and spiritual surplus, generated by societies deeply influenced by Christians views of justice, mercy, honesty, trust, compassion, non-violence and forgiveness, ebbs away, it would not be surprising to see increasingly authoritarian regimes impose arbitrary values on the populace, in order to prevent a descent into chaos.

Conclusion

The concern of this chapter has been to discuss how Christians, in accordance with the beliefs of the original communities, might view the relationship between their faith and public life. One way of clarifying this relationship has been to compare and contrast the ways in which Christians and Muslims perceive the political implications of their respective core convictions.

It has been important to emphasise that Christianity is not an e*soter*ic religion that proclaims withdrawal from worldly affairs as the highest good. On the contrary, the Christian community sees its mission today very much in terms of being immersed in the messy business of ordinary social and political life. However, contrary to its own long history at many points, but in conformity with its origin, it now advocates an approach that works from the bottom up. In other words, whilst recognising the necessity of political power, in order to take decisions and effect change, it does not as a body seek this for itself. It promotes the view that there are many ways of being political, that is engaging with the daily activities of the polis, at many different levels of action. History seems to suggest that the most fundamental and long-lasting social changes are almost always initiated from the grass-roots; they do not come from the top down.

One illustration of current Christian participation in the political realm is that of maintaining an 'open' society against those who wish to restrict fundamental freedoms, especially of belief and speech. This is a matter not just of individual rights, but more importantly of the gradual encroachment of the state into every nook and cranny of public and private life. What is at stake is the proper place of political activity. In light of the universal corrupting tendency of power, to struggle against state interference in realms where it has no legitimate right to be is a fundamentally political act. This, of course, is only one example of possible political engagement. It is, I believe, a profoundly prophetic way of being involved.

Chapter 11

The Quest for a Contemporary Prophetic Faith

Which Islam?

This study has attempted to reconsider the controversial thesis that, during the last few decades, a major clash of what Tariq Ramadan calls 'Universes of reference'[1] between the world of Islam and the West has been intensifying. Some evidence for this claim has to be admitted. Islam proposes an interpretation of reality from the perspective of a divine revelation alleged to be God's final word to a wayward humanity. It is at odds with a world-view that treats all such views as matters of private opinion and, therefore, of no public consequence. There is bound to be a conflict between a community convinced that human flourishing depends on listening to the maker's instructions and one that finds the intrusion of religious beliefs into the public realm at best an irritation and, at worst, an intolerable imposition.

The West, increasingly in the last half century, has adopted a similar attitude to its own religious mentor, Christianity. What Lesslie Newbigin has called 'a public doctrine',[2] or reigning cultural consensus, concerning the pre-eminence of the secular sphere as a religious-free zone, has now come to determine a population's rights and obligations. In other words, human flourishing is now established by principles which have deliberately been decoupled from any religious beliefs.[3] Christianity in the West has tended to acquiesce in this arrangement. It has bought into a tacit ideological treaty whereby Christians do not seek to insert their convictions into public life, for fear of the accusation of being unprofessional, of resorting to indoctrination or intellectual molestation. There is now, however, some evidence that, in the last few years, Christians are seeking to free themselves from such arbitrary secular shackles.[4]

---

[1] *Radical Reform: Islamic Ethics and Liberation* (Oxford: OUP, 2009), 315.

[2] *Truth to Tell: The Gospel as Public Truth* (Grand Rapids: Eerdmans, 1991), 78.

[3] Charles Taylor has notably and exhaustively chartered the history of this process; see, *A Secular Age, passim.*

[4] The intellectual case for the public expression of Christian belief is made by, amongst others, Terence Copley, *Indoctrination, Education and God: The Struggle for the Mind* (London: SPCK, 2005); Roger Trigg, *Religion in Public Life: Must Faith be Privatized?* (Oxford: OUP, 2007); Jonathan Chaplin, *Talking God: The Legitimacy of Religious Public Reasoning* (London: Theos, 2008).

Muslims have never capitulated to secularism to the same degree. They have maintained their confidence in the absolute priority of God's word over all human ideas. In so far, then, as the West collectively, through its opinion-formers (academics, intellectuals, politicians, artists, writers, celebrities and journalists) and through legislation, has turned its back on divine wisdom, Muslims have reacted in opposition. Sometimes the opposition has been virulent, particularly where the West is perceived as wishing to circumscribe or denigrate Islamic faith. Sometimes the opposition has been more circumspect; there are a good number of Muslims who view a so-called clash of civilisations as greatly exaggerated and alarmist.

How Muslims relate to the history and cultural heritage of Western nations will depend in large part on how they interpret and apply their beliefs to contemporary secular societies. This, in turn, will depend in part on whether the Muslims in question are living in Islamic nations or in the diaspora. Many authors (Muslim and non-Muslim) seem to agree in identifying three broad Islamic groupings in the modern world. They may be given different names, but in general terms they can be recognised as representing three distinct schools of thought.[5]

'Traditionalists' or 'conservatives' hold that change in society cannot affect the core religious traditions of the past. They tend to reject all innovations after the 3rd century of the Islamic era. They believe and practice the classic expressions of Islam (including a strict adherence to the 'five pillars', the wearing of distinctive dress and the right to practice polygamy). Above all, they advocate the introduction of Islamic law codes as the basis of all legislation. For this group, Islam is an absolute and self-sufficient body of thought, which has developed historically as a complete alternative to the current secularised, Hellenised, Judeo-Christian philosophy of Western society. Its identity, therefore, is quite distinct from modernity, which according to this interpretation is the child of the Christian world-view.[6]

A second group is known as 'modernists' or 'reconstructionists'. They are people who argue for a flexible interpretation of the foundation documents. They propose that a distinction should be drawn between the universal principles of Islamic belief and detailed legal injunctions, on the grounds that many of the latter were prescribed to meet particular circumstances, long since past. They also advocate a clear separation of the text of divine revelation from

---

[5] This division has to be rough and ready. It is important to distinguish different perspectives on Muslim thought and practice in order to demonstrate that Islam is not a monolithic creed. The danger, however, of any attempt at a typology is that some Muslims may well object that they do not fit into any of the categories chosen.

[6] See, Rippin, *Muslims: Their Religious Beliefs and Practice*, 183; Asad, *The Principles of State and Government in Islam*, 97; Armajani, *Dynamic Islam*, 11; Ruthven, *Islam in the World*, 327ff.

the reflections of subsequent interpreters, allowing for both a continuity and discontinuity of interpretation through time. Thus, for them, the true meaning of the Qur'an is not necessarily a rigidly understood literal meaning. Generally, they do not feel so threatened by modernity, allowing that it has brought some positive benefits (such as scientific rationality). They maintain a reverence for the Qur'an, the *sunnah* and the example of the first generation of Muslims, but also seek to re-evaluate their significance for contemporary living. Their reconstruction therefore takes the path of bringing together the underlying moral purpose of revelation with modern ideals, such as freedom of conscience, equality and social justice. They are, above all, critical of a view of Islam that has become wedded in an obscurantist way with a rigid, unreformable tradition: 'The self-inflicted death of intellect in Islam 1,000 years ago is the main cause of retrogressive and unenlightened mullah culture in Muslim societies today'.[7]

A third group has been given the name of 'Islamists', 'fundamentalists', 'radicals' or 'revivalists'. None of these labels does much to identify them properly, as they are used in a variety of ways and often as terms of offence. Generally, this group has been identified with the most militant wing of Islam. It calls for the reestablishment of a wholly Islamic regime, modelled on the Caliphate, without any deference to modern, Western notions of democracy, individual freedoms and human rights. Islamic law as codified in the first centuries after Muhammad should be implemented in full. Government would be administered by people with religious education, under the guidance of religious leaders. If necessary, violence can be used as a political tool to achieve the higher ends of an Islamic state. The division between 'the house of Islam' and 'the house of war' is pressed: Islam is the exclusive truth; other religions are false or of limited validity and the secular perspective of Western societies is antithetical to the true faith.[8] 'For those groups advocating violence the contemporary world resembles the one confronted by Muslims in Medina'.[9] Therefore, force may legitimately be used to overthrow regimes that do not, in the eyes of this group, practise the pure traditions of the early period of Islam (up to and including the four rightly-guided Caliphs).

It is this third group that so often hits the headlines. This is due to its apparent complete disregard for the conventions of 'civilised' society, such as the belief that ends do not justify means, that innocent people should not be targeted by acts of violence, that women should have equal access with men to

---

[7] Izrat Majeed, 'Open Letter to Osama bin Laden', *The Nation* (Pakistan), November 9th, 2001, quoted in Riddell and Cotterell, *Islam in Context,* 191; see also, Asad, 'Europe against Islam: Islam in Europe' in Abu-Rabi, *The Blackwell Companion to Contemporary Islamic Thought*, 309; Ramadan, *Western Muslims and the Future of Islam*, 109.

[8] See, Armajani, *Dynamic Islam*, 11.

[9] Riddell and Cotterell, *Islam in Context*, 164.

all the privileges and responsibilities of citizenship, that punishment should never take the form of the disfigurement of the human body (by amputation or flogging), that political power is not self-authenticated. Islamism arose in the twentieth century as a troubled response to what was perceived to be the triumphalist imperialism of certain Western nations towards Islamic majority territories, a deep sense of political, religious and intellectual malaise in the Arab world during the inter-war period and the abolition of the Caliphate in 1923.[10]

Approaching the Key Sources of Islam

These three groups represent in broad terms alternative ways of conceiving Islam in the contemporary world. They represent general categories, only approximating to specific types. Nevertheless, they exemplify particular attitudes both to the authoritative founding texts and traditions of Islam and to the questions raised by living in the modern world, to the extent that the views they express may be taken as distinctive and distinguishing.

Traditionalists and revivalists adopt a similar approach to the three main sources for determining an authentic interpretation of Islam - the Qur'an, the *hadith* of Muhammad and the lives of the *al-salaf al-salih* ('the Pious Forebears', comprising the three generations of the Companions of Muhammad, the Successors and the Successors to the Successors).[11] According to their understanding, within this early period of Islamic history and thought the true meaning of the revelations given to Muhammad and his authenticated sayings have been discerned by faithful interpreters, expounded and laid out in a systematic form in the teachings of the various law schools. Nothing needs to be added or taken away from this careful, systematic process of codification. Temporal closeness to the original events guarantees a bona fide, accurate account of the legitimate tradition springing from the primary revelatory events. (In passing, it might be noted that a similar conclusion has been drawn by the Orthodox tradition within the Christian faith regarding the normative status of the early councils and creeds. In essence the faith has been settled truly and for all time in this early period.) Thus, in the case of Islam, for example, the Penal Code (or *hudud*) has been fixed and may not be revoked. These stipulate punishments for specified crimes that are considered to have

---

[10] See Ibrahim M. Abu-Rabi, 'Contemporary Islamic Thought: One or Many?' in Ibrahim M. Abu-Rabi, *The Blackwell Companion to Contemporary Islamic Thought*, 9; Geaves, *Aspects of Islam*, 214; Ruthven, *Islam in the World*, 305-315, 363-369, 390-393.

[11] 'The Pious Forebears' comprise the generations that stretch from roughly 570-855 CE, see Asma Afsaruddin, *The First Muslims: History and Memory* (Oxford: One World, 2008), xiii.

been ordered directly by God, either in the Qur'an or through a genuine saying of Muhammad. Historical research, however, shows that many of the traditions have probably been elaborated at a later date, as they reflect situations outside of Muhammad's life-time. They represent, therefore, subsequent creedal interpretations of the prophet.[12] Thus, for example, the Muslim scholar Farid Esack 'broadly accepts non-Muslim opinion about the political shaping of Islam's second most authoritative source, the *hadith*'.[13] Only the Qur'an transmits unequivocally the will of Allah.

Reconstructionists, on the other hand, adopt a different approach to the sources. They base their arguments on criteria which call into question a dogmatic and rigid adherence to a millennial old usage and convention. First, as reliable first-hand accounts of Muhammad's sayings and practice, the *hadith* and sunna should be followed only with great caution. In spite of attempts to trace the genealogy of the traditions through trustworthy chains of transmitters (isnad) from Muhammad and his early companions onwards, many of the traditions are unreliable. Muhammad probably did not become a major source of authority for the community until the 9th century (CE). So, the biographical material may tell us more about developments in the later Muslim community than about Muhammad's own life time.

Secondly, even if the sunna and *hadith* were completely reliable in conveying the ipsissima verba of Muhammad, in the last resort, though he was undoubtedly a remarkable person, he was only a human being (Q. 18.110), and therefore capable of error. His words carry weight, but they cannot be considered in any way on a par with the immediate divine revelation given to Muhammad and recorded in the Qur'an. Moreover, there is no ruling in the Qur'an that says that the *hadith* must be followed.[14] The *hadith*, therefore, should not be regarded as sacred text, unchanged from the time of Muhammad and the Companions, but as a body of writings produced by gradual accumulation over many generations. They may, or may not, be a record of what Muhammad actually said and did; their primary value is in throwing light on the religious and political controversies of the first centuries of Islamic history.[15]

Thirdly, even if a completely reliable set of traditions, collected after a process of faithful transmission covering more than two centuries, were to constitute a guiding source of belief and behaviour for Muslims, having an authority only a little less than that of the Qur'an, they still have to be

---

[12] Rippin, *Muslims: Their Religious Beliefs and Practices*, 48-49; *The Historical Muhammad*, 2-6.

[13] Bennett, *Muslims and Modernity*, 97.

[14] Rippin, *Muslims: Their Religious Beliefs and Practices*, 206-212.

[15] This is the conclusion of the Islamic scholar Ignaz Goldziher as summarised in Hourani, *Islam in European Thought*, 38-39.

interpreted. Contemporary Muslims, with access to sophisticated tools of historical research, may be in a better position to extract from them pertinent and valuable lessons than 9th century jurists.

These arguments lead reconstructionists to the conclusion that there is no final, universally accepted, authorised and definitive rendering of the traditions. Every new generation has a right to do their own work of explanation, in accordance with their own understanding of the principles of historical investigation. This means, by logical progression, that only texts about which there can be no dispute are normative, not the traditions about them nor historically circumscribed interpretations. So, fruitful though it may have been, Islamic law does not have to refer back to a particular period of history; there is plenty of scope for a creative reinterpretation of the primary sources.

Fourthly, in the case of the Qur'an, the situation is somewhat different. It is taken as read that the text, finally compiled under the leadership of the third Caliph, Uthman, is utterly authentic. There is no question either of textual variations or mistaken identity. The Qur'an

> ...is considered to be the ultimate authority in all matters pertaining to religion. It furnishes the basic tenets of the faith, the principles of ethical behaviour, and guidance for social, political and economic activities.[16]

At the same time, as in the case of the *hadith*, the Qur'an has to be interpreted in order to bring out its many meanings. Reconstructionists assert that, subsequent to the time of the rightly-guided Caliphs (i.e. after the death of Ali ibn Abi Talib in 660 CE), there are, in principle, no interpreters who occupy a more privileged position vis-à-vis the text than any others. Some may be more esteemed for their insight, learning and wisdom, but they have no divine right to dictate the meaning. In this respect, whilst paying particular attention to the knowledge of the pious scholar, all Muslims have a right to discern for themselves what the text indicates or implies.

Fifthly, reconstructionists are careful to distinguish between eternally binding ethical norms and temporally relevant instructions given in response to the particular, and unrepeatable, historical situation of the first generation of believers. It is the task of interpreters of all eras to differentiate between the text itself and the accumulated layers of meaning assigned to it over the course of the centuries. This is a 'hermeneutical' task, which has two focal points: the text interpreted within its original context and the subsequent readings of the text interpreted as expressions of the circumstances of the time they were made.

For these people, then, the Qur'an has to be liberated from what Fazlur Rahman has called the myopic and tyrannical rule of religious and political leaders who influenced Islamic discourse and methods of education in such a

---

[16] Esposito (ed), *The Oxford Dictionary of Islam*, 256.

way that critical thinking and the free flow of ideas were discouraged.[17] This continues to be the principle bugbear of much of contemporary Islam, which is still located in a time-warp. It stifles the kind of free thought that would enable Muslims of this generation to develop meaningful and relevant solutions to contemporary challenges. Mohammed Arkoun believes that large parts of the Muslim world, because they are paralysed by a fear of chaos, long above all things for the order and stability of what is familiar.[18] He sets out in detail the process by which the authority of God, mediated through the Qur'an, was substituted by the authority of the traditions of interpretation, producing what he calls 'the Islamic Paradigm'.[19] Thus, if a tradition of interpretation or law-making is accepted as standard for long enough it easily becomes confused with the ultimate truth itself. Then, all thought stagnates into a mere repetition of what has already been thought and Islam, as a living tradition, has nothing constructive to contribute to the contemporary world order.[20]

This kind of criticism of a stale Islamic tradition has recently been taken up by Tariq Ramadan and Asma Afsaruddin in significant, scholarly treatments of original sources. Afsaruddin focuses her attention on the period of the 'Pious Forebears' (*al-salaf al-salih*), i.e. the development of the Islamic nation immediately following the death of Muhammad. She compares the two main ways in which this phase of Islamic life has been reconstructed. On the one hand, those who hold to an Islamist set of ideas tend to canonise the later traditions that arose sometime after the end of the initial government of the nation by Muhammad's original companions. According to this understanding, a distinctive Islamic political identity and a divinely mandated political agenda were established from the earliest years.[21] The early history has to be read through the eyes of those who collected together the traditions and spun them into a comprehensive set of rules and regulations. According to this tradition, a

[17] *Islam and Modernity*, 237, cited in Armajani, *Dynamic Islam*, 9.

[18] Armajani, *Dynamic Islam*, 11.

[19] Arkoun, *Islam: To Reform or to Subvert?* 215-227.

[20] It is worth pointing out that the modernist or reconstructionist approach to interpreting Islam in the contemporary world is not only a feature of the last few decades. At the turn of the twentieth century, there was a considerable reform movement, called Salafi, led by figures like Jamal al-Din al Afghani and Muhammad Abduh. In its origin, its 'prime objectives were to rid the Muslim *ummah* of the centuries-long mentality of taqlid (unquestioning imitation of precedent) and stagnation and to reform the moral, cultural and political conditions of Muslims… (It) sought reforms of Islamic law, education, and Arabic language. (It) viewed political reform as an essential requirement for (the) revitalization of the Muslim community', Esposito (ed), *The Oxford Dictionary of Islam*, 275. To avoid confusion, it is necessary to note that in the late twentieth century, the term Salafi came to denote reformers in the traditionalist, rather than modernist, tradition.

[21] Afsaruddin, *The First Muslims*, 148-152.

certain form of divine governance of the people (*al-hakimiyyah*), based on the unique divine sovereignty of Allah, was mandated from the beginning. Muhammad and his successors were commissioned directly by Allah to interpret the divine will. The Qur'anic text 4.59 is often cited in confirmation of this view: 'You who believe, obey God and the Messenger, and those in authority among you. If you are in dispute over any matter, refer it to God and the Messenger...'

Also mandated from the beginning was 'a practically immutable religious law, the *shari'ah*', derived from the Qur'an and the *sunnah*, and admitting of 'a single and uniform, often literal, interpretation, authoritatively established by the Prophet and upheld by his Companions, and thus valid for all times and places'.[22]

> Unlike classical Islamic jurisprudence which added analogical reasoning and consensus of the community as supplemental sources of jurisprudence in the absence of explicit texts, hard-line Islamists usually recognize no other authoritative sources besides the Qur'an and the sunna for legislative activity. For them the shari'a, simply put, is a legal code which 'enacted as it is by God, is unchangeable'.[23]

On the other hand, modernists view the history and significance of the salafis in an entirely different light. Employing a more discerning process of historical investigation of the source documents, they come to a quite different understanding of the status of an 'Islamic state' and of the *shari'ah*. The confusion that arose concerning the succession, as a result of Muhammad's sudden and unexpected death, demonstrates that Muhammad did not leave any specific instructions relating to the selection of his successor. It may be fairly assumed that the reason for this was that this issue and other matters of political rule

> ...were not considered to be within the purview of divine revelation and/or prophetic counsel. Political administration was a temporal matter and could be devised, changed, and launched according to the dictates of human deliberation and public utility.... Beyond offering broad moral and ethical guidelines for proper political conduct, no particular mode of governance was mandated...in Qur'anic prescriptions.[24]

The record of what actually transpired in the election of Abu Bakr and then Umar to succeed Muhammad would seem to bear out the somewhat improvised

---

[22] Afsaruddin, *The First Muslims*, 157.

[23] Afsaruddin, *The First Muslims*, 158, and quoting S. Abu'l-A'la Mawdudi, *Political Theory of Islam* (Lahore: 1976), 31.

[24] Afsaruddin, *The First Muslims*, 26.

nature of the process. The appointment of a six man advisory council called the *shura* points to Islam's inherent democratic principle and sets a precedent for consultative government that was repressed during the subsequent period of Umayyad (661-750 CE) and 'Abbasid (750-1258 CE) rule.[25]

Modernists have developed an Islamic-based version of democratic principles in the form of three cardinal tenets: *shura* (consultation); *bay'a* (ratification), and *ijma* (consensus). The first satisfies the principles of popular enfranchisement and accountability, the second gives expression to individual opinion in the election of a leader, and the third legitimises political decisions:

> While acknowledging God's sovereignty over all creation, modernists do not view this as impeding in any way human freedom in determining their course of action in particularly the political sphere under the guidance of broad moral imperatives...Fazlur Rahman stressed that the Qur'anic concept of God's sovereignty has nothing to do with political or legal sovereignty but rather means that 'God has bestowed a certain constitution both to this universe and to man.[26]

With regard to the issue of *shari'ah*, modernists make a number of distinctions: between the intent, overall objectives and application of religious law and a literal understanding of certain texts; between the Qur'an as a moral code from which a legal system may be derived and as a law-book, and between the science and study of the law (*fiqh*) and the law itself (*shari'ah*). Unfortunately, in the latter two cases, a fatal conflation has taken place. In considering legislation, Islamic law-makers should take into account what is required by the common good (*maslaha*), using their own independent reasoning (*ijtihad*). Modernists exalt the Qur'an over the *sunnah* as the only final, binding authority. Indeed, some go as far as to say that

> ...non-religious sunnaic rulings which have to do with civil, political and military matters, are the result of the Prophet's fallible personal *ijtihad* and are consequently non-binding on the believer.[27]

Tariq Ramadan strongly advocates a contemporary *fiqh*, which is able to distinguish between 'what in the texts is immutable and what may be changed'.[28] His project is to 'raise the issues of the sources of *usul al-fiqh*, of the categories that organize them, of the methodologies that result from them

---

[25] Afsaruddin, *The First Muslims*, 44-45.

[26] Afsaruddin, *The First Muslims*, 172, citing Fazlur Rahman, 'The Islamic Concept of State' in John J. Donohue and John L. Esposito (eds), *Islam in Transition: Muslim Perspectives*, 264.

[27] See, Afsaruddin, *The First Muslims*, 176 and also Wael Hallaq, *A History of Islamic Legal Theories: An Introduction to Sunni Usul al-Fiqh* (Cambridge: 1999), 214-220.

[28] Ramadan, *Radical Reform: Islamic Ethics and Liberation* (Oxford: OUP, 2009), 1.

and, finally, of the nature of the authority all those elements impart to text scholars (*'ulama* and especially fuqaha)'.[29] He proposes three fundamental propositions: (1) 'the contemporary Muslim world (both East and West), must reconsider the terms and modalities of the reform process (*islah, tajdid*)', distinguishing between 'adaptation reform' and 'transformation reform'; (2) the sources of usual *al-fiqh* must be reconsidered by, among other things, incorporating knowledge gained from disciplines other than the science of jurisprudence; (3) 'the centre of gravity of authority in the Islamic Universe of reference must be shifted by ranking more clearly the respective competences and roles of scholars in the different fields', combining the study of both text and context scholars (*'ulama an-nusus* and *'ulama al-waqi*).[30]

Ramadan Maintains that Islam is Inherently Open to Reform:

> The meaning of *tajdid*, as expressed in the Prophetic tradition, is indeed to 're-form' in the name of faithfulness.[31]

He argues strongly that the only way to remain faithful to the essence of the faith is by constantly seeking to reapply its essential message to new circumstances:

> In short, no faithfulness to Islamic principles through the ages can exist without evolution, without reform, without a renewal of intelligence and understanding.[32]

He contends that this has always been the mainstream Islamic approach to the original texts, the living tradition and the varying contexts in which Muslims find themselves:

> The eternal Word of God was revealed within a specific history, over twenty-three years, and if some texts or injunctions transcend the human History that receives them, some other verses cannot be understood without putting them within a particular time sequence. Human intelligence alone, then, can determine the contents of the timeless principle drawn from the text, while necessarily taking into account its relation to the social and historical context of its enunciation. This critical approach has been known and acknowledged since the beginning by all schools of Islamic law, and what was debated later on was not the legitimacy of the approach itself but the norms and limits of such contextualizing. The debate already involves the elaboration of applied hermeneutics.[33]

---

[29] Ramadan, *Radical Reform,* 3.
[30] Ramadan, *Radical Reform,* 3-4.
[31] Ramadan, *Radical Reform,* 13.
[32] Ramadan, *Radical Reform,* 13.
[33] Ramadan, *Radical Reform,* 16. The emphasis has been added to point out that there are similarities between this process within contemporary Islam and within Christian

For Ramadan what he calls 'the contemporary literalist approach' (as displayed by traditionalists and revivalists) is based on three fundamental confusions: 'between that which, in the Revelation, is immutable (*thabit*), absolute, and transhistorical, and that which is subject to change, linked to the temporal evolution and environmental changes (*mutaghayyir*);' between principles and models, and between a rule and its form'.[34] Thus, to take an example,

> The principles of justice, equality, rights, and human brotherhood that guided the Prophet of Islam indeed remain the references beyond history, but the model of the city of Medina founded by Muhammad in the seventh century is a historical realization linked to the realities and requirements of his time. Muslims must, in the course of history, try to remain faithful to those principles and strive to implement them as best they can according to the requirements of their time, but they cannot merely imitate, reproduce, or duplicate a historical model that was adapted for a particular time but no longer corresponds to the requirements of their own.[35]

Thus, finally, Ramadan advocates a process of interpretation and application that requires paying attention to what he calls the 'two Books' or 'the two Revelations'. This will demand,

> ...a new presentation of ethical goals...allying the comprehensive vision of the message with rigorous specialization in each area of human knowledge and action to grasp issues in their complexity and enable applied ethics to respond adequately to the inconsistencies and challenges of our time.[36]

Ramadan is well aware that between the traditionalists and the reformers 'the debate is sharp and the stakes are crucial'.[37] The way in which the sources are handled will determine the way in which Muslims, the world over, understand their role within their contemporary context.

The Community and the Political Order

Whether or not there already is, or is likely to be in the future, a conflict of civilisations between the West and Islam may well depend on how the debate, highlighted by Afsaruddin, Ramadan and others, works itself out. One of the key questions concerns the issue of whether Muslims today will continue to

---

theology. Hermeneutics has also been the focus of attention for some continental philosophers, most notably Hans-Georg Gadamer and Paul Ricoeur.

[34] Ramadan, *Radical Reform*, 17-20.

[35] Ramadan, *Radical Reform*, 19 (emphasis added).

[36] Ramadan, *Radical Reform*, 316.

[37] Ramadan, *Radical Reform*, 21.

insist on the ideal of an Islamic state. Bound up with this is the related question of whether Muslims can fully and faithfully fulfil all their obligations whilst living outside an Islamic state. We have already reviewed the suggestion that Islamic tradition allows for a situation which is not sharply divided between the concepts of the Territory of Islam and the Territory of War. This means, presumably, that Muslims may live in peace in a situation where political power is in the hands of non-Muslims. Does it also mean that Muslims are not necessarily under an obligation to seek power in the name of and for the sake of promoting their faith? This is a crunch question, for it has implications for how they see themselves as a community.

The Christian community has, by and large, already resolved this issue. As we have seen, from the very beginning it refused the temptation to interpret its mission in terms of wielding temporal power. The Constantinian shift, when it had power thrust upon it by a somewhat maverick emperor, was not on its horizon for the first 300 years of its existence. If the ideal for Muslims, following the example of Muhammad in Medina, has been to set up a godly state, governed by divine laws, the ideal for the first Christians was to realise a godly community of believers under law to Christ. The early church's vision of its vocation in the world was to be an alternative assembly of the people, striving to live in peace with all, and serve others with no other motives than care and compassion.

As the community was not allied to the state, it did not have to defend the interests of the state. Therefore, it was not obliged to go to war to save the state from external threats or internal subversion. It was free from manipulation by the political powers; no outside body could tell it what to believe or how to behave. Therefore, it was able to act as a prophetic people, insisting without compromise that the state pursue in all circumstances the justice that God requires. Above all, it was able to challenge the sacred pretensions of the state, resisting to martyrdom the claims of the state to represent the will of the gods. This was its ultimate political witness, as the etymology of the word martyr (*martur* = witness[38]) testifies.

Islam could have taken a similar path. There is nothing in the Qur'anic revelations that came to Muhammad in Mecca to suggest that this new community of believers in Allah was destined to become an empire. There is no hint that they were called to leave Mecca in order to set up a political order under the governance of the prophet. The change in the tone and content of the revelations given in Medina were ex eventu, after the purely human decision to escape from persecution by emigrating to another city. Once it was resolved to accept the invitation to become a leader elsewhere, the die was cast. All means, including considerable violence, had to be used to defend the interests of the city state and its new fledgling religion.

---

[38] See, Acts 1.8; 5.32.

It is not surprising, therefore, that there is no strong tradition of non-violence[39] in mainstream Islam. In Medina, to use an analogy from the Old Testament, Muhammad acted as both Nathan (the prophet) and David (the ruler).[40] The crux of the matter is, however, that these two roles cannot be combined. Nathan remained a prophet in so far as he was not co-opted by David, the ruler, into the governing regime. Had this happened, the prophetic message would have lost its cutting edge, as the history of the false prophets amply demonstrates.[41] The true prophets were independent agents, and therefore free to censure the rulers of Israel (and other nations) for abandoning the ways of God, not least for the unjustified violence that they committed against their own people and the unwarranted military adventures they undertook.

The Christian church has been characterised as a sign (pointing towards) and foretaste (a partial expression) of and a witness to (proclaiming it as good news) the rule of God. In each case it knows that it fails to live up to its high calling. During its history, the church has often betrayed its mission to be a light to the nations. It has descended into dark ways, such as the persecutions that took place on both sides at the time of the Reformation and the inter-state wars of the 17th century that were given a religious tinge. It, therefore, seeks forgiveness and the renewal of its inner life, in order to be able to do better. For the Christian faith the rule of God is always an aspiration. Christians pray for and long to see 'God's kingdom come' and 'his will be done on earth'. Their first task is to seek God's grace to implement this rule within their own assembly. There has to be, therefore, a discipline of life that upholds a pattern of behaviour that accords with the norms of the kingdom as set forth in the life of Jesus, the Messiah.

Such a pattern may be upheld within this community, because its members have voluntarily agreed to submit themselves to Jesus as the ruler of their lives. It cannot, however, be imposed upon the population in general, for people, who have not yet accepted their need for God's transforming power in their lives, cannot be expected to live by its standards. The Sermon on the Mount, for example, though reflecting the way of life under God's rule, is not a general ethic; it is a teaching to be obeyed by those who consciously desire to follow the one who has himself fully embodied it.

The notion that a universal divine law can be promulgated by a political regime and enforced upon an entire population is highly problematic. Unless there is a change of heart, so that people genuinely wish to delight in the law of

[39] By a tradition of non-violence I mean an interpretation of the foundation documents which understands them to forbid believers from taking the life of others, whatever the cause.

[40] See, 2 Samuel 12.1-15.

[41] For example, Jeremiah 28.15; Ezequiel 13. 1-12; Isaiah 9.15-16.

God, the only possibly effective strategy is coercion, backed up with the most severe sanctions. The harsh punishments meted out according to a strict interpretation of *shari'ah* are a logical conclusion of a religion that depends ultimately on law to achieve the ends of obedience to the will of God:

> As the Caliph al-Ma'mun (ruled 813-833) trenchantly observed, it is impossible, under the threat that overhangs society from *Shari'ah* political sanctions, to distinguish between political expedience and moral duty, between opportunism and sincerity. Threats corrupt, and absolute threats make absolute hypocrites...The lesson here is, if the state must procure the allegiance of believers, then religion cannot pretend that its truth claims have intrinsic persuasive merit, and so religion must disingenuously yield right of way to behavioural norms dispensed by the State.[42]

This is a powerful argument for separating out the demands of faith and the legally sanctionable stipulations of the state. The community of faith has to be able to tolerate, but not follow, a society whose laws, unfortunately, may leave much to be desired when compared with the ethical requirements of God's just and merciful rule.[43]

So much of the present, incipient and potential conflict between two political and social paradigms, Islam and the West, could be avoided, if the former were able to see itself as a community, called to give a trenchant witness to divine revelation, as it understands it, from within the wider non-believing community, but declining the allure of taking hold of the reigns of power. Is it feasible that Islam as a universal religion could possibly reinterpret its own original message, without compromising its essential nature, to distinguish between the absolute basic requirements of its walk with God and the contingent historical events that followed the *hijrah*? The evidence suggests that it can, for we have seen how some well-informed Muslim scholars are attempting to achieve this end.

Engaging the Powers

One of the main claims of this study has been that a close alliance between an inflexible, doctrinaire religious faith and the instruments of political power leads inevitably to a corruption of both. Like the 'theocratic' states of medieval Europe, an Islamic state is undesirable principally because the prophetic voice, which should hold power to account, is inevitably stifled. An Islamic state

[42] Lamin Sanneh, '*Shari'ah* Sanctions' in Geaves, *Islam and the West*, 161.

[43] In contemporary corporate life, a company may act wholly within the law, whilst also acting immorally. An example of such a case would be that, when one company takes over another, in order to make the savings necessary to service the enormous borrowing required to finance the take-over a number of workers lose their jobs.

cannot afford to allow opposition a free reign, for fear that its authority and credibility are undermined. There are numerous contemporary examples throughout the Islamic world of the crushing of dissent. Indeed, it could be argued that the notion of an Islamic state is itself a contradiction in terms, unless full provision is made for the voice of prophetic protest, whenever the fundamental moral principles of the faith – justice, equality, special concern for the poor and minority communities – are threatened.

Islam claims to be the last of the prophetic faiths, the final word of God to humanity. Such a contention needs to be tested by its being able to confront political rule, even when exercised in the name of the faith, whenever it deviates from the universal ethical precepts given in its founding revelation. Even more, the authenticity of an Islamic state should not be measured by whether it implements a particular, hard-line interpretation of *shari'ah*, but by whether it allows the prophetic voice to be heard within the political process. This is not un-Islamic, as there is a strong tradition, going back to Muhammad, of open consultation among the faithful. It would be hard to gainsay the principle of *shura* (consultation among the community), since it is prescribed in the Qur'an (Q, 3.158-159; 42.38) and was practised by Muhammad and his earliest successors:[44]

> The Quran confirms the principle of *shura*, consultation…: this Revelation is of crucial importance and states that the principle of deliberation, of majority decision-making, is not to be negotiated and must be respected beyond historical contingencies and human mistakes in decisions. Muslims are, therefore, those 'who conduct their affairs by mutual consultation…'[45]

Since Islam makes a useful distinction between the roots of its faith (*usul*) and the branches (*furu'*), and this can be translated into a distinction between fundamental values and procedures,[46] *shura* (the value) can legitimately be translated into 'democracy' (the procedure).[47]

Another value, relevant to the discussion, is that of *maslahah*, usually translated as 'public benefit'. The principle is that of the common good or overwhelming public interest. This is something that has to be decided in the absence of any explicit testimony in the foundation documents:

> The principle permits the addressing of social and legal issues that had not arisen previously, so that every new generation is able to interpret Muslim tradition and legal practice in the context of the needs of the time. Some of these issues relate to

---

44 See, Afsaruddin, *The First Muslims*, 44-45, 169-170; Northcliffe, *Islam Faith and Practice*, 22; Bennett, *Muslims and Modernity*, 46-49.

45 Ramadan, *The Messenger*, 127.

46 Ruthven, *Islam in the World*, 373; Ramadan, *Western Muslims*, 145-148.

47 An-Na'im, *Toward an Islamic Reformation*, 40.

> economic aspects, such as modern forms of banking, others to ethical issues, such as...political representation and human rights.[48]

The outcome of this discussion is to maintain that a state, wishing to promote Islamic values, should not be averse to implementing a democratic regime in some form. The problem within the current debate is that the radical wing of Islam has tried to hijack the notion of an Islamic state by driving a wedge between the so-called vox populi and the vox divina, between the will of the people and the will of God. This division, however, may well be artificial and unsubstantiated. Radicals maintain that a society must be governed according to the word of God, through which God's sovereignty over all human affairs is mediated. However, as has been pointed out in the course of this study, there are several difficulties with such an oversimplified notion.

In the first place, there is the problem of interpretation. By its very nature God's word is communicated to a specific group of people through a particular messenger, addressing concrete historical circumstances; for Muslims this all happened exactly 14 centuries ago. Clearly, since then, history has moved on. Though the essence of the message has not changed, the circumstances of the people to whom it is addressed have varied substantially. Given the historical distance, interpretation demands an imagination able to discern how the word of God, presumed to have been given in Arabia in the 7th century, is recognised as such in the twenty-first century. Some kind of literalist transposition of the text is unlikely to be faithful to the original intention.

In the second place, there is the problem of the interpreter. It goes without saying that there is no infallible interpreter. Within Islam there is no one centre of authoritative explanation, able to clarify the exact original meaning of the texts and their contemporary significance and relevance. If any were to make this claim, there would be plenty of other Islamic scholars who would dispute such an assertion. How the texts translate into modern situations is a matter of open discussion, often between different traditions. Dogmatic pronouncements, issuing in exclusive and excluding fatwas, undermine the principles of both *shura* (the process of adequate consultation of the faithful) and *ijma* (the process whereby consensus is reached on a matter of legal judgement).[49] Interpretation, therefore, if it is to be faithful to the intentions of the original revelation has to proceed by way of negotiation between different schools of

---

48 Nanji, *Dictionary of Islam*, 112.

49 Technically speaking, a *fatwa* is a legal opinion given by a legal scholar (a *mufti* in Sunni Islam; *mujtahid* among the *Shi'a*) in answer to a question not explicitly covered in the *fiqh* literature. It is advisory, not binding. An analogy might be the process of consultation that may go on in contemporary legal proceedings with barristers, known for their expertise in certain aspects of the law. A *fatwa* was never intended to act as a kind of mandatory and irreversible decision, in the way that it has sometimes been understood in recent years.

thought. It is difficult to see how such a process could possibly function within the modern concept of an Islamic state, where the presumed governance of God has to be immediate, unequivocal and swiftly implemented.

A process of dialogue, deliberation and mediation would be inimical to a government that wishes to claim a divine mandate. Such a government, to maintain its authority and credibility, must be able to have access to unquestionable interpretations and conclusive judgements. As proposed, at least theoretically in the literature,[50] there is only one way to understand the political implications of the faith and only one path to implementing 'God's eternal and immutable will for humanity'.[51] The problem, as many Islamic scholars have pointed out, is that *shari'ah* ('the total sum of duties, obligations and guidelines for Muslims'[52]) becomes confused with *fiqh* ('the total product of human efforts at understanding the divine will'[53]); the explication of the fundamental principles of Islamic law is made into the equivalent of the law itself. This leads inevitably to a rigid, static and ultimately anachronistic appropriation of the general precepts of divine revelation. To equate *shari'ah* with a specific body of law, elaborated at a particular moment of history, and then to seek to enact it in radically different situations, is to persist in sustaining this confusion.

In the third place, there is the problem of who governs. A further difficulty with the concept of an Islamic state is to ascertain who has the authority to pronounce the 'correct' guidance for the affairs of state. As can be seen in the recent history of Iran, the guardians of the law – the mullahs – are by no means agreed about many specific policies that have to do both with internal politics and with foreign relations. Who is to say which voice should be listened to? By what legitimate process is a supreme leader chosen? What constitutes the right relationship between the legal experts, the legislators and those appointed to administer the law?

It is well known that Mawlana Sayyid Abu al-Ala Mawdudi, the founder of the political organisation known as Jamaat-i-Islami in 1941, and prolific writer on aspects of Islamic governance, expounded a version of the 'Principles of an Islamic State' called by him a 'theo-democracy'.[54] This was an attempt to marry the absolute sovereignty of God over the affairs of state with a limited, but real, popular sovereignty, given that 'no one individual has special authority

---

[50] By people like Mawdudi and Qutb

[51] Esposito (ed), *The Oxford Dictionary of Islam*, 287.

[52] Nanji, *Dictionary of Islam*, 167.

[53] Esposito (ed), *The Oxford Dictionary of Islam*, p.87.

[54] The summary of his views follow the account given in Bennett, *Muslims and Modernity*, 49-53. His detailed ideas can be seen in his study, *Islamic Law and Constitution* (Karachi: Jamaat-i-Islami Publications, 1955) and 'Political theory of Islam' in Khurshid Ahmad (ed), *Islam: Its Meaning and Message* (Leicester: the Islamic Foundation, 1976), 147-171.

to determine what is or is not the Islamic position'. He argues that the institution of the caliphate, which he wishes to revive, is invested ultimately in the whole Muslim community. However, one person (the *kalif* or *amir*, the one who 'commands the confidence of the largest number of people in respect of his knowledge and grasp of Islam') has to be nominated to exercise supreme authority. He (only males can be appointed) may be assisted by an elected consultative assembly (*majlis-i-shura*), which collaborates in the framing of regulations not covered by specific injunctions of the *shari'ah*, and by a group of men learned in Islamic law, who 'would scrutinise all proposals to ensure their conformity with the *shari'ah*'.

Mawdudi's model for an Islamic state makes an attempt to combine rule by *shari'ah* with limited democratic principles. However, it has been criticised on at least four counts. First, there is no real mechanism for a democratic process of holding such a regime to account. Secondly, non-Muslim subjects must accept that they have no right 'to influence the basic policy of this ideological state'.[55] Thirdly, the notion of an ideological state, meaning a state that upholds a comprehensive code of guidance based on divine law, sounds many alarm bells ringing in the context of twentieth century geo-politics. Fourthly, the exact nature of an Islamic state is not specified in detail. This has been one of the main complaints voiced against those who advocate the implementation of *shari'ah* in the modern world: there is a studied vagueness about the details of how such a society would function. In spite of Mawdudi's promotion of the participation of the people, there is little discussion of how serious, popular dissent would be handled. The model may look superficially attractive in the face of so many absolutist Islamic regimes, but the devil is in the details.

[55] Ahmad (ed), *Islam: Its Meaning and Message*, 167. This was written in 1939. Later, he allowed a limited role for non-Muslims in the governance of the state; see the footnote to his article, on 167.

Epilogue

The West and Religious Faith

We return finally to the main conclusions of Huntingdon's celebrated study. In his own words,

> The futures of both peace and Civilization depend upon understanding and cooperation among the political, spiritual, and intellectual leaders of the world's major civilizations.... In the...global real clash, between Civilization and barbarism, the world's great civilizations, with their rich accomplishments in religion, art, literature, philosophy, science, technology, morality and compassion, will also hang together or hang separately. In the emerging era, clashes of civilizations are the greatest threat to world peace, and an international order based on civilizations is the surest safeguard against world war.[1]

I understand Huntingdon to be accentuating several different factors. In the first place, we must know ourselves and the others. If a clash of civilisations, leading to serious military conflicts, is to be avoided, the people who have enjoyed the constructive fruits of Western civilization need to have a right understanding of their place in world history. In Huntington's opinion this involves one positive and one negative assessment. Positively, Western peoples should reengage productively with the distinguishing core of their civilisation, which is the Christian faith. Negatively, they should abstain from seeking to impose the values of their cultures on all other inhabitants of the planet. Civilisations come in different versions. Each has strong and weak points; none is so superior to the rest that its protagonists should strive to mould the others into its image.

Secondly, therefore, people who really wish to live in conciliation and harmony will need to appreciate and emphasise the best aspects of other peoples' cultures and seek to eliminate the worst features of their own. Huntington's book is directed towards the peoples of the West. He tells them that, although Western civilisation is unique, it is not universal. Its value lies in its uniqueness, not in its being a prototype for every other culture. [2] In comparison with other cultures, there is much that is wrong with the West. In

---

[1] *The Clash of Civilizations*, 321.

[2] *The Clash of Civilizations*, 311.

the thought of Vinoth Ramachandra, the West is too inclined to live on the basis of myths that it has absorbed into its cultural bloodstream: the myths of terrorism, the religious legitimation of violence, human rights as the foundation of morality, multiculturalism, science as the all-encompassing explanation of life and the remedy for human disease and folly. [3]

Other myths could be added: the myths of democracy, of the capitalist system as the solution to poverty, of the current policies of development aid, of pre-emptive military interventions, of a serious commitment to combating climate change, of an ideological commitment to rationalism and secularism. Huntington and other commentators he cites believe that Western civilization is probably in a state of terminal decline; he mentions a number of indicators of internal decay, associated with what might be called amoral or immoral lifestyle choices leading to dysfunctional social units throughout society. [4] However, he adds the caveat that 'many things are probable but nothing is inevitable'.[5]

Thirdly, Huntington sees the threat of the resurgence of barbarism throughout the world, manifested in 'failed states...a global crime wave, transnational mafias and drug cartels, increasing drug addiction in many societies, a general weakening of the family, a decline in trust and social solidarity in many countries...and rule by the gun prevalent in much of the world'. Huntington ends his book in a deeply pessimistic mood:

> On a worldwide basis Civilization seems in many respects to be yielding to barbarism, generating the image of an unprecedented phenomenon, a global Dark Ages, possibly descending on humanity.[6]

It must be evident, therefore, that the last event that the present world order needs is a clash of civilisations.

Fourthly, as a consequence, remaking the world order will require a profound reality check. For Huntington the most pressing need at the moment is a re-evaluation of the beneficial contributions of systems of belief based on a reality beyond the material world, in other words the formative religions of the nations. The West, in particular, is in grave danger of throwing out the baby of distinctive Christian values with the bath water of its inclination to dismiss all Christian truth claims as incredible. What is needed, he believes, is the exploration of beliefs held in common across civilisations, emphasizing and seeking to inculcate the highest ideals of each. This is not necessarily a straightforward task, as projects on 'global ethics' have demonstrated. In this

---

[3] *Subverting Global Myths: Theology and Public Issues Shaping Our World.*

[4] *The Clash of Civilizations,* 304.

[5] *The Clash of Civilizations*, 303.

[6] *The Clash of Civilizations,* 321.

study there is no space to examine such an inter-civilisational project as such. However, within its limited scope we may draw out a few indicators as to how the subject-matter of this book could yield some positive results for mitigating conflict and engaging with the issue of remaking the present world order.

Islam, the West and Christian faith

Ever since the *hijrah* of Muhammad and his first companions, Islam has been committed to and reliant upon a marriage with political power. However, for 12 years (610-622), Islam was the religion of a group of people, totally devoid of influence in the state, persuaded to believe in Allah and his messenger by the intrinsic power of the message alone. In the light of this beginning, and noting the circumstances in which their own community originally came into being, Christians are bound to ask Muslims two fundamental questions: why is the situation in Medina considered to have priority in determining the essence of Islam? What role, if any, do the circumstances of the Islamic community in Mecca play in formulating Muslims' attitudes to the relevance of their faith in contexts where Medina cannot function as a realistic model?

As we have already indicated, the questions raise the issue of how Muslims handle the reading of the Qur'an. Is it possible that parts of the Qur'an can be considered to be no longer literally applicable, because the conditions of their communication have changed completely? It is difficult, for example, to suggest that today Muslims in non-Muslim environments are being systematically persecuted for their faith. The argument that only Islamic rule can properly ensure and safeguard Islamic faith is difficult to maintain, when one quarter of all Muslims live in non-Muslim majority states. Moreover, if a faith could only survive truly when supported by political institutions, that would be a sign of its weakness and deficiency. May not Cragg be right, when he says, 'Islam is truer as a religion, when it was tested by verbal contradiction in Mecca than when sanctioned in Medina against sedition?' [7]

One might contrast Muhammad's exodus from Mecca and subsequent strategy in Medina with Paul's reaction, when people refused his message in Damascus (Acts 9.23-25), Pisidian Antioch (Acts 13.46-52), Iconium (Acts 14.5-7), Lystra (Acts 14.19-20), Philippi (Acts 16.19-24) and so on. It is true that on occasions Paul defends himself by appealing to his Roman citizenship, but he never considers the possibility of using force to defend or promote the message of the Gospel. As Cragg says, the strength of prophecy in the Bible lies in the fact that the prophets did not belong to the corridors of power. In this sense, from a Biblical perspective, it is difficult to see how Islam could be a recapitulation of the whole prophetic tradition, as it claims. In the Biblical

[7] 'The Finality of the Qur'an and the Contemporary Politics of Nations' in *Islam and the West*, 57.

tradition the prophet is not, by definition, either a statesman or military commander.[8] One of the most fundamental disagreements between the two world religions is over the nature of prophecy.

Cragg points out the high percentage of Muslims who now live outside Islamic states. He points out that their migration is opposite to the one ordered by Muhammad from Mecca to Medina. They have moved from a protected to an unprotected status. They live as Muslims in a situation akin to that of the early years in Mecca (the reality of jahiliyyah or ignorance of a world ruled by the one Lord God), but without persecution. They practise their religion without recourse to political power. Why, then, he asks, is it not possible to realise the ideals of Islam in a non-Muslim society? State sponsorship of religion confirms secular suspicions that religious belief is too weak to stand alone. It appears to show a fear of criticism, of equal rights under the law and of heresy. Moreover, it does not acknowledge fully the human integrity of other believers. If the state must procure the allegiance of believers, the truth claims of religion have no intrinsic, persuasive merit.

Finally, in the context of the discussion so far, we may ask whether there should be any limits to the extension of a secular culture. If one understands secular culture in terms of the operation of justice as impartiality towards all, irrespective of religious belief, social status, financial power, age, gender or ethnic identity then this has to be a fundamental value in an open and pluralist society. The state should not be seen to favour one set of beliefs over another; it should allow a conflict of interpretations to happen, but without violence, harassment or gratuitous offence. By the same token, it has no mandate for favouring secularism by promoting through legislation and publicity beliefs or values antagonistic to religion, implying that they are more acceptable in contemporary society than religious ones.

In the context of the tensions between religious faith and secular culture, Christians and Muslims may seek alliances in continuously challenging the fallacious belief, widely maintained in the West, that non-religious standpoints and attitudes are neutral and religious ones are, by definition, sectarian, partisan and narrow-minded.[9] On the contrary, as I have argued elsewhere, the underlying convictions that drive secular societies possess many of the

[8] The prophets represented an alternative mode of power in the world: the divine word of judgement against the abuse of political power and economic exploitation, and the willingness to *suffer violence without retaliation* in the cause of the message of justice, judgement, mercy and forgiveness. In the New Testament, the supreme example was the Messiah, Jesus, followed closely by his cousin John.

[9] See the concluding argument of Roger Trigg, 'The Illusion of Neutrality' in *Religion in Public Life*, 230-236.

hallmarks of belief systems. [10] This point has to be vigorously pressed home in Western societies, in order to overturn the default belief in the neutrality of a secular stance and to establish in the public mind the true nature of secularism's ideological status.

Terence Copley takes the discussion one stage further by arguing that the educational processes of Western nations are being used to indoctrinate young people into the tacit assumptions of secularism. [11] In other words, this latter has replaced Christianity as the assumed consensus belief of Western societies. Religions can be accommodated and tolerated as long as they abide by the implicit, cardinal code of behaviour of such societies, namely to reserve their beliefs and practices wholly to the personal and private world of voluntary organisations. [12] However, for different reasons, neither Christianity nor Islam can agree to such a convention. If Christianity tacitly allows itself to be neutralised by secularism, it is finished as a community with a prophetic message of judgement, grace and hope. Its own present conflict with the West, at the least, has to do with its being marginalised as a valid partner in the current debates about human flourishing, the shape of society and valid ethical norms. It has to be allowed to contribute its cumulative wisdom that springs from the existence of a reality beyond the material world. If the West is to avoid the same fate as other civilisations, namely a slow descent into an increasing ignorance about what constitutes the greatness and dignity of human beings, it should be willing to listen to critical voices that offer good reasons for not sharing the secular consensus.

The current dispute between sectors of Islam and Western secular culture highlights afresh a profound conflict of perspectives that, for the sake of the integrity of the respective ideologies involved, has to be played out. Muslims, it appears, can go in one of two directions. They can maintain an implacable hostility to the whole Western enterprise, and seek to undermine it, either from the outside by selective acts of *jihad*, aimed at symbolic targets of Western domination (cultural, economic and military) or from the inside by strengthening its own participation in the instruments of power. They may be tempted to believe that secular society, left to its own devices, will slowly eat its own tail and gradually drift into either anarchy or authoritarianism, neither of which would be sustainable in the long term. Muslims may surmise that by trying to live on the basis of the death of the gods or an unreflective agnosticism a secular society will eventually implode. Its moral and spiritual bankruptcy will ultimately overtake it. Whereupon, the community with the

---

[10] See, J. Andrew Kirk, 'Mission as dialogue: the case of secular faith', in *Mission under Scrutiny: Confronting Current Challenges.*

[11] See, *Indoctrination, Education and God: The Struggle for the Mind* (London: SPCK, 2005)

[12] See also, *Religion in Public Life,* 190-208.

most coherent response to the crisis will have the opportunity to direct its future path.

On the other hand, Muslims as a whole can revert to what can be interpreted as a purer version of their faith, by maintaining a strong witness to the liberating power of belief in one God, and to the destructive consequences for human life of all forms of idolatry. Can they see themselves, then, in their situation as a minority faith in the West, acting as a community that offers a better alternative to human living than that practised by the largely godless population in which they find themselves? Are they capable of discovering a political role in society, whose chief ambition, however remote, may not be the assumption of power?

From a Christian perspective, Muslims have both genuine and spurious reasons for criticising the West. In the case of democracy, to take one example, they would be right to find fault with the arrogant belief that the current Western form represents the best that is available. There is much that is wrong with Western democracy: for example, its lack of structures of accountability; the restricted means of accessing power; its tendency to centralisation; the lack of genuine representation; its culture of secretiveness; its proneness to over-legislation, and the perceived self-regard of its political class. Western democracy is in great need of a radical overhaul. Muslims, perhaps, can find within their own tradition, as we have been exploring, democratic principles that could aid such a renovation.

On the other hand, they would be wrong to dismiss democracy altogether, in the mistaken belief that it is totally incompatible with rule by God. There is also much that is laudable about democracy as an institution in its own right: for example, the equality it accords to all citizens; its putative openness to scrutiny; the opportunities it gives theoretically for participation and representation, and its denial of a distinction between rulers and ruled ('government of the people, by the people, for the people'). Can Muslims, then, participate fully, freely, and yet critically in the democratic processes that have come to fruition in the West, without any whiff of nostalgia for another kind of governance? There is evidence that a good number are already doing so.

The proposition that there is now, or may be in the not too distant future, a clash of civilisations cannot be dismissed lightly. It should not, however, be overstated. If such a clash is to be avoided or mitigated, for fear of the unpredictable destructive consequences that might ensue, the West has to re-negotiate its negative reaction to allowing, let alone encouraging, religiously inspired views to be fully aired in the public square. The present trend of constricting and constraining beliefs, held by self-appointed guardians of public value to be unacceptable, often without understanding or debate, is historically naive and, paradoxically, undemocratic. Both Muslims and Christians, sometimes for the same reasons and sometimes for different ones, have excellent grounds for finding current Western, secular assumptions to be superficial, unsophisticated and unsustainable. They long to find secularists and humanists who are genuinely willing to discuss the issues that divide contemporary societies (such as the existence of so-called 'faith' schools), without first having to clear away the kind of ignorant, prejudiced, distorted and one-sided anti-religious propaganda that usurps the place of proper, unbiased debate.

By the same token, Muslims will have to learn to live in a genuinely plural society. Convinced though they may be about the truth of their faith and its application to every aspect of life, they need to recognise that other people are equally assured of the truth and relevance of their divergent beliefs. Disputes are rarely settled satisfactorily through confrontation and combat. Muslims put themselves in danger of increasing hostility towards themselves by adopting what are perceived to be belligerent stances. It may be hard for people with strong convictions to live alongside or in contact with people who ignore or deny them. Nevertheless, it is part of sustaining a mature faith to learn how to accept the reality that other people, because they are people, have been given the freedom to choose their own way, even though it may cause them damage.

To fulfil their mission today in the West Christians, with renewed intellectual vigour and ethical integrity, have to reappraise the nature of the context in which they are called to bear witness to the enduring message of Jesus, the Messiah. To achieve this end they need to rediscover, as we have been intimating, their true prophetic heritage. The prophet's task is to discern the signs of the times, warn people of the dangers of ignoring God's liberating plan for his creation and tell the story of God's sacrificial love for every individual person.

Now, amongst some Christians, the prophetic message is restricted almost wholly to matters of social and political concern. Thus the prophetic task is interpreted to mean advocacy for policies, programmes and strategies of justice for the vulnerable outsiders of society. That is well and good; however, prophecy in its Biblical setting also deals with other issues. Its undertaking is to probe to the heart of a culture and engage it at the level of its deepest sentiments. It is charged with discerning the beliefs and activities that a people cherish most, and engaging with them, whether positively or negatively.

Prophetic ministry is not for the faint-hearted or for those who wish to experience a quiet life. It wishes to know and affirm the truth as the only force capable of arresting the long, slow descent into the anarchy of irresolvable, conflicting beliefs, ideas, theories and notions. Part of the process of engaging with the truth is by unmasking the illusions, fantasies, myths, fallacies and plain lies by which a people, individually or collectively, deceive themselves about the nature of reality. Western culture is increasingly inclined to invest in deceptions about its place and role in the world that need to be rigorously uncovered and contested. Naturally, first and foremost, Christians need to be entirely honest about themselves; God's judgement begins with the church. Repentance (the willingness to admit the truth of one's error) is, I believe, a necessary part of a new world order of understanding and forbearance.

Confession of mistakes and wrong-doing is not a sign of weakness, but of courage. The emancipating rule of God on earth begins with repentance:

> Jesus came…proclaiming the good news of God, and saying, 'The time is fulfilled, and the kingdom of God has come near; repent, and believe in the good news (Mark 1.14-15).

The Western world may still avert the catastrophe of a descent into a new barbarism, predicted by Huntington and others, if it is willing to take seriously the double truth of the prophetic message which proclaims,

> You felt secure in your wickedness; you said, 'No one sees me'. Your wisdom and your knowledge led you astray, and you said in your heart', I am, and there is no one besides me'. But evil shall come upon you, which you cannot charm away; disaster shall fall upon you, which you will not be able to ward off; and ruin shall come on you suddenly, of which you know nothing (Isaiah 47.10-11).

And, at the same time, it also announces,

> Thus says the Lord…:Do not fear, for I have redeemed you; I have called you by name, you are mine…You are precious in my sight, and honoured, and I love you (Isaiah 43.1, 4).

Selected Bibliography

Abu-Rabi, Ibrahim M. *The Blackwell Companion to Contemporary Islamic Thought.* Oxford: Blackwell, 2006.

Afsaruddin, Asma. *The First Muslims: History and Memory*. Oxford: One World, 2008.

Ahmad, Barakat. *Muhammad and the Jews: A Re-examination*. New Delhi: Vikas, 1979.

Ahmad, Khurshid. Ed. *Islam: Its Meaning and Message*. Leicester: The Islamic Foundation, 1980.

Ahmed, Akbar S. *Discovering Islam: Making Sense of Muslim History and Society.* London, Routledge, 1988.

Anderson, Norman. *Islam in the Modern World: A Christian Perspective*. Leicester: IVP, 1990.

Arkoun, Muhammad. *Islam: To Reform or to Subvert?* London: Saqi Books, 2006/2.

Armajani, Jon. *Dynamic Islam: Liberal Muslim Perspectives in a Transnational Age.* Lanham: University of America Press, 2004.

Armstrong, Karen. *Islam: A Short History*. London: Weidenfeld and Nicolson, 2000.

Asad, Muhammad. *The Principles of State and Government in Islam.* Gibraltar: Dar al-Andalus, 1980/2.

Asamoah-Gyadu, K. 'Prophecy'. In *Dictionary of Mission Theology: Evangelical Foundations*. John Corrie. Ed. Nottingham: IVP, 2007, 319-321.

Barnett, Paul. *Jesus and the Rise of Early Christianity: A History of New Testament Times*. Downers Grove: IVP, 1999.

Bauckham, Richard. *Jesus and the Eyewitnesses: The Gospels as Eyewitness Testimony.* Grand Rapids: Eerdmans, 2006

Beasley-Murray, George R. *John*. Word Biblical Commentary. Volume 36. Dallas: Word Incorporated, 1991.

Bell, Richard. *The Origin of Islam in Its Christian Environment.* London: Macmillan, 1926.

Bennett, Clinton. *Muslims and Modernity: An Introduction to the Issues and Debates.* London: Continuum, 2005.

Boase, Roger Ed. *Islam and Global Dialogue: Religious Pluralism and the Pursuit of Peace*. Aldershot: Ashgate Publishing, 2010.

Bosch, David. *Transforming Mission: Paradigm Shifts in Theology of Mission.* Maryknoll: Orbis Books, 1991.

Brown, Daniel. *A New Introduction to Islam*. Oxford: Blackwell, 2004.

Bryan, Christopher. *Render to Caesar: Jesus, the Early Church and the Roman Superpower*. Oxford: OUP, 2005.

Cameron, A. Ed. *The Byzantine and Early Islamic Near East.* Princeton: The Darwin Press, 1995.

Carson, D.A. *The Gospel according to John.* Leicester: Inter-Varsity Press, 1991.

Carter, Warren. *The Roman Empire and the New Testament: An Essential Guide.* Nashville: Abingdon Press, 2006.

Chaplin, Jonathan. *Talking God: The Legitimacy of Religious Public Reasoning.* London: Theos, 2008.

Charlesworth, J.H. *Jesus within Judaism*. London: SPCK, 1989.

Cooper, John, Nettler, Ronald and Mohamed Mahmoud. Eds. *Islam and Modernity: Muslim Intellectuals Respond*. London: I.B.Taurus, 1998.

Copley, Terence. *Indoctrination, Education and God: The Struggle for the Mind*. London: SPCK, 2005.

Corrie, John. Ed. *Dictionary of Mission Theology: Evangelical Foundations*. Nottingham: IVP, 2007.

Cragg, Kenneth. *The House of Islam*. Belmont, CA: Wadsworth, 1975.

_____. *Muhammad and the Christian: A Question of Response*. London: Darton, Longman and Todd, 1984.

_____. *Muhammad in the Quran: The Task and the Text*. London: Melisende, 2001.

_____. *The Qur'an and the West: Some Minding Between*. London: Melisende, 2005.

Davidson, Ivor J. *The Birth of the Church: From Jesus to Constantine (AD 30-312)*. Vol. I. Grand Rapids: Baker Books, 2004.

D'Costa, Gavin. 'Engaging with a "Clash of Civilisations": Liberal Views of Religion in the Public Domain and Catholic Approaches'. *Studies in Interreligious Dialogue* 17: 1 (2007), 36-39.

Donohue, John J. and Esposito, John L, Eds. *Islam in Transition: Muslim Perspectives*. New York: OUP, 1982.

El-Affendi, Abdelwahab. 'Hasan Turabi and the Limits of Modern Islamic Reformism'. In *The Blackwell Companion to Contemporary Islamic Thought*. Ibrahim M. Abu-Rabi. Ed. Oxford. B;ackwell. 2006. 145-156.

Elias, Norbert. The Civilizing Process. Vol. I: The History of Manners. Oxford: Basil Blackwell, 1978.

Engineer, Asghar Ali. 'Islam and Secularism'. *The Blackwell Companion to Contemporary Islamic Thought*. Ibrahim M. Abu-Rabi. Ed. Oxford. Blackwell. 2006. 338-344.

Esack, Farid. *Qur'an, Liberation and Pluralism: An Islamic Perspective of Interreligious Solidarity against Oppression*. Oxford: One World, 1997.

Esposito, John L. *Islam: The Straight Path*. Oxford: OUP 1991/2.

_____. Ed. *The Oxford Dictionary of Islam*. Oxford: OUP, 2003.

Finley, M. I. *The Legacy of Greece: A New Appraisal*. Oxford: Clarendon Press, 1981.

Flusser, David. *Jesus*. New York: Herder and Herder, 1969.

Forrest, Robert, 'Love of Enemies in the Age of Constantine'. Craig A. Smith. Ed. *The Cross at the Crossroads: Loving our Enemies in the Twenty-first Century*. Manila: OMF, 2008.

Fukuyama, Francis. *The End of History and the Last Man*. London: Hamish Hamilton, 1992.

Geaves, Ron. *Aspects of Islam*. London: Darton, Longman and Todd, 2005.

Geaves, Ron, Gabriel Theodore, Haddad, Yvonne and Smith, Jane Idleman, Eds. *Islam and the West Post 9/11*. Aldershot: Ashgate Publishing, 2004.

Gorringe, T.J. *Furthering Humanity: A Theology of Culture*. Aldershot: Ashgate Publishing, 2004.

Haleem, M.A.S. Abdel. *The Qur'an: A New Translation*. Oxford, OUP, 2004.

Hallaq, Wael. *A History of Islamic Legal Theories: An Introduction to Sunni Usul al-fiqh*. Cambridge: CUP, 1999.

Hawthorne, Gerald F., Martin, Ralph P., Reid Daniel G., Eds. *Dictionary of Paul and His Letters*. Leicester: IVP, 1993.

Hazlett, Ian. *Early Christianity: Origins and Evolution to AD 600*. London: SPCK, 1991.

Hiebert, Paul G. *Anthropological Insights for Missionaries*. Grand Rapids: Baker Book House, 1985.

Hinnells, John R., Ed. *A Handbook of Living Religions*. London: Penguin Books, 1991.

Hitti, Philip K. Islam: *A Way of Life*. Minneapolis: University of Minnesota Press, 1970.

Hollenweger, Walter J. 'Prophecy'. *Dictionary of Mission: Theology, History, Perspectives*. Karl Muller, Theo Sundermeier, Stephen Bevans, and Richard Bliese, Eds. Maryknoll: Orbis Books, 1998.

Horsley, Richard A. Ed. *Paul and Empire: Religion and Power in Roman Imperial Society*. Harrisburg: Trinity Press International, 1997.

_____. Ed. *Paul and Politics: Ekklesia, Israel, Imperium, Interpretation*. Harrisburg: Trinity Press International, 2000.

Hourani, Albert. *Islam in European Thought*. Cambridge: CUP, 1991.

Huntington, Samuel P. *The Clash of Civilisations and the Remaking of World Order*. London: Simon and Schuster, 1998.

Ishaq, Ibn. *The Life of Muhammad: Apostle of Allah*. London: The Folio Society, 2003.

Judge, E .A. 'Rank and Status in the World of the Caesars and St Paul'. *Social Distinctive of the Christians in the First Century: Pivotal Essays by E.A. Judge*. David M. Scholer. Ed. Peabody, MA: Hendrickson, 2008.

Kaldun, Ibn. *The Muqaddimah: An Introduction to History*. Princeton: Princeton University Press, 1967.

Kamali, M.H. 'The Limits of Power in an Islamic State'. *Islamic Studies* 28:4 (1989).

Kim, Seyoon. *Christ and Caesar: The Gospel and the Roman Empire in the Writings of Paul and Luke*. Grand Rapids: Eerdmans, 2008.

Kirk, J. Andrew. *The Meaning of Freedom: A Study of Secular, Muslim and Christian Views*. Carlisle: Paternoster Press, 1998.

_____. *Mission under Scrutiny: Confronting Current Challenges*. London: Darton, Longman and Todd, 2006.

_____. *The Future of Reason, Science and Faith: Following Modernity and Post-modernity*. Aldershot: Ashgate, 2007.

Kreider, Alan. Ed. *The Origins of Christendom in the West*. Edinburgh: T and T Clark, 2001.

E. Landau-Tasseron. 'Features of the Pre-Conquest Muslim Army in the time of Muhammad'. In A. Cameron. Ed. *The Byzantine and Early Islamic Near East*. Princeton: The Darwin Press, 1995.

Lane, Jan-Erik and Redissi, Hamadi. *Religion and Politics: Islam and Muslim Civilization*. Aldershot: Ashgate Publishing, 2009.

Leirvik, Oddbjorn. *Images of Jesus Christ in Islam*. Uppsala: Swedish Institute of Missionary Research, 1999.

Lyons, Jonathan. *The House of Wisdom: How the Arabs transformed Western Civilization*. London: Bloomsbury, 2008.

Martin, David. *On Secularization: Towards a Revised Grand Theory*. Aldershot: Ashgate Publishing, 2005.

Martin, Richard C. *Approaches to Islam in Religious Studies*. Oxford: One World, 2001/2.

Mawdudi, Syed Abu'l A'la. *The Islamic Way of Life*. Leicester: The Islamic Foundation, 1986.

McAuliffe, Jane Dammen. Ed. *The Cambridge Companion to The Qur'an*. Cambridge: CUP, 2006.

McCarthy, Justin. *The Population of Palestine*. New York: Columbia University Press, 1990.

McKechnie, Paul. *The First Christian Centuries: Perspectives on the Early Church*. Leicester: IVP. 2001.

Merk, Frederick and Bannister, Kerm Lois. *Manifest Destiny and Mission in American History*. Grand Rapids: Eerdmans, 1995.

Moltmann, Jurgen. *The Way of Jesus Christ: Christology in Messianic Dimensions*. London: SCM Press, 1990.

Muller, Karl, Sundermeier, Theo, Bevans, Stephen B., Bliese, Richard H. Eds. *Dictionary of Mission: Theology, History, Perspectives*. Maryknoll: Orbis Books, 1998.

Murray, Stuart. *Post-Christendom: Church and Mission in a Strange New World*. Milton Keynes: Paternoster, 2004.

Nanji, Azim. *The Penguin Dictionary of Islam*. London: Penguin Books, 2008.

Nasr, Seyyed Hossein. *Ideals and Realities of Islam*. ABC International Group, 2000.

_____. *The Heart of Islam: Enduring Values for Humanity*. New York: HarperCollins, 2002.

Nazir Ali, Michael. *Conviction and Conflict: Islam, Christianity and World Order*. London: Continuum, 2006.

Newbigin, Lesslie. *Foolishness to the Greeks: The Gospel and Western Culture*. London: SPCK, 1986.

_____. *Truth to Tell: The Gospel as Public Truth*. Grand Rapids: Eerdmans, 1991.

Norcliffe, David. *Islam: Faith and Practice*. Brighton: Sussex Academic Press, 1999.

Northcott, Michael. *An Angel Directs the Storm: Apocalyptic Religion and American Empire*. London: SCM Press,2007.

O'Donovan, Oliver. *The Desire of the Nations: Rediscovering the Roots of Political Theology*. Cambridge: CUP, 1996.

Orwell, George. *Nineteen Eighty-Four*. London: Secker and Warburg, 1949.

Peters, R. *Jihad in Classical and Modern Islam*. Princeton, NJ: Princeton University Press, 1996.

Rahman, Fazlur. *Islam*. London: 1961.

_____. *Islam and Modernity: Transformation of an Intellectual Tradition*. Chicago: University of Chicago Press, 1982.

_____. *Revival and Reform in Islam*. Ebrahim Moosa. Ed. Oxford: Oneworld Publications, 1999.

_____. 'The Islamic Concept of the State'. *Islam in Transition: Muslim Perspectives*. John J. Donohue and John L. Esposito. Eds. New York: OUP, 1982.

Ramachandra, Vinoth. *Subverting Global Myths: Theology and the Public Issues Shaping our World*. London: SPCK, 2008.

Ramadan, Tariq. *Western Muslims and the Future of Islam*. Oxford: OUP, 2004.

_____. The Messenger: The Meanings of the Life of Muhammad. London: Allen Lane, 2007.

_____. *Radical Reform: Islamic Ethics and Liberation*. Oxford: OUP, 2009.

Rees, Phil. *Dining with Terrorists: Meetings with the World's Most Wanted Militants*. Basingstoke: Pan Books, 2006.

Reuther, Rosemary Radford. *America, Amerikkka: Elect Nation and Imperial Violence.* London: Equinox, 2007.

Riches, J. *Jesus and the Transformation of Judaism.* London: Darton, Longman and Todd, 1980.

Riddell, Peter G. and Cotterell, Peter. *Islam in Context: Past, Present and Future.* Grand Rapids: Baker Academic, 2003.

Rippen, Andrew. *Muslims: Their Religious Beliefs and Practices.* London: Routledge, 2001.

Rowland, Christopher. *Christian Origins: The Setting of the Character of the Most Important Messianic Sect of Judaism.* London: SPCK, 2002/2.

Ruthven, Malise. *Islam in the World.* London: Granta Books, 2006/3.

Sadri, Mahmoud and Sadri, Ahmad. *Reason, Freedom and Democracy in Islam: The Essential Writings of Abdolkarin Soroush.* Oxford: OUP, 2000.

Saeed, Abdullah. *Interpreting the Qur'an: Towards a contemporary approach.* London: Routledge, 2006.

Said, Edward W. *Orientalism.* New York: Pantheon Books, 1978.

Sanders, E.P. *Jesus and Judaism.* London: SCM Press, 1985.

Sanneh, Lamin, '*Shari'ah* Sanctions and State Enforcement: A Nigerian Islamic Debate and an Intellectual Critique'. *Islam and the West Post 9/11.* Ron Geaves, Theodore Gabriel, Yvonne Haddad and Smith, Jane Idleman, Eds. Aldershot: Ashgate Publishing, 2004. 146-165.

_____. *Whose Religion is Christianity? The Gospel Beyond the West.* Grand Rapids: Eerdmans, 2003.

Scholer, David M. Ed. *Social Distinctive of the Christians in the First Century: Pivotal Essays by E.A. Judge.* Peabody, MA: Hendrickson, 2008.

Sen, Amartya. *Identity and Violence: The Illusion of Destiny.* London: Penguin Books, 2007.

Singh, David Emmanuel. Ed. Jesus and the Cross: Reflections of Christians from Islamic Contexts. Oxford: Regnum Books, 2008.

Schnabel, Eckhard. *Paul the Missionary: Realities, Strategies and Methods.* Downers Grove: Intervarsity Press, 2008.

Sobrino, Jon. *Christology at the Crossroads: A Latin American Approach.* London: SCM Press, 1978.

Spengler, Oswald. *The Decline of the West.* Arthur Helps, and Helmut Werner. Eds. Trans. Charles F. Atkinson. New York: OUP, 1991.

Stanton, Graham. *Jesus and the Gospel.* Cambridge: CUP, 2004.

Stark, Rodney. *The Rise of Christianity: A Sociologist Reconsiders Christianity.* Princeton: Princeton Univ. Press, 1996.

Storkey, Alan. *Jesus and Politics: Confronting the Powers.* Grand Rapids: Baker Academic, 2005.

Taji-Faraki, Suha and Nafi, Basheer M. *Islamic Thought in the Twentieth Century.* London: I.B. Taurus, 2004.

Tallentyre, S.G. *The Friends of Voltaire.* London: G.P. Putnam's Sons, 1910.

Taylor, Charles. *A Secular Age.* Cambridge, MA: Harvard University Press, 2007.

Tidball, D.J. 'Social Setting of Mission Churches'. *Dictionary of Paul and His Letters.* Gerald F. Hawthorne, Ralph P. Martin and Daniel G. Reid. Eds. Leicester: IVP, 1993. 883-892.

Toynbee, Arnold. *A Study of History.* Oxford: OUP, 1946.

Trigg, Roger. Rationality and Religion: Does Faith need Reason? Oxford: Blackwell, 1998.

_____. *Religion in Public Life: Must Faith Be Privatized*? Oxford: OUP, 2007.

Tucker, Robert C. *The Marx-Engels Reader*. New York: W.W. Norton, 1972.

Turabi, H. 'Principles of Governance, Freedom and Responsibility in Islam'. *The American Journal of Islamic Social Sciences* 4:1 (1987).

Vermes, G. *Jesus the Jew*. London: Collins, 1973.

Watt, Montgomery. *Islam and the Integration of Society*. London: Routledge and Kegan Paul, 1961.

Witherington III, Ben. *New Testament History: A Narrative Account*. Carlisle: Paternoster Press, 2001.

Wright, N.T. *The New Testament and the People of God*. London: SPCK, 1992.

_____. *Jesus and the Victory of God*. London: SPCK, 1996.

_____. *The Resurrection of the Son of God*. Minneapolis: Fortress Press, 2003.

_____. Paul: Fresh Perspectives. London: SPCK, 2005.

Yoder, John Howard. *The Politics of Jesus: Vicit Agnus Noster*. Grand Rapids: Eerdmans, 1972.

Zayd, Nasr Hamid Abu. 'Divine Attributes in the Qur'an: Some Poetic Aspects'. *Islam and Modernity: Muslim Intellectuals Respond*. John Cooper, Ronald Nettler and Mohamed Mahmoud. Eds. London: I.B.Taurus, 1998.

Zeitlen, Irving M. *The Historical Muhammad*. Cambridge: Polity Press, 2007.

Index

REGNUM EDINBURGH 2010 SERIES
Series Listing

David A. Kerr, Kenneth R. Ross (eds.)
Edinburgh 2010
Mission Then and Now
2009 / 978-1-870345-73-6 / xiv + 343pp (paperback)
2009 / 978-1-870345-76-7 / xiv + 343pp (hardback)

No one can hope to fully understand the modern Christian missionary movement without engaging substantially with the World Missionary Conference, held at Edinburgh in 1910. As the centenary of the Conference approaches, the time is ripe to examine its meaning in light of the past century and the questions facing Christian witness today. This book is the first to systematically examine the eight Commissions which reported to Edinburgh 1910 and gave the conference much of its substance and enduring value. It will deepen and extend the reflection being stimulated by the upcoming centenary and will kindle the missionary imagination for 2010 and beyond.

Daryl M. Balia, Kirsteen Kim (eds.)
Edinburgh 2010
Witnessing to Christ Today
2010 / 978-1-870345-77-4 / xiv +301pp

This volume, the second in the Edinburgh 2010 series, includes reports of the nine main study groups working on different themes for the celebration of the centenary of the World Missionary Conference, Edinburgh 1910. Their collaborative work brings together perspectives that are as inclusive as possible of contemporary world Christianity and helps readers to grasp what it means in different contexts to be 'witnessing to Christ today'.

Claudia Währisch-Oblau, Fidon Mwombeki (eds.)
Mission Continues
Global Impulses for the 21st Century
2010 / 978-1-870345-82-8 / 271pp

In May 2009, 35 theologians from Asia, Africa and Europe met in Wuppertal, Germany, for a consultation on mission theology organized by the United Evangelical Mission: Communion of 35 Churches in Three Continents. The aim was to participate in the 100th anniversary of the Edinburgh conference through a study process and reflect on the challenges for mission in the 21st century. This book brings together these papers written by experienced practitioners from around the world.

Brian Woolnough and Wonsuk Ma (Eds)
Holistic Mission
God's plan for God's people
2010 / 978-1-870345-85-9

Holistic mission, or integral mission, implies God is concerned with the whole person, the whole community, body, mind and spirit. This book discusses the meaning of the holistic gospel, how it has developed, and implications for the the church. . It takes a global, eclectic approach, with 19 writers, all of whom have much experience in, and commitment to, holistic mission. It addresses critically and honestly one of the most exciting, and challenging, issues facing the church today. To be part of God's plan for God's people, the church must take holistic mission to the world.

REGNUM STUDIES IN GLOBAL CHRISTIANITY

(Previously GLOBAL THEOLOGICAL VOICES series)

Series Listing

David Emmanuuel Singh (ed.)

Jesus and the Cross

Reflections of Christians from Islamic Contexts

2008 / 978-1-870345-65-1 / x + 226pp

The Cross reminds us that the sins of the world are not borne through the exercise of power but through Jesus Christ's submission to the will of the Father. The papers in this volume are organised in three parts: scriptural, contextual and theological. The central question being addressed is: how do Christians living in contexts, where Islam is a majority or minority religion, experience, express or think of the Cross? This is, therefore, an exercise in listening. As the contexts from where these engagements arise are varied, the papers in drawing scriptural, contextual and theological reflections offer a cross-section of Christian thinking about Jesus and the Cross.

Sung-wook Hong

Naming God in Korea

The Case of Protestant Christianity

2008 / 978-1-870345-66-8 / xiv + 170pp

Since Christianity was introduced to Korea more than a century ago, one of the most controversial issue has been the Korean term for the Christian 'God'. This issue is not merely about naming the Christian God in Korean language, but it relates to the question of theological contextualization—the relationship between the gospel and culture—and the question of Korean Christian identity. This book examines the theological contextualization of the concept of 'God' in the contemporary Korean context and applies the translatability of Christianity to that context. It also demonstrates the nature of the gospel in relation to cultures, i.e., the universality of the gospel expressed in all human cultures.

Hubert van Beek (ed.)

Revisioning Christian Unity

The Global Christian Forum

2009 / 978-1-870345-74-3 / xx + 288pp

This book contains the records of the Global Christian Forum gathering held in Limuru near Nairobi, Kenya, on 6 – 9 November 2007 as well as the papers presented at that historic event. Also included are a summary of the Global Christian Forum process from its inception until the 2007 gathering and the reports of the evaluation of the process that was carried out in 2008.

Paul Hang-Sik Cho
Eschatology and Ecology
Experiences of the Korean Church
2010 / 978-1-870345-75-0/ 260pp (approx)

This book raises the question of why Korean people, and Korean Protestant Christians in particular, pay so little attention (in theory or practice) to ecological issues. The author argues that there is an important connection (or elective affinity) between this lack of attention and the other-worldly eschatology that is so dominant within Korean Protestant Christianity. Dispensational premillennialism, originally imported by American missionaries, resonated with traditional religious beliefs in Korea and soon came to dominate much of Korean Protestantism. This book argues that this, of all forms of millennialism, is the most damaging to ecological concerns.

Dietrich Werner, David Esterline, Namsoon Kang, Joshva Raja (eds.)
The Handbook of Theological Education in World Christianity
Theological Perspectives, Ecumenical Trends, Regional Surveys
2010 / 978-1-870345-80-4/ 759pp

This major reference work is the first ever comprehensive study of Theological Education in Christianity of its kind. With contributions from over 90 international scholars and church leaders, it aims to be easily accessible across denominational, cultural, educational, and geographic boundaries. The Handbook will aid international dialogue and networking among theological educators, institutions, and agencies. The major objectives of the text are (1) to provide introductory surveys on selected issues and themes in global theological education; (2) to provide regional surveys on key developments, achievements, and challenges in theological education; (3) to provide an overview of theological education for each of the major denominational / confessional traditions; and (4) to provide a reference section with an up-to-date list of the regional associations of theological institutions and other resources.

David Emmanuel Singh & Bernard C Farr (eds.)
Christianity and Education
Shaping of Christian Context in Thinking
2010 / 978-1-870345-81-1/ 244pp (approx)

Christianity and Education is a collection of papers published in *Transformation: An International Journal of Holistic Mission Studies* over a period of 15 years. It brings to life some of the papers that lay buried in shelves and in disparate volumes of *Transformation,* under a single volume for theological libraries, students and teachers. The articles here represent a spectrum of Christian thinking addressing issues of institutional development for theological education, theological studies in the context of global mission, contextually aware/informed education, and academies which deliver such education, methodologies and personal reflections.

REGNUM STUDIES IN MISSION
Series Listing

Kwame Bediako

Theology and Identity

The Impact of Culture upon Christian Thought in the Second Century and in Modern Africa

1992 / 1-870345-10-X / xviii + 508pp

The author examines the question of Christian identity in the context of the Graeco–Roman culture of the early Roman Empire. He then addresses the modern African predicament of quests for identity and integration.

Christopher Sugden

Seeking the Asian Face of Jesus

The Practice and Theology of Christian Social Witness in Indonesia and India 1974–1996

1997 / 1-870345-26-6 / xx + 496pp

This study focuses on contemporary holistic mission with the poor in India and Indonesia combined with the call to transformation of all life in Christ with micro-credit enterprise schemes. 'The literature on contextual theology now has a new standard to rise to' – Lamin Sanneh (Yale University, USA).

Hwa Yung

Mangoes or Bananas?

The Quest for an Authentic Asian Christian Theology

1997 / 1-870345-25-8 / xii + 274pp

Asian Christian thought remains largely captive to Greek dualism and Enlightenment rationalism because of the overwhelming dominance of Western culture. Authentic contextual Christian theologies will emerge within Asian Christianity with a dual recovery of confidence in culture and the gospel.

Keith E. Eitel

Paradigm Wars

The Southern Baptist International Mission Board Faces the Third Millennium

1999 / 1-870345-12-6 / x + 140pp

The International Mission Board of the Southern Baptist Convention is the largest denominational mission agency in North America. This volume chronicles the historic and contemporary forces that led to the IMB's recent extensive reorganization, providing the most comprehensive case study to date of a historic mission agency restructuring to continue its mission purpose into the twenty-first century more effectively.

Samuel Jayakumar

Dalit Consciousness and Christian Conversion

Historical Resources for a Contemporary Debate

1999 / 81-7214-497-0 / xxiv + 434pp

(Published jointly with ISPCK)

The main focus of this historical study is social change and transformation among the Dalit Christian communities in India. Historiography tests the evidence in the light of the conclusions of the modern Dalit liberation theologians.

Vinay Samuel and Christopher Sugden (eds.)

Mission as Transformation

A Theology of the Whole Gospel

1999 / 0870345133/ 522pp

This book brings together in one volume twenty five years of biblical reflection on mission practice with the poor from around the world. The approach of holistic mission, which integrates proclamation, evangelism, church planting and social transformation seamlessly as a whole, has been adopted since 1983 by most evangelical development agencies, most indigenous mission agencies and many Pentecostal churches. This volume helps anyone understand how evangelicals, struggling to unite evangelism and social action, found their way in the last twenty five years to the biblical view of mission in which God calls all human beings to love God and their neighbour; never creating a separation between the two.

Christopher Sugden

Gospel, Culture and Transformation

2000 / 1-870345-32-0 / viii + 152pp

A Reprint, with a New Introduction, of Part Two of Seeking the Asian Face of Jesus

Gospel, Culture and Transformation explores the practice of mission especially in relation to transforming cultures and communities. - 'Transformation is to enable God's vision of society to be actualised in all relationships: social, economic and spiritual, so that God's will may be reflected in human society and his love experienced by all communities, especially the poor.'

Bernhard Ott

Beyond Fragmentation: Integrating Mission and Theological Education

A Critical Assessment of some Recent Developments
in Evangelical Theological Education

2001 / 1-870345-14-2 / xxviii + 382pp

Beyond Fragmentation is an enquiry into the development of Mission Studies in evangelical theological education in Germany and German-speaking Switzerland between 1960 and 1995. The author undertakes a detailed examination of the paradigm shifts which have taken place in recent years in both the theology of mission and the understanding of theological education.

Gideon Githiga

The Church as the Bulwark against Authoritarianism

Development of Church and State Relations in Kenya, with Particular Reference to the Years after Political Independence 1963-1992

2002 / 1-870345-38-x / xviii + 218pp

'All who care for love, peace and unity in Kenyan society will want to read this careful history by Bishop Githiga of how Kenyan Christians, drawing on the Bible, have sought to share the love of God, bring his peace and build up the unity of the nation, often in the face of great difficulties and opposition.' Canon Dr Chris Sugden, Oxford Centre for Mission Studies.

Myung Sung-Hoon, Hong Young-Gi (eds.)

Charis and Charisma

David Yonggi Cho and the Growth of Yoido Full Gospel Church

2003 / 1-870345-45-2 / xxii + 218pp

This book discusses the factors responsible for the growth of the world's largest church. It expounds the role of the Holy Spirit, the leadership, prayer, preaching, cell groups and creativity in promoting church growth. It focuses on God's grace (charis) and inspiring leadership (charisma) as the two essential factors and the book's purpose is to present a model for church growth worldwide.

Samuel Jayakumar

Mission Reader

Historical Models for Wholistic Mission in the Indian Context

2003 / 1-870345-42-8 / x + 250pp

(Published jointly with ISPCK)

This book is written from an evangelical point of view revalidating and reaffirming the Christian commitment to wholistic mission. The roots of the 'wholistic mission' combining 'evangelism and social concerns' are to be located in the history and tradition of Christian evangelism in the past; and the civilizing purpose of evangelism is compatible with modernity as an instrument in nation building.

Bob Robinson

Christians Meeting Hindus

An Analysis and Theological Critique of the Hindu-Christian Encounter in India

2004 / 1-870345-39-8 / xviii + 392pp

This book focuses on the Hindu-Christian encounter, especially the intentional meeting called dialogue, mainly during the last four decades of the twentieth century, and specifically in India itself.

Gene Early

Leadership Expectations

How Executive Expectations are Created and Used in a Non-Profit Setting

2005 / 1-870345-30-4 / xxiv + 276pp

The author creates an Expectation Enactment Analysis to study the role of the Chancellor of the University of the Nations-Kona, Hawaii. This study is grounded in the field of managerial work, jobs, and behaviour and draws on symbolic interactionism, role theory, role identity theory and enactment theory. The result is a conceptual framework for developing an understanding of managerial roles.

Tharcisse Gatwa

The Churches and Ethnic Ideology in the Rwandan Crises 1900-1994

2005 / 1-870345-24-X / approx 300pp

Since the early years of the twentieth century Christianity has become a new factor in Rwandan society. This book investigates the role Christian churches played in the formulation and development of the racial ideology that culminated in the 1994 genocide.

Julie Ma

Mission Possible

Biblical Strategies for Reaching the Lost

2005 / 1-870345-37-1 / xvi + 142pp

This is a missiology book for the church which liberates missiology from the specialists for the benefit of every believer. It also serves as a textbook that is simple and friendly, and yet solid in biblical interpretation. This book links the biblical teaching to the actual and contemporary missiological settings with examples, making the Bible come alive to the reader.

Allan Anderson, Edmond Tang (eds.)

Asian and Pentecostal

The Charismatic Face of Christianity in Asia

2005 / 1-870345-43-6 / xiv + 596pp

(Published jointly with APTS Press)

This book provides a thematic discussion and pioneering case studies on the history and development of Pentecostal and Charismatic churches in the countries of South Asia, South East Asia and East Asia.

I. Mark Beaumont

Christology in Dialogue with Muslims

A Critical Analysis of Christian Presentations of Christ for Muslims from the Ninth and Twentieth Centuries

2005 / 1-870345-46-0 / xxvi + 228pp

This book analyses Christian presentations of Christ for Muslims in the most creative periods of Christian-Muslim dialogue, the first half of the ninth century and the second half of the twentieth century. In these two periods, Christians made serious attempts to present their faith in Christ in terms that take into account Muslim perceptions of him, with a view to bridging the gap between Muslim and Christian convictions.

Thomas Czövek,

Three Seasons of Charismatic Leadership

A Literary-Critical and Theological Interpretation of the Narrative of Saul, David and Solomon

2006 / 978-1-870345484 / 272pp

This book investigates the charismatic leadership of Saul, David and Solomon. It suggests that charismatic leaders emerge in crisis situations in order to resolve the crisis by the charisma granted by God. Czovek argues that Saul proved himself as a charismatic leader as long as he acted resolutely and independently from his mentor Samuel. In the author's eyes, Saul's failure to establish himself as a charismatic leader is caused by his inability to step out from Samuel's shadow.

Jemima Atieno Oluoch

The Christian Political Theology of Dr. John Henry Okullu

2006 / 1-870345-51-7 / xx + 137pp

This book reconstructs the Christian political theology of Bishop John Henry Okullu, DD, through establishing what motivated him and the biblical basis for his socio-political activities. It also attempts to reconstruct the socio-political environment that nurtured Dr Okullu's prophetic ministry.

Richard Burgess

Nigeria's Christian Revolution

The Civil War Revival and Its Pentecostal Progeny (1967-2006)

2008 / 978-1-870345-63-7 / xxii + 347pp

This book describes the revival that occurred among the Igbo people of Eastern Nigeria and the new Pentecostal churches it generated, and documents the changes that have occurred as the movement has responded to global flows and local demands. As such, it explores the nature of revivalist and Pentecostal experience, but does so against the backdrop of local socio-political and economic developments, such as decolonisation and civil war, as well as broader processes, such as modernisation and globalisation.

David Emmanuel Singh & Bernard C Farr (eds.)
Christianity and Cultures
Shaping Christian Thinking in Context
2008 / 978-1-870345-69-9 / x + 260pp

This volume marks an important milestone, the 25th anniversary of the Oxford Centre for Mission Studies (OCMS). The papers here have been exclusively sourced from Transformation, a quarterly journal of OCMS, and seek to provide a tripartite view of Christianity's engagement with cultures by focusing on the question: how is Christian thinking being formed or reformed through its interaction with the varied contexts it encounters? The subject matters include different strands of theological-missiological thinking, socio-political engagements and forms of family relationships in interaction with the host cultures.

Tormod Engelsviken, Ernst Harbakk, Rolv Olsen, Thor Strandenæs (eds.)
Mission to the World
Communicating the Gospel in the 21st Century:
Essays in Honour of Knud Jørgensen
2008 / 978-1-870345-64-4 / 472pp

Knud Jørgensen is Director of Areopagos and Associate Professor of Missiology at MF Norwegian School of Theology. This book reflects on the main areas of Jørgensen's commitment to mission. At the same time it focuses on the main frontier of mission, the world, the content of mission, the Gospel, the fact that the Gospel has to be communicated, and the context of contemporary mission in the 21st century.

Al Tizon
Transformation after Lausanne
Radical Evangelical Mission in Global-Local Perspective
2008 / 978-1-870345-68-2 / xx + 281pp

After Lausanne '74, a worldwide network of radical evangelical mission theologians and practitioners use the notion of "Mission as Transformation" to integrate evangelism and social concern together, thus lifting theological voices from the Two Thirds World to places of prominence. This book documents the definitive gatherings, theological tensions, and social forces within and without evangelicalism that led up to Mission as Transformation. And it does so through a global-local grid that points the way toward greater holistic mission in the 21st century.

Bambang Budijanto

Values and Participation

Development in Rural Indonesia

2009 / 978-1-870345-70-5 / x + 237pp

Socio-religious values and socio-economic development are inter-dependant, inter-related and are constantly changing in the context of macro political structures, economic policy, religious organizations and globalization; and micro influences such as local affinities, identity, politics, leadership and beliefs. The three Lopait communities in Central Java, Indonesia provide an excellent model of the rich and complex negotiations and interactions among all the above factors. The book argues that the comprehensive approach in understanding the socio-religious values of each local community is essential to accurately describing their respective identity which will help institutions and agencies, both governmental and non-governmental, to relate to these communities with dignity and respect.

Young-hoon Lee

The Holy Spirit Movement in Korea

Its Historical and Theological Development

2009 / 978-1-870345-67-5 / x + 174pp

This book traces the historical and theological development of the Holy Spirit Movement in Korea through six successive periods (from 1900 to the present time). These periods are characterized by repentance and revival (1900-20), persecution and suffering under Japanese occupation (1920-40), confusion and division (1940-60), explosive revival in which the Pentecostal movement played a major role in the rapid growth of Korean churches (1960-80), the movement reaching out to all denominations (1980-2000), and the new context demanding the Holy Spirit movement to open new horizons in its mission engagement (2000-). The volume also discusses the relationship between this movement and other religions such as shamanism, and looks forward to further engagement with issues of concern in wider society.

Alan R. Johnson

Leadership in a Slum

A Bangkok Case Study

2009 / 978-1-870345-71-2 xx + 238pp

This book looks at leadership in the social context of a slum in Bangkok from an angle different from traditional studies which measure well educated Thais on leadership scales derived in the West. Using both systematic data collection and participant observation, it develops a culturally preferred model as well as a set of models based in Thai concepts that reflect on-the-ground realities. This work challenges the dominance of the patron-client rubric for understanding all forms of Thai leadership and offers a view for understanding leadership rooted in local social systems, contrary to approaches that assume the universal applicability of leadership research findings across all cultural settings. It concludes by looking at the implications of the anthropological approach for those who are involved in leadership training in Thai settings and beyond.

Titre Ande

Leadership and Authority

Bula Matari and Life - Community Ecclesiology in Congo

2010 / 978-1-870345-72-9 xvii + 189pp

This book proposes that Christian theology in Africa can make significant developments if a critical understanding of the socio-political context in contemporary Africa is taken seriously. The Christian leadership in post-colonial Africa has cloned its understanding and use of authority on the Bula Matari model, which was issued from the brutality of colonialism and political absolutism in post-colonial Africa. This model has caused many problems in churches, including dysfunction, conflicts, divisions and a lack of prophetic ministry. Titre proposes a Life-Community ecclesiology for liberating authority, where leadership is a function, not a status, and 'apostolic succession' belongs to all the people of God.

Frank Kwesi Adams

Odwira and the Gospel

A Study of the Asante Odwira Festival and its Significance for Christianity in Ghana

2010 /978-1-870345-59-0

The study of the Odwira festival is the key to the understanding of Asante religious and political life in Ghana. The book explores the nature of the Odwira festival longitudinally - in pre-colonial, colonial and post-independence Ghana - and examines the Odwira ideology and its implications for understanding the Asante self-identity. The book also discusses how some elements of faith portrayed in the Odwira festival could provide a framework for Christianity to engage with Asante culture at a greater depth. Theological themes in Asante belief that have emerged from this study include the theology of sacrament, ecclesiology, eschatology, Christology and a complex concept of time. The author argues that Asante cultural identity lies at the heart of the process by which the Asante Christian faith is carried forward.

Bruce Carlton

Strategy Coordinator

Changing the Course of Southern Baptist Missions

2010 / 978-1-870345-78-1 xvii + 268pp

In 1976, the Southern Baptist Convention adopted its Bold New Thrusts in Foreign Missions with the overarching goal of sharing the gospel with every person in the world by the year 2000. The formation of Cooperative Services International (CSI) in 1985 and the assigning of the first non-residential missionary (NRM) in 1987 demonstrated the Foreign Mission Board's (now International Mission Board) commitment to take the gospel message to countries that restricted traditional missionary presence and to people groups identified as having little or no access to the gospel. Carlton traces the historical development along with an analysis of the key components of the paradigm and its significant impact on Southern Baptists' missiology.

Julie Ma & Wonsuk Ma
Mission in the Spirit:
Towards a Pentecostal/Charismatic Missiology
2010 / 978-1-870345-84-2 xx + 312pp

The book explores the unique contribution of Pentecostal/Charismatic mission from the beginning of the twentieth century. The first part considers the theological basis of Pentecostal/Charismatic mission thinking and practice. Special attention is paid to the Old Testament, which has been regularly overlooked by the modern Pentecostal/Charismatic movements. The second part discusses major mission topics with contributions and challenges unique to Pentecostal/Charismatic mission. The book concludes with a reflection on the future of this powerful missionary movement. As the authors served as Korean missionaries in Asia, often their missionary experiences in Asia are reflected in their discussions.

GENERAL REGNUM TITLES

Vinay Samuel, Chris Sugden (eds.)
The Church in Response to Human Need
1987 / 1870345045 / xii+268pp

Philip Sampson, Vinay Samuel, Chris Sugden (eds.)
Faith and Modernity
Essays in modernity and post-modernity
1994 / 1870345177 / 352pp

Klaus Fiedler
The Story of Faith Missions
1994 / 0745926878 / 428pp

Douglas Peterson
Not by Might nor by Power
A Pentecostal Theology of Social Concern in Latin America
1996 / 1870345207 / xvi+260pp

David Gitari
In Season and Out of Season
Sermons to a Nation
1996 / 1870345118 / 155pp

David. W. Virtue
A Vision of Hope
The Story of Samuel Habib
1996 / 1870345169 / xiv+137pp

Everett A Wilson
Strategy of the Spirit
J.Philip Hogan and the Growth of the Assemblies of God Worldwide, 1960 - 1990
1997 /1870345231/214

Murray Dempster, Byron Klaus, Douglas Petersen (eds.)
The Globalization of Pentecostalism
A Religion Made to Travel
1999 / 1870345290 / xvii+406pp

Peter Johnson, Chris Sugden (eds.)
Markets, Fair Trade and the Kingdom of God
Essays to Celebrate Traidcraft's 21st Birthday
2001 / 1870345193 / xii+155pp

Robert Hillman, Coral Chamberlain, Linda Harding
Healing & Wholeness
Reflections on the Healing Ministry
2002 / 978-1- 870345-35- 4 / xvii+283pp

David Bussau, Russell Mask
Christian Microenterprise Development
An Introduction
2003 / 1870345282 / xiii+142pp

David Singh
Sainthood and Revelatory Discourse
An Examination of the Basis for the Authority of Bayan in Mahdawi Islam
2003 / 8172147285 / xxiv+485pp

For the up-to-date listing of the Regnum books see www.ocms.ac.uk/regnum

regnum

Regnum Books International

Regnum is an Imprint of The Oxford Centre for Mission Studies
St. Philip and St. James Church
Woodstock Road
Oxford, OX2 6HR
Web: www.ocms.ac.uk/regnum

THE THREE ETHOLOGIES

Animal Lives

Jane C. Desmond, Series Editor; Barbara J. King, Associate Editor for Science; Kim Marra, Associate Editor

BOOKS IN THE SERIES

Displaying Death and Animating Life: Human-Animal Relations in Art, Science, and Everyday Life
by Jane C. Desmond

Voracious Science and Vulnerable Animals: A Primate Scientist's Ethical Journey
by John P. Gluck

The Great Cat and Dog Massacre: The Real Story of World War Two's Unknown Tragedy
by Hilda Kean

Animal Intimacies: Interspecies Relatedness in India's Central Himalayas
by Radhika Govindrajan

Minor Creatures: Persons, Animals, and the Victorian Novel
by Ivan Kreilkamp

Equestrian Cultures: Horses, Human Society, and the Discourse of Modernity
by Kristen Guest and Monica Mattfeld

Precarious Partners: Horses and Their Humans in Nineteenth-Century France
by Kari Weil

Crooked Cats: Beastly Encounters in the Anthropocene
by Nayanika Mathur